TRUTH AND POWER IN
AMERICAN ARCHAEOLOGY

Critical Studies
in the History of
Anthropology

SERIES EDITORS

Regna Darnell
Robert Oppenheim

Alice Beck Kehoe

TRUTH AND POWER IN AMERICAN ARCHAEOLOGY

University of Nebraska Press | Lincoln

Chapter 3 originally printed in *Current Anthropology*,
vol. 22, no. 5, 1981.
Chapter 5 originally printed in *Research in Economic
Anthropology*, vol. 14, JAI Press, 1993.
Chapter 6 reprinted from Volume 30, *Reprints in
Anthropology*, J and L Reprint Company, 1985.
Chapter 10 originally printed in *Exploring Gender
Through Archaeology*, Prehistory Press, 1992.

The University of Nebraska Press is part of a land-grant
institution with campuses and programs on the past,
present, and future homelands of the Pawnee, Ponca,
Otoe-Missouria, Omaha, Dakota, Lakota, Kaw, Cheyenne,
and Arapaho Peoples, as well as those of the relocated
Ho-Chunk, Sac and Fox, and Iowa Peoples.

∞

Publication of this work was assisted by the Murray-Hong
Family Trust, to honor and sustain the distinguished
legacy of Stephen O. Murray in the History of
Anthropology at the University of Nebraska Press.

Library of Congress Control Number: 2024002393

Set in in Arno Pro by A. Shahan.

Frontispiece: Alice Kehoe at Osage Tribal Museum,
Pawhuska, Oklahoma, November 11, 2007. Behind her is
the museum's painting of Cahokia, which Osage history
says they ruled. James Elsberry, Osage Tribal Museum.

Contents

Dramatis Personae   vi

Greetings!   1

PART 1. Archaeology Makes Histories   5

    1. Constructing Data   9

    2. Excluded from History: The Albertans Who Really "Opened the West"   25

    3. Revisionist Anthropology: Aboriginal North America   39

    Interpolation: Metis and Rationality, a Classical Class Struggle   89

PART 2. Archaeology Is a Historical Science   91

    4. Looking at Landscapes: Disciplinary Boundaries and Unrecognized Precursors   97

    5. How the Ancient Peigans Lived   121

    6. The Direct Ethnographic Approach to Archaeology on the Northern Plains   143

PART 3. Archaeology Lives in Social Contexts   159

    7. Chiefdoms   165

    8. Cahokia from a Postcolonial Standpoint   193

PART 4. Postcolonial: Scientific Standpoint and Moral Imperative   221

    9. Delgamuukw   223

    10. The Muted Class: Unshackling Tradition   229

PART 5. The Themes that Bind   249

    Acknowledgments   265

    References   271

    Index   279

Dramatis Personae

Ac ko mok ki (Akai Mokti) . . . Blackfoot alliance leader

William Adams . . . . Anthropologist and writer on the philosophy of science in archaeology

Edwin Ardener . . . . British social anthropologist who introduced syntagm/paradigm terms

Shirley Ardener . . . . British anthropologist and feminist leader

Aristotle . . . . Greek philosopher and scientist

Anthony Aveni . . . . Writer on archaeoastronomy

Barry Barnes . . . . British sociologist of science

Juliana Barr . . . . American colonial historian

Lowell Bean . . . . Californian anthropologist

Lewis Binford . . . . Prominent archaeological theorist of 1970s–1990s

Junius Bird . . . . Expert on ancient American fabrics

Glenn Black . . . . Taught fieldschools

Donald Blakeslee . . . . Archaeologist and researcher of dispersed towns

Henri (Abbé) Breuil . . . . . . Paleolithic art specialist

Robert Carneiro . . . . Archaeological theorist

Sarah Carter . . . . Canadian historian

V. Gordon Childe . . . . British archaeologist and theorist

Andrew Christenson . . . . . . Archaeologist organizing history of archaeology work

Cheryl Claassen . . . . American archaeologist (Southeast) and feminist leader

Grahame Clark . . . . British prehistorian archaeologist

Felix Cohen . . . . Coauthor (with Lucy Kramer Cohen) of 1934 Indian New Deal

Lucy Kramer Cohen . . . . . . Coauthor (with Felix Cohen) of 1934 Indian New Deal

R. G. Collingwood . . . . Archaeologist and philosopher

Bruce Alden Cox . . . . Ecological anthropologist

Carole Crumley . . . . Historical ecology archaeologist

Dara Culhane . . . . Anthropologist working with British Columbia First Nations

Adrian Currie . . . . Philosopher of historical sciences

William Denevan . . . . Cultural landscape geographer

Dena Dincauze . . . . Archaeologist and former president of the Society for American Archaeology

Roland Dixon . . . . AAA president, 1913

Georges Dumézil . . . . Scholar of Indo-European cultural heritage

Timothy Earle . . . . American archaeologist and student of Elman Service

Umberto Eco . . . . Semiotic linguist

John A. (Jack) Eddy . . . . . . Astronomer

Cynthia Eller . . . . Scholar of religion

Jaco Finlay . . . . Fur trader, the son of a Canadian trader and a Saulteau woman

James A. Ford . . . . Leading Southeastern archaeologist

Morton Fried . . . . Anthropologist who critiqued the "tribes" category

Joan Gero . . . . Feminist archaeologist

Guy Gibbon . . . . Archaeologist and writer on the philosophy of science

Steven Gimbel . . . . Philosopher of science

Laurie Godfrey . . . . Anthropologist combating anti-evolutionism

Jane C. Goodale . . . . Revisionist anthropologist working with Tiwi in Australia

Robert Goodvoice . . . . Dakota historian and religious leader

Marjorie Glicksman Grene . . . Philosopher

James B. Griffin . . . . Prominent North American archaeologist and expert on sherds

Norwood Russell Hanson . . . . Philosopher of science

Donna Haraway . . . . Iconoclastic analyst of American culture

Jon Hather . . . . Archaeobotanist

Johann Herder . . . . Famous German Enlightenment philosopher

James H. Howard . . . . Ethnohistorian, especially of Siouan First Nations

Anne Ingstad . . . . Archaeologist who excavated Norse site in Canada

Helge Ingstad . . . . Anthropologist who excavated Norse site in Canada

Barry Isaac . . . . Economic anthropologist

Carl Johannessen . . . . Cultural geographer, student of Carl Sauer

Thomas F. (Tom) Kehoe . . . . Northern Plains archaeologist

David H. Kelley . . . . Mayanist and researcher in pre-Columbian voyages

Jane Kelley . . . . Archaeologist and theorist

J. Charles Kelley . . . . Excavated in northwest Mexico

Susan Kent . . . . Ethnoarchaeologist who worked in southern Africa

Dorothy Keur . . . . Anthropologist who studied a Dutch peasant community

Darrell Robes Kipp . . . . Amskapi Pikuni (Blackfeet) language revitalization leader

Patrick Kirch . . . . Oceanic archaeologist

Madeline Kneberg . . . . Southeastern archaeologist

Karin Knorr-Cetina . . . . Sociologist of science

Kristian Kristiansen . . . . . . Danish archaeologist studying Bronze Age Europe

Alfred Kroeber . . . . Boas student, anthropology leader in the first half of the twentieth century

Donald Lathrap . . . . Archaeologist working in the Upper Amazon

Bruno Latour . . . . Anthropologist-sociologist of science

Claude Lévi-Strauss . . . . French anthropological theorist and Amazon River nations ethnographer

Meriwether Lewis . . . . Captain of U.S. Corps of Discovery, 1804–1806

John Locke . . . . Political advisor for British colonial enterprises, known as a philosopher

John Lubbock . . . . Armchair archaeologist, banker, and leader for British imperialism

Nancy Lurie . . . . Anthropologist who suffered patriarchal rejection

Maureen Lux . . . . Canadian historian and writer on Canadian policy for its Indians

William Marquardt . . . . Archaeologist and historical ecologist, Southeast and Europe

John Marshall . . . . Chief Justice of the United States, 1801–1835

Washington Matthews . . . . . Army doctor and ethnographer

Allan McEachern . . . . Prominent Canadian jurist

Bob McGhee . . . . Canadian archaeologist and Arctic researcher

Tony Merchant . . . . Canadian lawyer considering lawsuit against Indian boarding schools

John H. Moore . . . . Ethnohistorian of Plains nations, Marxist anthropologist

Lewis Henry Morgan . . . . . . Nineteenth-century uniliniear evolutionist

William Mulloy . . . . Northern Plains archaeologist

Joseph Needham . . . . Biochemist, historian of Chinese science, and supporter of UNESCO

Patricia O'Brien . . . . Central Plains archaeologist who argued for interpreting Cahokia as a state

Gerald Oetelaar . . . . Alberta archaeologist working with Blackfoot on ecology and history

Thomas Patterson . . . . Marxist archaeologist

Timothy Pauketat . . . . Archaeologist specializing in theory about Cahokia

C. S. Peirce . . . . Philosopher of science, also noted as a researcher on ocean height

Valerie Pinsky. . . . . Analyst of archaeology

J. H. Plumb . . . . British social historian

(Major) John Wesley Powell . . Director of U.S. Geological Survey and founder of Bureau of American Ethnology, Smithsonian

David H. Price . . . . Anthropologist and historian of anthropological involvement, U.S. military intelligence

Arthur J. Ray . . . . Ethnohistorian on First Nations' histories

Thomas Reid . . . . Scottish Enlightenment philosopher

Marshall Sahlins. . . . . Anthropolitical theorist

Carl O. Sauer . . . . Cultural landscape geographer

Claude E. Schaeffer . . . . Ethnohistorian (Kutenai, Blackfoot)

James Schoenwetter . . . . Archaeologist and paleobotanist

Elman Service . . . . Professor at the University of Michigan who taught unilinear cultural evolution

Steven Shapin. . . . . Historian of science

George Gaylord Simpson. . . . . Twentieth-century paleontologist and evolution scientist

Bruce D. Smith . . . . Archaeologist and researcher of plant domestication in Americas

Donald B. Smith . . . . Canadian historian and writer on First Nations and Canadian policies

Mark Solovey . . . . Historian of science, especially the National Science Foundation

Albert Spaulding. . . . . Teacher of statistics for archaeology

Frank Speck . . . . Boas student who found and studied Eastern Algonkian nations

Herbert Spencer . . . . British social philosopher

Julian Steward . . . . Anthropologist theorizing ecological adaptations stimuli to cultural developments

George Stocking, Jr. . . . . Historian of anthropology in Victorian and Boas's times

William Sturtevant . . . . Ethnologist and researcher of U.S. Southeast and northern South America

David Thompson. . . . . Canadian explorer linking eastern Canada to the Pacific

Bruce Trigger . . . . Historian of archaeology, archaeologist

Justin Trudeau . . . . Prime minister of Canada

Pierre Trudeau . . . . Former prime minister of Canada

Jim Tuck . . . . Archaeologist who worked in the Northeast

Frederick Jackson Turner . . . . American historian

Edward Tylor . . . . English armchair anthropologist

C. C. Uhlenbeck . . . . Dutch linguist who recorded and studied Algonkian and Basque languages

Joan Vincent . . . . Political anthropologist

David Wake . . . . Evolutionary biologist

Marvalee Wake . . . . Evolutionary biologist

Patty Jo Watson . . . . Midwestern archaeologist and follower of Binford

Waldo Wedel . . . . Plains archaeologist

Annette Weiner . . . . Revisionist anthropologist who worked in Trobrian Islands

Leslie White . . . . Anthropologist and theorist

Daniel Wilson . . . . Pioneering scientific archaeologist

Stephen Wolfram . . . . Authority in computational science

Richard Woodbury . . . . American archaeologist who taught Alice Kehoe

Victoria Claflin Woodhull . . . . Nineteenth-century radical

Alison Wylie . . . . Philosopher of science in archaeology

John Yellen . . . . Archaeologist and program director for archaeology at the National Science Foundation

John Ziman . . . . Physicist and analyst of science

TRUTH AND POWER IN AMERICAN ARCHAEOLOGY

Greetings!

You are looking at a challenge to the power that, after World War II, unseated American archaeology's basic science. Through National Science Foundation funding, mainstream American archaeology fell into mere scientism. It rejected local culture histories perniciously in favor of slotting sites into nineteenth-century imperialist racism. Manifest Destiny ideology and the Doctrine of Discovery were taken for granted. We who knew better had our papers rejected, did not get hired at research universities, were not invited to lecture or join discussion groups. As some Canadian archaeologists phrased it, we were out on the tundra in the chilly climate.

Slowly, the ground has been shifting. A superficial cause was the decline into dementia and then death of charismatic Lewis Binford. A much stronger cause is the tidal current carrying real demands and efforts to respond to the gross inequities built into the United States' Manifest Destiny ideology. In the sense of Aristotle's "efficient cause," NAGPRA, the Native American Graves Protection and Repatriation Act of 1990, was the tipping point.

My professional life began as a Barnard student in the 1950s, taking courses in Columbia's Department of Anthropology and working as a student aide in the anthropology department of the American Museum of Natural History. Richard Woodbury taught me how to work through archaeological data, and Glenn Black taught me field techniques, excavating not at Angel Mounds that summer, but salvaging bundle burials eroding into the Ohio River from the high bluff overlooking the Green River's mouth. In the museum, Junius Bird taught me to recognize and deeply respect twining as a fabric technique, I helped James Ford sort his collection from Point Barrow, Alaska (reeking each day of seal oil a thousand years old), I helped doctoral candidates Walter Fairservis and Frank Saul with their sherds and bones, respectively. Empirical went without saying; hands on artifacts, eyes on site maps, profiles, soil analyses—what Edwin Ardener termed the syntagms in the field.

Woodbury taught his World Prehistory course by bringing in the doctoral students to present, visually, their dissertation excavations: Ralph

Solecki showed us Shanidar Cave, Robert Suggs his Marquesas work, Rose Lillien (soon to be Rose L. Solecki) her work with Duncan Strong in Peru, part of the Viru Project. The exception to empirical was a course taught by the "brilliant young" postdoc Marshall Sahlins on Leslie White's cultural evolution theory. Each week Sahlins deconstructed a chapter of White's then-forthcoming *Evolution of Culture* (published 1959). I was so impressed at how cogently Sahlins revealed the many flaws in each chapter. Just before final exams, I said this in a little study group. The grad students around me were amused—"Alice, we all see this as you do, but beware, Sahlins *believes* White is *correct*! Watch what you write in the exam!"

Between the museum, the still-Boasian Columbia anthropology department, and my summer field experiences with Black, J. Charles Kelley in Durango, Mexico, and Melvin Fowler at Modoc Rockshelter in southern Illinois, I was richly grounded in archaeological sites, data, artifacts, and logical inferences. Of all, the critical moment was in Woodbury's office where he explained why my classmate Dena Ferran (Dincauze) earned an A on her seminar paper, and I only a B+. Dena focused clearly on the site, site data, and logical chain to her concluding interpretation. That, our mentor said, was science. I brought in some ethnohistory, it was true enough, but it was not part of the *archaeological* data set. I understood.

This practice of culture-histories was then bombed by the Cold War policy of focusing America's resources on maintaining military power. Leslie White was the prophet, insisting that mankind's progress depended on harnessing ever-increasing sources of energy. America's nuclear bombs climaxed this evolution, inevitable once human brains had evolved in their capacity to capture extrasomatic energy. Dedication to the physical sciences had carried us to this pinnacle of power. The National Science Foundation was established in 1950 "to secure the national defense" as well as promote health and prosperity. Statistics were touted as the essence of science. Laws of cultural evolution were set forth and validated deductively. First Nations people had no place in this universe of discourse.

Meanwhile, back on the northern prairies, I was living and working with First Nations on their reserves and in the prairie cities. I was forced to do a dissertation in ethnography (see my memoir, *Girl Archaeologist*), and the archaeology I shared with my husband was culture-historical, in Blackfoot and Cree territories. Tom was trained on the Blackfeet Reservation by a student of Frank Speck to respectfully listen to the local people, especially First Nations, and to develop research strategies through their knowledge. Professionally, I was disdained as "soft," of course, I was a woman; Tom's work on the chronologies of point styles in our deep bison-pound excavations and our analyses of bison butchering was "hard" enough to get some respect, and he was a man.

Tom's career took him to Saskatchewan as its first Provincial Archaeologist, then—when a political upset brought in a conservative government defunding heritage work—to Lincoln, Nebraska, where I was hired to teach at the University of Nebraska, and finally to Milwaukee, Wisconsin, where he was Curator of Archaeology at Milwaukee Public Museum. I got a faculty position teaching anthropology at Marquette University, a Jesuit institution. Although I applied, when openings occurred, at University of Wisconsin–Milwaukee and later also at UW–Madison, neither public university was ever interested in adding me to its faculty. Women were not seen as archaeologists, nor was my work in ethnohistory seen as anthropology.

For the forty years of my professional employment, two factors militated against what would be recognized as professional success: teaching in an institution unknown outside Midwest Catholic circles, and working within the premises and methodology of the historical sciences. NSF scientism ruled during those years, from the 1960s to 2000. Papers I researched and wrote in the framework of historical science were rejected, or sometimes published obscurely and not cited. My one apparent breakthrough, *The Land of Prehistory: A Critical History of American Archaeology* (Kehoe 1998), does get cited without, so far as I've seen, changing anyone's practice.

History of American archaeology is a tag I've carried since the breakthrough conference of 1987, organized by Andrew Christenson, that created a subfield out of disparate interests. This, at last, gave me my niche. From this standpoint, I could look at both the history of power in American archaeology and the history of concepts of science in American archaeology. From this standpoint I could justify what I wrote about Cahokia, about ethnohistorical aspects of American archaeology, and about using the methodology of historical sciences. My final book, I expected, would be a memoir of my life in American archaeology, presented as a contribution to the history of the discipline. *Girl Archaeologist* is not autobiographical, in that readers know nothing about my three kids or extended family or activities irrelevant to my professional life. After months of discussing what is included in that book, not included in that book, and why, my editor at the University of Nebraska Press, Matthew Bokovoy, suggested I should support my memoir, as a disciplinary history, with publication of my principal rejected or unnoticed papers. Text around these papers explain how I see their fate illuminating power versus "truth" in American archaeology.

Introduction to the Papers

Part 1, Archaeology Makes Histories, begins with the result of my years reading philosophies of science and of history. Both fields are contentious, toward which I could bring my field experiences and analyses of archaeological and ethnohistorical data. Part 2, Archaeology is a Historical Science, more directly utilizes my field-based, foundational knowledge to counter narrow, fashionable archaeological practices. There is a body of practice and interpretation for historical sciences—geology, paleontology, archaeology, and historically-oriented cultural geography—that is clear on methods and principles of interpretation. Part 3, Archaeology Lives in Social Contexts, takes as its standpoint the principle that historical sciences look wide to reach inferences to the best explanation. "Evolutionary" schemes slotting societies by population size into Western categories and interpretations rejecting data that interfere with easy slotting are each critiqued in this section. Part 4, Postcolonial, exhibits probably the most blatant example of the powerfully ingrained Western disdain for other societies: the 1991 ruling of the Chief Justice of British Columbia against two small First Nations, petitioning against wholesale robbery of their timber. During the long hearing of this case, the Chief Justice wanted to mute these nations' own histories, a practice of dominant classes against those lower than them—including men muting women as a class. Lastly, in Themes that Bind, I present ideological and political positions that empowered leaders of the profession of American archaeology and contrast these with my own cultural and political positions. As a woman born in the 1930s, not WASP but a Jew, not from a wealthy family, and a married mother of three, I have been muted. More important, *mainstream American archaeology from the 1960s on has rejected method and principles of historical science.* This book illuminates the much broader range of data and interpretive standpoint that American archaeology ought to embrace.

PART 1. Archaeology Makes Histories

Speak Truth to Power?

A man named Yeshua from Nazareth tried it and got crucified. My grand-father fled Lodz, Poland, before dawn to Germany before the Czar's police could take him to Siberia. Power has only contempt for Truth.

Archaeology might seem so unimportant, so simplistic in North America that it could be a refuge from Power's cruelties. Archaeology is a science—there are standard ways to work out Truth. This book is about archaeology as a historical science, beset and betrayed by power struggles. It was sociology of science, a standpoint I discovered in 1981, that gave coherency to the confusions that bedeviled me as a young archaeologist. Tellingly, Barry Barnes, the sociologist of science whose work opened that door for me, moved from studying science to studying power. "According to him, problems to do with knowledge and those to do with power are in fact two sides of one coin" (Hwang et al. 2010, 601).

When I entered archaeology in the 1950s, the field of archaeology was ostensibly a means to discover unwritten histories, particularly in colonized nations. Their pasts were conceptualized as simple developments, from Paleolithic bands dependent on wild foods, to domesticating a few prime resources to maintain on farms, then increasing technologies and coalescing populations in cities, inventing writing, and crossing the border into civilization. Prehistory was impenetrably separate from History, the first professed by few persons and the second by thousands in well-supported university departments. Literacy was the touchstone.

Literacy is essential for institutionalized power today as the basis for our recognized nation-states, for businesses, and for regulating citizenry. Literacy customarily separated directors of archaeological projects from their laborers and communities around their sites. Literacy provided frameworks and scenarios for interpreting pasts, privileging Western European dicta supporting conquests and colonization. From proposing projects through recording field and laboratory data to publishing, literacy is the sine qua non for practicing archaeology. Even when Peter Schmidt and I produced

Archaeologies of Listening in 2019, literacy was the means to propound the value of listening to collaborators and the actual worlds they live in.

The history of American archaeology depends upon documents produced by literate participants. Those who write, and whose writings are archived, are few in the profession. Inevitably they are biased by their language structure, by their education and experiences, and by their practical interests. What primarily concerns me in this book are the unacknowledged ideologies behind archaeological work and their gate-keepers. These produce and maintain what is accepted as the histories of America's First Nations.

How Archaeology Makes Histories

The discipline and profession of archaeology developed during the nineteenth century in European and European-immigrant nations. Admiring ruins and collecting artifacts had been carried on by formally educated people since the Renaissance, continuing the elevation of Greek and Roman cultures as models of civilization. The rise of modern nation-states professing locally-rooted populations as their "people" led to dissatisfaction with universal admiration for classical ideals, the antiquarian being contrasted with the local historian (Scott 1815). Prehistoric archaeology was codified by Christian Thomsen in his 1836 exposition of Denmark's deep roots in its soil, witnessed in the sequences of artifacts from Stone Age to Bronze Age to Iron Age. Geology, a natural science, was the model for stratigraphy. Thus, archaeology sits as a science, rather than with humanities as history.

Lewis Binford's 1960s assault upon archaeology for culture histories (Kehoe 1998, 115–41) ostensibly confirmed the place of archaeology as a science. Culture histories were denounced as unscientific. At the same time, the Society for Historical Archaeology was organized in 1967, as CRM (Cultural Resource Management) was growing as employment for archaeologists. Usually part of projects protecting and often restoring documented sites, historic archaeology initially saw itself as furnishing material to supplement documents; as it grew over the decades, it realized that its data can be powerful in expanding and correcting conventional histories (see http://npshistory.com/publications/afbg/index.htm, the website for African Burial Ground National Monument). Work on culture histories was not going to disappear.

For my own concern as a field archaeologist, and for my obligations teaching a regular course on prehistory and archaeology, I sought to understand Binford's New Archaeology. I read histories and philosophy of science, trying to apply them to published archaeology and my own work. By the 1980s, I had come to focus on a basic question: what are data? Binford did not address this, other than following his teacher Albert Spaulding in claiming that statistics can reveal more than can conventionally eyeballing and describing site features and artifacts. By the 1980s, I had thirty years of field and reports experience, twenty years of teaching and of learning from keen, well-grounded, ethical scholars, both Western and First Nations. I felt ready to enter the lists, armed with solid scholarship. I submitted "Constructing Data" to our leading journal, *American Antiquity*. It was summarily rejected.

Reading the paper thirty years later, I see it is too long. The journal editor could have said this and recommended drastic cutting. He— W. Raymond Wood—did not. He simply rejected it. Ray knew me as Tom's wife from when we were all finishing grad work (in different schools). The River Basin Surveys were still going on, the common experience of the men, from which women were excluded (but see Knudson 2014). Its program was positivist and very colonial, brutally displacing First Nations from their agricultural bottomlands, their villages, and their graves. Archaeological data were what the men dug up. Women cleaned and cataloged in the labs, and as Knudson pointed out, typed up. No need for philosophers.

I disagreed then, and I still disagree. Here, at last, as Chapter 1, my effort can be read.

1. Constructing Data

In the celebratory volume *American Archaeology Past and Future*, Patty Jo Watson decries, "for the first time in the history of Americanist archaeology, . . . a few practicing archaeologists . . . who do not believe the real past is accessible" (Watson 1986, 441). Exactly half a century earlier, the practicing archaeologist Robin Collingwood—who as R. G. Collingwood has been the only professional archaeologist who is also a major philosopher—asserted, expounding upon Oakeshott (1933), "The historical past is the world of ideas which the present evidence creates in the present. In historical inference we do not move from our present world to a past world; the movement in experience is always a movement within a present world of ideas. . . . history is not the past as such" (Collingwood 1956, 154; cf. Piggott 1981, 187). The real past, the past-in-itself, *Dinge an sich*, is infinitely detailed beyond human comprehension.

Archaeologists undertake to build pasts from recoverable data. The crux of our task is to realize, in both senses of the word, what is humanly possible in our task. Most discussions of the science of archaeology have focused on techniques, on the logics of explanation (e.g., Watson, LeBlanc, and Redman 1971, 1984; Salmon and Salmon 1979; Gibbon 1989), or on the issue of empirical validation (Dunnell 1971; Kelley and Hanen 1988). The semiotics of archaeological discourse have been rather neglected. This paper addresses the question of how we recognize, re-cognize, archaeological data. My argument concerns the epistemological naïveté that is a legacy of our Common-Sense metaphysic inherited from nineteenth-century American science.

Common-Sense

Thomas Jefferson is popularly held to have been the first person to have conducted proper archaeological investigations in America (Willey and Sabloff 1980, 28; but see Schávelzon 1983). Jefferson and his colleagues held some truths to be self-evident, as they declared in 1776. That Age of Enlightenment was engrossed by epistemological analyses; Joseph

Agassi (1981, 386) casts a cold eye upon those valiant assays upon Truth, and concludes, "positivism, inductivism, pure rationality, scientific proof, and all that, are parts of a myth." More conservatively, Larry Laudan (1981, chap. 7) traces the formation of what might be termed Common-sense science to a contemporary of Jefferson, Thomas Reid, a Scottish natural philosopher (1710–1796). Praising Francis Bacon but relying principally upon Newton, Reid urged induction of general laws from observation of particulars, and held that the "Baconian method" was open to anyone who would take the pains to observe with meticulous care. God had ordained a universe embodying principles of order, and endowed men with capacity to search to discover these principles. This was a revolutionary metaphysic allied to Protestantism and deeply implicated in the English, American, and French Revolutions (Jacob 1976; Shapin and Schaffer 1985).

American science and engineering have been strongly influenced by the Scottish Enlightenment and especially by Reid's Common-Sense Realism (Bozeman 1977). Not only were Scots a significant proportion of immigrants to colonial America and the early United States, Reid's philosophy was highly compatible with American egalitarianism. Joseph Henry's direction of the Smithsonian Institution, idealistically encouraging lay science, clearly reflects this disposition (Hinsley 1981). Observation, measurement (Washington, Jefferson, and Lincoln all practiced the sophisticated applied science of land surveying [Dupree 1972]), experiment and inductive generalization were codified in the American System of manufacturing (Boorstin 1978, 3–4) culminating in an "engineering ideology" (Rosenberg 1976, 267), a scientism (Putnam 1981, 113), the "science of management" (Braverman 1974, Noble 1977, chap. 10). Reid was referring to Newton's *regulae* but was as well summing up Common-Sense Realism when he wrote of "principles which, though they have not the same kind of evidence that mathematical axioms have; yet have such evidence that every man of common understanding readily assents to them" (quoted in Laudan 1981, 109).

A groundswell of research rising since the 1970s brings an instauration of that Pyrrhonic skepticism that Reid rejected. Collingwood believed the cogent philosophical analyses he and Oakeshott presented in the 1930s had dealt the death-blow to positivism, but in the event, it has taken a convergence of sociology of knowledge and sociology of science to undermine that positivist program that Collingwood summed up as, "in principle, vicious" (Collingwood 1956, 131; cf. Gibbon 1989, 140): "first, ascertaining facts; secondly, framing laws. The facts were immediately ascertained by sensuous perception. The laws were framed by generalizing from these facts" (Collingwood 1956, 126–27). Cognitive studies have substantiated the power of metaphor in molding perception (Lakoff 1987), and the sociology (and anthropology [Latour 1990]) of science exposes the real viciousness of much scientific practice (e.g., Collins 1985). It now seems inescapable that facts are, in a word, factitious.

Where does that leave the practicing archaeologist? It does *not* push us into a reader-makes-the-text deconstructionism. Out of an informed and reflective survey of contemporary science and philosophy, we can build what Pickering (1989; cf. Woolgar 1988) terms *pragmatic realism*. His reading of ethnographies of laboratory life leads him to suggest that a matter of fact is achieved at the moment of coherence of material procedure, experimenter's conceptual understanding of the instrumentality of the experiment, and experimenter's phenomenal model of relevant "nature." Rather than accept a simple correspondence theory of realism, in which facts are so because they correspond to fixed aspects of a natural world, Pickering sees the material world *resistant* to our understanding, with scientists manipulating material procedures and reconceptualizing instrumental principles and the phenomenal world until the three seem to cohere. This is pragmatic realism, postulating a "real" world effectively beyond our ken, "actual" phenomena arising from the real world, and "empirical observations" performed upon phenomena in accordance with socially monitored concepts (Gibbon 1989, 144–45). What we know is contingent upon both the "real" world and our socially transmitted conventions of apprehending experience. The archaeologist should be concerned with techniques of discovery *and* methods of categorization and argumentation.

John Ziman, a physicist, put it this way: "The objectivity of well-established science is thus comparable to that of a well-made map, drawn by a great company of surveyors.... The objectivity of scientific knowledge resides in its being a social construct" (Ziman 1978, 107). We can take as given, as a primitive postulate, that there exist sources of sensory impressions experienced as similar by most humans. Which sense impressions, *experientia*, are recognized to be data are not inherent in the phenomena but are, in the final analysis, consensual. The difference between pragmatic realism and Reid's Common-Sense realism lies in Reid's belief that the real world directly *compels* consensus, whereas contemporary analyses of science emphasize socially constituted convention producing consensus. In practice, that means language and rhetoric. The crucial role of language in the formulation of knowledge demands that scientific analyses consistently be concerned with epistemology.

Years ago, Norwood Russell Hanson remarked, "We observe objects, processes, and events. . . . We do not observe facts (what would they look like?). Facts are not objects or collections of objects or constellations of objects. Facts are [a statement] *to the effect that. . . . Facts are what true statements state* . . . not simple existence" (Hanson 1971, 9–10, his italics). Observations and facts are "logically different . . . different kind[s] of" denotata, he pointed out (Hanson 1971, 9). Observations are translated into (statements of) facts. Our preceptors channeled our attention to particular sensory impressions—*experientia*—and by speaking of them, labeled them (Barnes 1982, 27; Pickering 1989, 276). Sense experience is thus coded into symbols, and through the domains of these symbols, extended by analogy and metaphor (Hesse 1980, xvii, chap. 4). "Matters of fact" are established within "a disciplined space, where experimental, discursive, and social practices were collectively controlled by competent members" (Shapin and Schaffer 1985, 39, 51–72, 78). Knorr-Cetina's ethnographic record confirms this view, leading her to conclude that "scientific enquiry" is "*constructive* . . . in terms of the decision-laden character of knowledge production, [marked by] *indeterminacy* and . . . *contextual contingency*— rather than non-local universality—[and by] *analogical reasoning* which orients the opportunistic logic of research" (1981, 152, her italics).

Examples of Syntagm and Paradigm in Archaeology

Let me illustrate this abstruse discourse with some pertinent examples. In simple, we can suppose an archaeologist perceiving a discoloration in the soil. (Note that the excavator may fail to notice the discoloration: see next paragraph.) This discoloration is part of the *syntagm* presented upon excavation to the observer. Our experienced archaeologist has learned by ostension, as a student in the field, to recognize the soil discoloration as significant and to label it "postmold." This label commits the archaeologist to a *paradigm* of wood-framed structures. The researcher compares the discoloration pattern to ethnographically described wood-framed structures and hypothesizes a particular form of structure—"wigwam," "scaffold," etc. Semiotically, a soil discoloration became a sign signifying "wood post," which then became a sign signifying "structure" and functioning as a paradigmatic set including "wigwam," "scaffold," etc. The *experientia* of soil color is turned into a demonstration that a wooden structure existed at this site.

Robert Dunnell's (1983) reworking of data from a 1939–1940 WPA excavation is a textbook case of distinction between syntagm and paradigm. The original field director failed to label percepts that Dunnell recognized to be empty pits and sheet midden. Presumably the excavator, lacking Dunnell's extensive formal training and experience, had never learned to perceive as significant the colorations and patterns that to Dunnell constitute data. Unrecognized, unlabeled, the features were not matters of fact. Verbalized by the original excavator, the site appeared to lack (empty) pits and sheet midden, and the paradigm modeling the prehistoric occupation is thereby ill-founded. The original report is not merely incomplete, it failed to identify probable similar sites and its analogies were not as cogent as they could have been, were the author cognizant of all the visible data in the syntagm he exposed. His paradigm could not incorporate similarity relations to other sites and to ethnographic descriptions of sites with the features "(empty) pits" and "sheet midden." Because the excavator did follow standard scientific archaeological procedure for demonstrating *experientia*, his records of the actual syntagms at the site permitted Dunnell to recover by recognition the neglected data, to construct a new, richer, and probably more valid (better-founded) paradigm that proves more useful in comparative studies.

Cahen and Keeley (1980) present a virtuoso performance of a logic of discovery. Concentration C-IV at Meer is a syntagm in which the authors perceive a high proportion of lithic material allowing refitting within the designated area (Cahen and Keeley 1980, 169–70). They then reference (171–74) additional syntagms constituting microwear analyses, add the syntagm C-IV in contiguity with other concentrations within the site (174–77), and conclude with an explicit chain of significations (177–79) leading to a paradigmatic model or interpretation of C-IV as representing the workshop of two craftsmen. The paper may seem idiographic in the extreme, reconstructing a few hours in the lives of two Belgian Mesolithic flintknappers, but it created a paradigm with clear extensions to ethnographic, economic, and technological analogies. It is soundly scientific in the careful distinctions between observations and facts, and the authors' presentation of their chain of signification permits the reader to replicate the process producing their conclusion.

Contrast Cahen and Keeley's paper with a more conventionally presented lithics study, for example Michael Schiffer's 1976 *Behavioral Archeology*. Schiffer reports (101–2) that he spent 285 +/− 25 person/hours eyeballing the stone artifacts recovered from the Joint site, but eschewed the use of any magnifying lens. He hypothesized possible technology and uses for the artifacts, based on naked-eye morphological criteria. For a work published in the 1970s, failure to make edge-wear observations (cf., e.g., from the same year, Dincauze 1976, 25: "all precolonial artifacts . . . were subjected to . . . magnifications between 10x and 30x") stands as a disjunction in a contemporary archaeological standard chain of signification and makes his conclusion poorly founded. Omitting an expected description of a set of attributes in his syntagm counts as an experimental flaw in his establishment of matters of fact. Careful reading indicates that Schiffer's interpretative summary rested less on the data preceding it than upon an analogy with Hill's site nearby (Schiffer 1976, 176, 177–78). The jump to Hill's paradigm is logically weak; perhaps edge-wear data on Joint site lithics would have strengthened the relation of similarity to Hill's project.

Another example of the syntagm/paradigm distinction and its utility in archaeological interpretation may be offered from my own work at DkMq-2, the Moose Mountain Medicine Wheel (Saskatchewan). Astronomer John A. Eddy, with whom we worked at the site in 1975, concluded that there is a high probability that the boulder configuration on the site was an astronomical observatory about two thousand years ago. Our excavations the following year confirmed Eddy's estimated age for the boulder construction, and yielded a collection of artifacts of which three-quarters (403 out of 555) are stone endscrapers (Kehoe and Kehoe 1979, 48). The syntagm was of a relatively dense scatter of artifacts, preponderantly crude endscraper blades, along the western portion of the central cairn area, with other artifacts more sparsely scattered in the other excavated sectors. None of the portable artifacts were within the till subsoil, although the basal rocks of the cairns and boulder lines were embedded in the top of this subsoil. We labeled the lithic objects using morphological and edge-wear attributes. The chain of signification begun with labeling the artifacts could proceed into either of two plausible paradigms: the artifacts could have been utilized in activities (ritual?) connected with the astronomical observations, or they could have been utilized independently of the boulder configuration. We chose the second alternative, privileging the observation that no artifacts appeared depositionally associated with the construction of the boulder figure. This choice made, inference to the best explanation (Kelley and Hanen 1988, 329) linked the preponderance of endscrapers to a postulated post-observatory occupation of the hilltop by people scraping hides, taking advantage of its constant cooling wind to mitigate that sweaty, stinking work. (The constant wind is part of the syntagm.) We now had two or more occupations of the site, one two thousand years ago (radiocarbon and astronomical best-fit dating) for astronomical observations, one or more later for scraping hides. There remained an additional feature of the syntagm that called for interpretation: the distribution of the portable artifacts. The chain of signification here included the curious presence of two gnawed pencils between rocks in the cairn. An experienced field naturalist identified the pattern of gnawing as small rodents seeking salt from sweat-stained wood; he told us that gophers steal sweat-stained artifacts and take them into their burrows to lick the salt. This *experientia* explained the pencils and created a taphonomic paradigm into which we could link the prehistoric scrapers (Kehoe and Kehoe 1979, 54). I make no claim that our report is innovative in its presentation—to the contrary, the controversies over archaeoastronomy in the 1970s impelled us to adhere to an innocuous standard format—but we did explicate (in narrative style) our logic of discovery, recording both syntagm and chains of signification to paradigms. In this manner we establish matters of fact in archaeology, substituting the published description for laboratory demonstration (cf. Shapin and Schaffer 1985, 51–72, 78).

Syntagms and Paradigms

The upshot of contention over the vulnerability of facts is that archaeologists ought to carefully explicate the chain of signification between initial observation and the constitution of a matter of fact. Neither blind imitation of standard presentations nor cursorily asserted interpretations will pass muster; clear explication is the sine qua non of good science. I wish to suggest a methodology that facilitates explication. This method comes from linguistics via the anthropological linguist Edwin Ardener, who addressed the question of epistemology in ethnography in his 1971 Malinowski Lecture.

Ardener took the terms *paradigm* and *syntagm* from Hjelmslev ([1943] 1961), who applied them to Saussure's distinction between *langue* and *parole*. Paradigm is by now a familiar term, derived from the Greek *para deiknumi*, "shows beyond." Syntagm derives from the Greek *syntaxis*, "layout" or "arrangement," as of soldiers in battle formation on a field. Syntagms are data as givens, actually ostensible. (In formal language: syntagms are sets of percepts in actual contiguity.) Paradigms, in contrast, are concepts related to one another by similarity (as opposed to contiguity). Paradigms are the means by which syntagms are placed in wider domains. Because paradigms are relations of similarity, they are constructed by analogy or metaphor. Models are paradigms. So are words, in a most basic sense, for words are not directly "real," they are symbols. Therefore, when a sense percept is talked about, a word put to it, it is assimilated into a symbolic domain, a paradigm. Like Moliere's bourgeois gentleman, we have been using syntagms and paradigms all along, and we thought we were just talking.

Archaeologists assign percepts to paradigmatic classes whenever they label artifacts and features. Most of us keenly realize the decision-laden character of this operation. The prominence, in archaeological reports, of visual presentations of data, by photographs, drawings, maps, profiles, accords primacy to percepts and their relations of contiguity (context)—-i.e., syntagms. Replication of visual data in publications is the principal means by which archaeologists demonstrate matters of fact (Kehoe 1992). We cannot repeat each other's excavations, but by examining collections and records we can replicate the excavator's observations and the chain of signification from syntagm to conclusive interpretation. "Experience" and "experiment" have the same Latin root, *experientia*. We may disagree over the initial labeling of percepts ("This is not an endscraper, it's a postdepositional chance flake") or over similarity relations (Do the five precincts recognized at Kaminaljuyú signify a conical clan chiefdom? [Kehoe 1982,

117–18]). So long as evidence is retained and available for examination, consensus may be reached, archaeological data can become matters of fact, interpretations can be characterized as well-founded (cf. Laudan 1983; Kelley and Hanen 1988).

Labeling

Umberto Eco (1979, 7) makes the interesting point that "If something cannot be used to tell a lie, conversely it cannot be used to tell the truth: it cannot in fact be used 'to tell' at all." Speaking as a linguist, he emphasizes (1979, 16) that signification exists only in social context, consequent upon the establishment of a social convention. Natural languages are, in Lotman's term, "primary modelling systems" (Lotman et al. 1975), not straightforward coding from object to label. Archaeologists' language is overwhelmingly natural language, wonderfully rich but teasingly ambiguous. Common-sense interpretation is locked into its natural language; if it seems unambiguous, that is because auditor/readers do not contest the primary modeling system. It is scientists' business to be skeptical of the modeling system uncritically accepted by ordinary users of a natural language.

When Berger and Luckmann (1966) wrote of the "social construction of reality," they emphasized the role of social convention in the transformation of observations into facts. Scientific communities profess, and teach, "principles which . . . every man of common understanding readily assents to." As it inculcates a scientific community's primary modeling system, whether in a natural or mathematical language, professional training may subvert science's avowed ideal of a hypertrophied critical faculty. Where pragmatic realism engages the researcher in struggle with a material world tacitly accepted as existing, common-sense realism orients the researcher only to the consensual community. A scientific stance should subject language to a critical deconstruction that will disengage the syntagm existing in the material world from the theory-laden terminology commonly applied to it.

Labeling data place them into conceptual categories that may heavily weight interpretation. A telling example is the label "projectile point." Our preceptors taught us, by ostension (Barnes 1982, 27), to categorize under this label bifacial stone artifacts with acute-angled distal ends and proximal ends prepared for hafting. "Knives" have largely been a residual category

of stone bifaces with wider-angled distal ends and/or lacking basal prepa-
ration for hafting. Even so careful a researcher as Dincauze restricted the
term "knives" to a subcategory of "casual flake tools . . . compar[able] to
similar unstandardized tools" (Dincauze 1976, 68–69), a procedure that left
the ratio of "projectile points" to "knives" at 4:1 (106), which seems odd
for a fishing station. The majority of bifacially flaked stone artifacts illustrated in American archaeological reports are labeled "projectile points,"
in spite of having been discovered in what are agreed to be domestic
contexts—habitation sites. The morphological criterion of symmetry
along the longitudinal axis, which should be critical if a projectile is to be
thrown at a target, was largely ignored although as easily observed as base
and tip shape. It is difficult to explain the ubiquity of the label "projectile
point" in prehistoric archaeology except through the dominance of the
Enlightenment paradigm of the Savage as Hunter (Kehoe 1990, 25–26).
There can be few clearer illustrations of the power of what Kuhn (1970,
24–25, 37) terms "normal science" than the generations of archaeologists
pigeonholing artifacts into "projectile point types."

Explicating the criteria for decisions at each step of the chain of signification exposes the paradigms—models or paradigmatic sets—that have
been invoked, always to the exclusion of other paradigms. Explication is
likely to suggest empirical tests to confirm, or disconfirm, the validity of
the labeling choice. In the example of projectile point versus knife, the
edge-wear criterion, supported by experiment, is itself an empirical test of
validity. Our generations-old social convention of applying the label "projectile point" on the basis of two morphological criteria, unsupported by
experiment, is no better than Common-Sense Realism, and that is obsolete.

Concluding Discussion

Does stringent explication of chains of signification from syntagm to paradigm, with discussion of labeling decisions as alternate working hypotheses and attention to the potential for empirical testing of each decision's
validity, give us access to the real past? Stuart Piggott (1965, 5), quoting
Carr, charged that the notion "is a preposterous fallacy." The alternative is
not despair but a fundamentally scientific methodology, a commitment
to a rigorous logic. The probabilism that, for some, passes for scientific
methodology (Gibbon 1989, 115; Kelley and Hanen 1988, 195, 199, 303–9)

is simply inadequate for the range of phenomena encompassed in archaeological research.

Pasts-as-known are sets of maps drawn by many cartographers, each bringing particular talents, skills, and predilections to the enterprise. A striking example of two cartographers' contrasting predilections is provided in Schoenwetter's (1990, 106) analysis of the disagreement between him and Flannery over Guila Naquitz data. Practicing archaeologists are markedly eclectic in welcoming additional sciences to collaborate, expecting to simultaneously use the several maps that will be produced. Schoenwetter illustrates the hidden pitfall in failing to explicate the guiding assumptions (Laudan, Laudan, and Donovan 1988, 9–10) directing various workers' chains of signification.

American archaeologists, as Americans, are heir to Common-Sense Realism and to Positivistic Progress (Trigger 1989, 100; Restivo 1989), the cultural tradition that culminated in the immortal slogan of the 1933 Chicago Exposition, "Science Finds—Industry Applies—Man Conforms" (Goldman 1989, 294). The former philosophy, with its essentially democratic principle of the accessibility of knowledge, allows each researcher to construct a past-as-known and postulates a readily achieved consensus on the validity of maps; the latter premises a constantly improved map. Postmodern criticism and its spin-off, post-processual archaeology, valiantly attacked the easy rejection of epistemology inherent in positivist science. It remains to build a more reflective methodology: I have found a version of Ardener's "New Anthropology" useful and robust.

Ambiguity and indeterminacy are inherent in the sense perceptions from which we form our data. There is no etic classificatory system out there to be discovered, only the many primary modeling systems that are the languages of human communities including scientific communities (Latour 1987, 208–10). There are no infallible or incorrigible methodologies in science, as science is understood today. Archaeology's peculiarly impoverished data base, which further suffers appallingly inevitable and irrevocable destruction during recovery, demands that our syntagms, the sets of percepts in actual contiguity, be recorded as fully and directly as techniques permit, so that they remain available as demonstrations. Every labeling act performed upon the syntagmatic data base is a relational statement; every relational statement lies within a paradigm. Validity of interpretation depends upon explicating the chain of signification from syntagm to paradigm, permitting readers to judge the basis for each decision on similarity relations.

Common understanding is not appropriate for science. Elaboration of techniques must be matched by critical attention to the cognitive process through which discovery becomes data, and these, matters of fact.

Acknowledgments

I am grateful to the late Edwin Ardener (Oxford), Michael McNulty, S.J. (Department of Philosophy, Marquette), and Arthur Donovan (Visiting Fellow, Institute for Advanced Studies in the Humanities, Edinburgh) for discussions clarifying issues I had wrestled with. Earlier versions of this paper were presented at the Conference on Structuralism and Symbolism in Archaeology, Cambridge, April 1980, where I appreciated encouragement from Alison Wylie and Susan Kus, and at the 49th annual meeting, Society for American Archaeology, April 1984.

REFERENCES

Agassi, J. 1981. *Science and Society*. Dordrecht: D. Reidel.

Ardener, E. 1971. "The New Anthropology and Its Critics." *Man* 6: 449–67.

Barnes, B. 1982. *T. S. Kuhn and Social Science*. New York: Columbia University Press.

Berger, P. L. and T. Luckmann. 1966. *The Social Construction of Reality*. Garden City NY: Doubleday.

Boorstin, D. J. 1978. *The Republic of Technology*. New York: Harper and Row.

Bozeman, T. D. 1977. *Protestants in an Age of Science*. Chapel Hill: University of North Carolina Press.

Braverman, H. 1974. *Labor and Monopoly Capital*. New York: Monthly Review Press.

Cahen, D. and L. H. Keeley. 1980. "Not Less than Two, Not More than Three." *World Archaeology* 12 (2): 166–80.

Collingwood, R. G. 1956. *The Idea of History*. New York: Oxford University Press.

Collins, H. B. 1985. *Changing Order*. Newbury Park CA: Sage.

Dincauze, D. F. 1976. *The Neville Site*. Cambridge: Peabody Museum Monographs No. 4.

Dunnell, R. C. 1971. *Systematics in Prehistory*. New York: Free Press.

———. 1982. "Science, Social Science, and Common Sense: the Agonizing Dilemma of Modern Archaeology." *Journal of Anthropological Research* 38 (1): 1–25.

———. 1983. "Aspects of the Spatial Structure of the Mayo Site (15-JO-14), Johnson

County, Kentucky." In *Lulu Linear Punctated: Essays in Honor of George Irving Quimby*, edited by R. C. Dunnell and D. K. Grayson, 109–65. Ann Arbor: Museum of Anthropology, University of Michigan, Anthropological Paper no. 72.

———. 1985. "Methodological Issues in Contemporary Americanist Archaeology." PSA 1984 (2): 717–44. East Lansing MI: Philosophy of Science Association.

Dupree, A. H. 1972. "The Measuring Behavior of Americans." In *Nineteenth-Century American Science*, edited G. Daniels, 22–37. Evanston: Northwestern University Press.

Eco, U. 1979. *A Theory of Semiotics*. Bloomington: Indiana University Press.

Gibbon, G. 1989. *Explanation in Archaeology*. Oxford: Basil Blackwell.

Goldman, S. L., ed. 1989. *Science, Technology and Human Progress*. Bethlehem PA: Lehigh University Press.

Hanson, N. R. 1971. *Observation and Explanation: A Guide to Philosophy of Science*. New York: Harper and Row.

Hesse, M. 1980. *Revolutions and Reconstructions in the Philosophy of Science*. Bloomington: Indiana University Press.

Hinsley, C. M., Jr. 1981. *Savages and Scientists*. Washington DC: Smithsonian Institution Press.

Hjelmslev, L. [1943] 1961. *Prolegomena to a Theory of Language*. Translated by F. J. Whitfield. Madison: University of Wisconsin Press.

Jacob, M. C. 1976. *The Newtonians and the English Revolution*. Ithaca: Cornell University Press.

Kehoe, A. B. 1982. "Evolution, Cultural Evolutionism, and Human Societies." *Canadian Journal of Anthropology* 3 (1): 113–21.

———. 1990. "Points and Lines." In *Powers of Observation: Alternate Views in Archeology*, edited by S. M. Nelson and A. B. Kehoe, 23–37. Washington DC: Archeological Papers of the American Anthropological Association No. 2.

———. 1992. "The Paradigmatic Vision of Archaeology: Archaeology as a Bourgeois Science." In *Rediscovering Our Past: Essays in the History of American Archaeology*, edited by J. Reyman. Glasgow: Worldwide Archaeology.

Kehoe, A. B. and T. F. Kehoe. 1979. *Solstice-Aligned Boulder Configurations in Saskatchewan*. Ottawa: Canadian Ethnology Service Paper No. 48, Mercury Series, National Museum of Man.

Kelley, J. H. and M. Hanen. 1988. *Archaeology and the Methodology of Science*. Albuquerque: University of New Mexico Press.

Knorr-Cetina, K. D. 1981. *The Manufacture of Knowledge*. Oxford: Pergamon.

Kuhn, T. S. 1970. *The Structure of Scientific Revolutions*. 2nd ed. Chicago: University of Chicago Press.

Lakoff, G. 1987. *Women, Fire, and Dangerous Things*. Chicago: University of Chicago Press.

Latour, B. 1987. *Science in Action.* Milton Keynes: Open University Press.

———. 1990. "Postmodern? No, Simply Amodern! Steps Toward an Anthropology of Science." *Studies in the History and Philosophy of Science* 21 (1): 145–71.

Laudan, L. 1981. *Science and Hypothesis.* Dordrecht: D. Reidel.

———. 1983. "The Demise of the Demarcation Problem." *Working Papers,* Virginia Tech Center for the Study of Science in Society 2 (1): 7–35.

Laudan, R., L. Laudan, and A. Donovan. 1988. *Scrutinizing Science.* Dordrecht: Kluwer.

Lotman, Ju. M., B. A. Uspenskij, V. V. Ivanov, V. N. Toporov, and A. M. Pjatigorskij. 1975. "Theses on the Semiotic Study of Cultures (as Applied to Slavic Texts)." In *The Tell-Tale Sign,* edited by T. A. Sebeok, 57–83. Lisse: Peter de Ridder Press.

Noble, D. F. 1977. *America By Design.* New York: Alfred A. Knopf.

Oakeshott, M. B. 1933. *Experience and its Modes.* Cambridge: Cambridge University Press.

Piggott, S. 1965. *Ancient Europe.* Chicago: Aldine.

———. 1981. "Summary and Conclusions." In *Towards a History of Archaeology,* edited by G. Daniel, 186–89. London: Thames and Hudson.

Pickering, A. 1989. "Living in the Material World." In *The Uses of Experiment,* edited by D. Gooding, T. Pinch, and S. Schaffer, 275–97. Cambridge: Cambridge University Press.

Putnam, H. 1981. "Philosophers and Human Understanding." In *Scientific Explanations,* edited by A. F. Heath, 99–120. Oxford: Clarendon Press.

Restivo, S. 1989. "In the Clutches of Daedalus: Science, Society, and Progress." In *Science, Technology and Human Progress,* edited by S. L. Goldman, 145–76. Bethlehem PA: Lehigh University Press.

Rosenberg, C. E. 1976. *No Other Gods.* Baltimore: Johns Hopkins University Press.

Salmon, M. H. and W. C. Salmon. 1979. "Alternative Models of Scientific Explanation." *American Anthropologist* 81 (1): 61–74.

Schávelzon, D. 1983. "La Primera Excavación Arqueológica de América." *Anales de Antropología* XX (I): 121–34.

Schiffer, M. B. 1976. *Behavioral Archeology.* New York: Academic Press.

Schoenwetter, J. 1990. "Lessons from an Alternate View." In *Powers of Observation: Alternate Views in Archeology,* edited by S. M. Nelson and A. B. Kehoe, 103–12. Washington DC: Archeological Papers of the American Anthropological Association No. 2.

Shapin, S. and S. Schaffer. 1985. *Leviathan and the Air-Pump.* Princeton: Princeton University Press.

Watson, P. J. 1986. "Archaeological Interpretation." In *American Archaeology Past and Future,* edited by D. J. Meltzer, D. D. Fowler, and J. A. Sabloff, 439–57. Washington DC: Smithsonian Institution Press.

Watson, P. J., S. A. LeBlanc, and C. L. Redman. 1971. *Explanation in Archaeology: An Explicitly Scientific Approach.* New York: Columbia University Press.

———. 1984. *Archeological Explanation: The Scientific Method in Archeology.* New York: Columbia University Press.

Willey, G. R. and J. A. Sabloff. 1980. *A History of American Archaeology.* 2nd ed. San Francisco: W. H. Freeman.

Woolgar, S. 1988. *Science: The Very Idea.* Chichester: Ellis Horwood.

Ziman, J. 1978. *Reliable Knowledge.* Cambridge: Cambridge University Press.

2. Excluded from History
The Albertans Who Really "Opened the West"

Archaeology makes History, as Collingwood insisted in my quote in "Constructing History" (Chapter 1): not one Enlightenment-assumed universal history, but many. No matter how grounded we are in fieldwalking and testing, we necessarily are clued in also by what we are told and read about an area. Researching François's House, the 1768–1773 fur trade post in eastern Saskatchewan (Kehoe 1978, 2000), I became very aware of large lacunae in Canadian history—independent traders ("pedlars"), First Nations persons, and women. Not only were hundreds of significant figures ignored, their work might be attributed to heroic white men such as David Thompson (who made his heroic passage to the Pacific, mirroring Lewis and Clark, accompanied by his Métis wife Charlotte and their children). When my Calgary friend Donald B. Smith invited me to present a lecture to the University of Calgary's history department, I enjoyed speaking about significant excluded people. Don himself wrote biographies of three men strangely involved with Canadian First Nations and of nineteenth-century Ontario Native leaders who dealt with the British government. In his book *Seen But Not Seen*, he also wrote rich essays about "influential Canadians" dealing with Indian policy—figures more or less blind to the men and women they meant to help (Smith 2021).

"Excluded from History," following here, is the lecture I gave in 2001 in Calgary, unrevised because I want to awaken realization that not only when but also where historical research is presented will influence what is included and what is excluded. My audience in the University of Calgary knew Sarah Carter as their colleague sitting in the audience, the Sweet Grass Hills southeast of Calgary as their environment, and the Okanagan Valley southwest as where Nkwala maintained a trading post. None of these would have been mentioned if I were speaking to a U.S. Midwestern audience. Worlds within worlds, not only local histories, but also national and global histories, fit within frames. They are like theater pieces: the audience expects a frame and expects to ignore what isn't lighted. Lighted or not, people and action were on those stages.

A postscript to the paper is that Jaco Finlay founded Spokane House as a Nor-wester and then Hudson's Bay Company post in 1810 and lived there with his family until he died in 1828. He was buried under one of its bastions, by special permission of the company, verified by archaeology in 1951 (https://www.historylink.org/File/8409). The archaeological report mentions that the student crew member who excavated the grave was named Ray Carlson; Ray? Might it have been *Roy?* Roy Carlson, who became a professor at University of British Columbia, worked for years in Northwest archaeology with his wife Maureen as his assistant, and father of archaeologist Catherine Carlson? I asked Catherine, long a friend and colleague, and yes, it was Roy who unearthed Jaco. Small world of archaeology.

Excluded from History
The Albertans Who Really "Opened the West"

When in 1807 David Thompson crossed the Rockies over Howse Pass to begin his exploration of the Columbia, he followed a trail literally blazed by a North West Company employee named Jaco Finlay. Jaco—Jacques Raphael Finlay—had built a post on Kootenai Plain, near the headwaters of the Saskatchewan, in 1806. From this staging ground, he and his Indian friends not only prepared Thompson's route, but kindly left a canoe on the B.C. side for Thompson to use in traveling down the tributary to the main river. Does Jaco Finlay, prairie-born Métis son of a Montreal trader, get the credit for pioneering the crossing of the Rockies?

When David Thompson searched for routes feasible for packhorses, he was obliged to stay north of Piegan territory, because on July 27, 1806, Captain Meriwether Lewis had needlessly killed a young Piegan man at a camp on the Two Medicine River. The Piegan thereafter, understandably, would not tolerate any more white explorers in their lands. Now, the reason Captain Lewis and three of his men were in Blackfoot territory in the first place was because they had been ordered by Thomas Jefferson to utilize a map showing in considerable detail the Missouri Basin from the Mandan towns in central North Dakota, west to the mountains, the intermontane valleys, and the Snake River to its end, merged with the Columbia at the Pacific coast. North to south, this map runs from the Cypress Hills into Wyoming. Who drew this map? Ac ko mok ki [Akai Mokti], Old Swan, principal chief of the Blackfoot. He drew maps during two winter visits in 1801 and 1802 to Peter Fidler's post at the mouth of the Red Deer. Fidler annotated the maps according to Ac ko mok ki's information, sent them to the Hudson's Bay Company headquarters in London, they were incorporated in the professional cartographer Arrowsmith's map quickly published, obtained by Jefferson, and given to Lewis and Clark to follow. Thus Old Swan "opened the West" to American imperialism and, as a result of Lewis committing murder in Piegan territory, diverted northward the Canadian trade and the nation it built. Every Alberta schoolchild should know the name of this prominent Alberta leader of the early 1800s. Do they?

Europeans on the margins of modern empires were excluded from Canadian histories until very recently. One of the funniest stories in archaeology is that of Red Bay, Labrador. National Museum of Man archaeologists Bob McGhee and Jim Tuck carried out an intensive foot survey of the southern Labrador coast, recording many Indian sites. Afterward, an English historian working in the archives of Bilbao in Spain wrote the archaeologists, inquiring on the location of the Basque whaling station used in the 1540s. She pointed out that tons of broken Mediterranean red roof tiles had been shipped over as ballast, then used to cover the sheds on the Labrador shore where whales had been rendered into oil. McGhee and Tuck realized they had crunched this red tile scrap underfoot at Red Bay without recognizing how very odd it is to see tons of Mediterranean clay tiles in a Labrador village. Thanks to the English researcher, the Basque component in Canadian maritime history is retrieved.

A few historians, Laurier Turgeon of Laval is one, see evidence that Basques may have sailed on trading voyages to Canada as early as the 1380s, a full century before Columbus. We now accept that even earlier, Norse attempted settlement at the tip of Newfoundland at L'Anse aux Meadows. Until the National Geographic Society sponsored Anne Ingstad's excavations at the site, initially identified through her husband Helge's evaluations of sailing descriptions, chronicles of American trips and colonization in Icelandic sagas were dismissed as myth. National Geographic publicity overcame scholars' reluctance to admit evidence of Norse west of Green-land; scholars had not seriously considered how the Greenlanders got the timbers they used to build their houses and churches. Parks Canada are happy to use L'Anse aux Meadows and Red Bay to draw tourists to the depressed northern Maritimes, so now Norse and Basque are squarely in Canadian history.

That one short-lived village at the tip of Newfoundland, and limited trips in what are now Labrador and Nunavut, is all the standard histories allow the Norse. A large stone found in northwestern Minnesota in 1898, inscribed with 62 rune letters, is labeled a hoax. In 1910, three highly-regarded geologists reported that the runes appeared weathered, not recent; their testimony was disregarded. Last year [2000], the stone was examined by scanning microscope in a petrographic laboratory, apparently confirming the 1910 opinion. At the same time, a Danish-speaking avocational linguist presented detailed argument concerning alleged errors in the runes and language on the stone: he found European manuscripts attesting use of variant runes and dialect Norse conforming to that on the stone. My opinion is that the stone probably is valid, inscribed as a memorial to murdered members of a Norse expedition traveling in 1362 up the St. Lawrence, through the Great Lakes, and beyond, or south from York Factory on Hudson's Bay, to seek furs. A critical point is that in 1360, the German Hanseatic League imposed a stranglehold on Scandinavia, cutting its kingdoms off from the lucrative Russian fur trade. Setting the date and text of the Kensington Runestone in context of Scandinavian history, which includes Norse in the Maritimes and Eastern Arctic for already three and a half centuries, seems to me to weigh probability in favor of authenticity. This would mean Norse were following the long trade routes developed by First Nations and later used by the Canadian fur trade, from Montreal through Sault Ste. Marie and Lake Superior, or down from Hudson's Bay, to the interior West, Manitoba, and Minnesota. Iroquois who appear at the very forefront of the documented fur trade, here with David Grant in 1794, and themselves settling in Alberta and just south in the Flathead Valley early in the nineteenth century, knew the route. Possibly it was Iroquois who left the pair of late-prehistoric Mississippian shell masks in that rockshelter in the Sweet Grass Hills—the location fits an Iroquois creation legend. Cultural changes in Manitoba and Minnesota in Indian sites during the late fourteenth and the fifteenth centuries suggest intensification of trade and warfare in the region. Perhaps the Norse and the Iroquois should no longer be excluded from Prairie prehistory.

Not only First Nations people, Métis, and marginal Europeans have customarily been excluded: many of you will recognize the name of Sir Daniel Wilson, first president of the University of Toronto. Few realize it was Daniel Wilson, long before he reluctantly accepted a knighthood, who assembled the principles and methods of scientific archaeology, introducing the word "prehistory" into the English language in 1851. Wilson came from a lower-middle-class Scottish family; his father and uncle ran a liquor shop on Leith Walk, frequented by sailors. Too poor to matriculate at university, Wilson worked at the Society of Antiquaries of Scotland with Robert Chambers, a publisher and avocational geologist, to re-order the society's collections on the model of pioneering Danish professional archaeology. Settled in Toronto to teach at the new University College, Wilson researched American antiquities and traveled with Ojibwe on Lake Superior, culminating in an 1862 book, *Prehistoric Man*. Wilson's substantial work on prehistoric archaeology was co-opted and plagiarized by the wealthy English politician Sir John Lubbock, Baronet, FOD (Friend of Darwin) and leader, like his daddy before him, of the Royal Society and the British Association for the Advancement of Science. It matters that Wilson's work was ignored and Lubbock's secondhand stuff enshrined, because Wilson argued for recognition of the abilities and accomplishments of First Nations, while Lubbock was a racist calling American Indians "savages." Lubbock's prejudices, both class and racial, buried Wilson's enlightened descriptions; it is Lubbock's ideas that inform Justice McEachern's disastrous judgment in *Delgamuukw*, just ten years ago (see Chapter 9).

Acknowledging the contributions of those excluded from conventional histories is more than politically correct, more than affirming diverse peoples' self-esteem. Acknowledging those who have been excluded is necessary to understand the treaties that by law govern the conduct of Canada and the First Nations within her dominion. We need to understand Old Swan's West, where the Backbone of the World was fronted and crossed by well-known roads, the valleys inhabited by recognized nations cultivating indigenous food plants and managing livestock on the hoof. Jaco Finlay was born into this West, not a servant to white men but a family man carrying on his hereditary business of trading. We need to understand Anglo-Canadians insisting that plow agriculture "precedes all civilization; with it is connected rest, peace and domestic happiness, of which the wandering savage [read "Indian"] knows nothing"—a quote Sarah Carter found, from a deputy superintendent general of Indian affairs (Hayter Reed) during the 1890s.

Sarah's deputy superintendent cited the book *Bible Teachings in Nature.* The real source for Anglo policy, in both Canada and the United States, was an extraordinary spin doctor named John Locke. Locke earned his living in the political entourage of England's Earl of Shaftesbury, tutoring the Earl's grandson and accepting such benefices as the post of secretary to the Board of Trade of Great Britain, in 1689, and, later, secretary to the proprietors of the Carolina Colony. During his Board of Trade tenure, when his patron's maneuvers had landed their party in power with William of Orange, Locke published his *Two Treatises on Government,* declaring, "in the beginning all the World was *America*," "wild woods and uncultivated waste." Locke equated plow agriculture with civilization, claiming that property is created through labor value, as men invest in clearing and cultivating land: "As much land as a man tills, plants, improves, cultivates, and can use the product of, so much is his Property."

According to Locke, transforming common land into private property is of great general benefit:

> He who appropriates land to himself by his labour, does not lessen but increase the common stock of mankind. For the provisions serving to support human life, produced by one acre of inclosed and cultivated land, are (to speak much within compasse) ten times more, than those, which are yielded by an acre of land, of an equal richnesse, lyeing waste in common. And therefore he, that incloses land and has a greater plenty of the conveniences of life from ten acres, thus he could have from a hundred left to nature, may truly be said, to give ninety acres to mankind. (quoted in Williams 1990, 248)

Note that Locke shot two unhappy birds with this stone, justifying both British landlords' enclosure of what had been peasant commons, and European takeovers of American lands. Somehow, this marvelously glib, self-serving politician's hack is celebrated as a philosopher.

Locke's thesis is directly repeated by Chief Justice McEachern in his *Reasons for Judgment* in Delgamuukw, referring to "a vast country in which there are none but erratic nations . . . in establishing the obligation to cultivate the earth, . . . these nations cannot exclusively appropriate to themselves more land than they . . . are able to settle and cultivate." Back in 1926, anthropologist Bronislaw Malinowski described how political power is legitimated by myths about past conditions. Disregarding not only Gitksan and Wet'suwet'en oral histories and contemporary anthropologists' accounts, the Justice ignored a century of landmark ethnographic studies from Franz Boas through Claude Lévi-Strauss, studies such as Lévi-Strauss' 1982 monograph arguing that Gitksan and other Tsimshian societies were organized much like the noble houses of medieval France: highly territorial, anything but "erratic." Locke's myth chartering British expropriation of First Nations' lands led to a catch-22 argument for Indian removal. The governor of the state of Georgia, during the efforts to legitimate expulsion of the First Nations, explained to his legislative assembly that treaties honored Indian title only so long as the Indians hunted: "Fixed habits of agriculture . . . violated the treaties"! Benjamin Franklin had remarked, "So convenient a thing it is to be a reasonable creature, since it enables one to find or to make a reason for everything one has a mind to do."

Excluded from history have been not only prominent indigenous people, Métis, and sons—and of course daughters—of the lower classes; excluded also have been significant economic data. John Moore, an anthropologist, estimates that the production of buffalo robes in the Missouri Valley alone during the nineteenth century contributed fifty million dollars into the U.S. economy, channeled through a few trading companies, notably that of John Jacob Astor. The Canadian fur trade was provisioned by Indian, and later also Métis, hunters, some working directly for a post, others selling processed pemmican by the bag. The costs to the posts are difficult to assess: providers were sometimes paid in kind, sometimes by extension of credit, and sometimes a standard price augmented by "gifts," to circumvent management dictates from London or Montreal. Bruce Alden Cox examined Harold Innis's classic work on the fur trade in Canada and found apparent anomalies in tables prepared from Innis's data. Cox resolved the anomalies by taking account of the Indians' pursuit of their own economic interests. Given the basic purpose of the Bay and the Nor'Westers, to make money out of transactions, employees and Indian customers alike were likely to be short-changed. Nkwala, an Okanagan leader, agreed in about 1812 to maintain an independent post over the winter, including receiving furs; for his months of work, Nkwala was paid ten guns and ammunition. Sir George Simpson, in 1823, called "the Plains tribes" "insolent and independent" when they insisted he compensate them fairly for their labor.

After the bison herds were exterminated in the early 1880s, Indians were compelled to accept reserves. Sarah Carter, of this history department, documented the systematic undermining of Indian agricultural enterprise by the Department of Indian Affairs (and south of the line, similarly by the U.S. Bureau of Indian Affairs). John Moore emphasizes that concomitant with the crippling restrictions placed on Indian farming was a need for cheap seasonal labor by the white farmers who homesteaded what had been Indian land, or leased what remained on the reserves. Indians became a reserve labor pool for so-called family farms and also for agribusiness such as the sugar beet industry. By excluding the economic value of small-scale subsistence farming, hunting, fishing, and manufacture and sale of so-called handicrafts such as axe handles and potato-harvest baskets, official economic statistics hide the real contributions of Indian labor: Indian subsistence pursuits subsidized the labor costs of extractive industries and agriculture, enabling these to post profits. If seasonal Indian labor had been paid a living wage, account ledgers would have looked quite dismal.

Bureaucratic structure segregates the welfare economy fostered by the Indian Act from larger regional economics. Non-Indians in towns near reserves have profited for over a century by providing professional and commercial services to reserve dwellers hamstrung by Department of Indian Affairs regulations and restricted access to investment capital. Non-Indians leasing reserve land generally have paid less than would be demanded for private land, not to mention illegal encroachment upon reserves—one of my archaeological projects was on a ranch the operator's grandfather had taken from the band assigned to it, and when in the 1970s the band went to court to retrieve their property, the operator connived with a Regina lawyer to appeal the case at every level up to the Supreme Court, meanwhile running his cattle without paying either rent or property taxes. I can still see the line of fat yearling steers, thousands of dollars on the hoof, that came each evening to our camp to watch me brush my teeth. Between shady dealings and legitimate enterprises benefiting from quasi-captive clienteles on reserves, a not-insignificant portion of the Canadian economy prospers from the peculiar conditions imposed on status Indians—a factor usually excluded from economic history.

Western Canada lacks stupendous monumental architecture like that built by Hopewell and Mississippian societies in Midwestern United States—for example, at Cahokia, occupying what is now St. Louis, are pyramids surpassed only by Mexico's two largest in Teotihuacán and Cholula, and at Newark, Ohio, is a perfect geometric octagon plus circle embankments, so huge an entire golf course with country club is now inside the octagon. Canadian prairies do have innumerable ruins such as tipi rings accumulating over at least twelve thousand years of occupations, and some sites testify to sophisticated knowledge. The Majorville Cairn here is a landmark of spiritual significance recognized for several thousand years. Gordon and Phyllis Freeman, of this university, argue on the basis of field measurements that it is the center of extensive stone alignments recording celestial observations. Moose Mountain, in southeastern Saskatchewan, is a more compact boulder construction, two thousand years old, pinpointing summer solstice sunrise and the risings at that season of the bright stars Sirius, Aldebaran, Capella, and Fomalhaut. A number of other boulder constructions incorporate alignments for determining solstice and correlated risings of Sirius or Capella. At Minton in south-central Saskatchewan is a turtle figure with solstice, Sirius, and Capella alignments: the turtle enclosing these reminds us of the Siouan image of the earth as a giant turtle. At Writing-on-Stone, I noticed a panel with pecked circles representing the Big Dipper and an adjacent constellation identified for me by George Kicking Woman, of the Southern Pikuni (Blackfeet) Nation, as the Winter Path, indication of the coming of the cold winter. A circle below the Big Dipper may represent the North Star.

First Nations' scientific knowledge, based on repeated painstaking observations, has been slighted to the extent that when I interviewed Indian people about Moose Mountain, I was told how Cree bands designated someone to keep a daily calendar tally based on beginning the year at summer solstice. This custom enabled bands to rendezvous at predetermined times, but the custom is not recorded in the standard ethnographies. No one asked about knowledge that was assumed, a priori, to be beyond the understanding of aborigines. Most people today realize that indigenous plant remedies are often efficacious. In rural municipalities, white as well as Indian people may seek medicine from First Nations herb doctors. Maureen Lux's recent book on the appalling postconquest medical conditions on Alberta and Saskatchewan reserves details the government policy of rendering the bands destitute to force them into peasant farming, supposedly that first step on the road to civilization. Many quotes Lux presents from First Nations leaders makes clear their correct understanding of the factors responsible for health or disease. Here again, the imperialist myth of less-evolved, weak, or backward "races" was invoked to legitimate, in this case, criminal cruelty approaching that of the Nazis. Would that we could exclude these passages of the "opening of the West" from history! To be fair, there were Victorians, for example Herbert Spencer, advocating similar policies of letting the poor in Britain die out, attributing their stunted bodies and diseases also to racial inferiority. Among the myths distorting history was the contention that rational scientific research validated such genocidal policies.

British historian J. H. Plumb said, a few years ago, that "True history [is] destructive, for by its very nature it dissolves those . . . deceiving visions [derived from] created ideology." Considering some of the historical situations buried in those heroic, deceiving visions of the "opening of the West," conventional history looks like alchemy, transforming base metals into allegedly golden "progress." Our perspective now opens the West in a different way, broadening our vision to encompass much more of humanity. Daniel Wilson quoted an essay by Thomas Carlyle celebrating Walter Scott's historical novels: "To teach all men this truth, which looks like a truism, and yet was as good as unknown to writers of history and others, till so taught—that the bygone ages of the world were actually filled by living men."

RESOURCES FOR TOPICS DISCUSSED IN TEXT

Jaco Finlay: [Posted Note #1] Bond 1970:60–63; Giraud 1986:348; Morton 1939; Thompson 1971:237, 242, 289.

Ac ko mok ki: Dempsey 1985; Moodie and Kaye 1977; Ruggles 1991:63–64; Binnema

Norse, Kehoe 2000; Basques, Barkham 1978

Iroquois, Nicks and Morgan 1985.

Daniel Wilson: Kehoe 1998.

Carter 1990 quote, p. 15; Locke quotes, Williams 1990:248.; McEachern quote, p. 80 (Culhane 1998:239); Boas, e.g., 1970[1916], Lévi-Strauss 1982; Governor of Georgia quote in Weinberg 1935:87, Franklin quote p. 86.

Economics: Carstens 1991, Carter 1990, 1999, Cox 1993, Dyck 1991:101, Hedley 1993, Lux 2001, Moore 1996, Ray 1974 (quote from Simpson, page 207).

Plumb (1970:11–17) quoted in Molho and Wood 1998:16.

Wilson 1851:xi, quoting *Carlyle's Miscellanies*, 2nd ed., vol. V:301

REFERENCES

Barkham, Selma. 1978. "The Basques: Filling a Gap in Our History Between Jacques Cartier and Champlain." *Canadian Geographical Journal* 96 (1): 8–19.

Binnema, Theodore. 1996. "Old Swan, Big Man, and the Siksika Bands, 1794–1815." *Canadian Historical Review* 77:1–32.

———. 2001. "How Does a Map Mean?" In *From Rupert's Land to Canada*, edited by Theodore Binnema, Gerhard J. Ens, and R. C. Macleod, 201–24. Edmonton: University of Alberta Press.

———. 2001. *Common and Contested Ground: A Human and Environmental History of the Northwestern Plains*. Norman: University of Oklahoma Press.

Boas, Franz. [1916] 1970. *Tsimshian Mythology*. New York: Johnston Reprint.

Bond, Rowland. 1970. *The Original Northwester David Thompson*. Nine Mile Falls WA: Spokane House Enterprises.

Carstens, Peter. 1991. *The Queen's People: A Study of Hegemony, Coercion, and Accommodation among the Okanagan of Canada*. Toronto: University of Toronto Press.

Carter, Sarah. 1990. *Lost Harvests: Prairie Indian Reserve Farmers and Government Policy*. Montreal: McGill-Queen's University Press.

———. 1999. *Aboriginal People and Colonizers of Western Canada to 1900*. Toronto: University of Toronto Press.

Cox, Bruce Alden. 1993. "Natives and the Development of Mercantile Capitalism: A New Look at 'Opposition' in the Eighteenth-Century Fur Trade." In *The Political Economy of North American Indians*, edited by John H. Moore, 87–93. Norman: University of Oklahoma Press.

Culhane, Dara. 1998. *The Pleasure of the Crown: Anthropology, Law and First Nations*. Burnaby BC: Talon.

Dempsey, Hugh A. 1985. A-CA-OO-MAH-CA-YE (Ac ko mok ki, Ak ko mock ki, A'kow-muk-ai, known as Feathers and Old Swan). *Dictionary of Canadian Biography*, volume VIII, 1851 to 1860, 3–4. Toronto: University of Toronto Press.

Dickason, Olive Patricia. 1992. *Canada's First Nations*. Norman: University of Oklahoma Press.

Dyck, Noel. 1991. *What is the Indian "Problem:" Tutelage and Resistance in Canadian Indian Administration*. St. John's: Institute of Social and Economic Research, Memorial University of Newfoundland.

Giraud, Marcel. 1986. *The Métis in the Canadian West*. Translated by George Woodcock. Lincoln: University of Nebraska Press.

Hedley, Max J. 1993. "Autonomy and Constraint: The Household Economy on a Southern Ontario Reserve." In *The Political Economy of North American Indians*, edited by John H. Moore, 184–213. Norman: University of Oklahoma Press.

Kehoe, Alice Beck. 1971. "Small Boats Upon the North Atlantic." In *Man Across the Sea*, edited by C. Riley, et al., 275–92. Austin: University of Texas Press.

———. 1981. "Revisionist Anthropology: Aboriginal North America." *Current Anthropology* 22 (5): 503–17.

———. 1993. "How the Ancient Peigans Lived." *Research in Economic Anthropology* 14, edited by Barry Isaac, 87–105. Greenwich CT: JAI Press.

———. 1998. *The Land of Prehistory: A Critical History of American Archaeology*. New York: Routledge.

Kehoe, Alice Beck, and Barry Hanson. 2000. "The Kensington Runestone Reexamined." Paper presented at the annual meeting of the Midwest/Plains Conference, St. Paul MN, November 10, 2000.

Klein, Kerwin Lee. 1997. *Frontiers of Historical Imagination: Narrating the European Conquest of Native America, 1890–1990*. Berkeley: University of California Press.

Lévi-Strauss, Claude. 1982. *The Way of the Masks*. Translated by Sylvia Modelski. Seattle: University of Washington Press.

Lux, Maureen K. 2001. *Medicine That Walks: Disease, Medicine, and Canadian Plains Native People, 1880–1940*. Toronto: University of Toronto Press.

Molho, Anthony and Gordon S. Wood, eds. 1998. "Introduction." In *Imagined Histories: American Historians Interpret the Past*, 3–20. Princeton: Princeton University Press.

Moore, John H. 1996. "Cheyenne Work in the History of U.S. Capitalism." In *Native Americans and Wage Labor*, edited by Alice Littlefield and Martha C. Knack, 122–43. Norman: University of Oklahoma Press.

Morton, Arthur S. 1939. *A History of the Canadian West to 1870–71*. London: Thomas Nelson and Sons.

Moodie, D. W. and Barry Kaye. 1977. "The Ac Ko Mok Ki Map." *The Beaver* Outfit 307 (4): 5–15.

Nicks, Trudy and Kenneth Morgan. 1985. "Grande Cache: The Historic Development of an Indigenous Alberta Métis Population." In *The New Peoples: Being and Becoming Métis in North America*, 163–81. Winnipeg: University of Manitoba Press.

Ray, Arthur J. 1974. *Indians in the Fur Trade: Their Role as Hunters, Trappers and Middlemen in the Lands Southwest of Hudson Bay, 1660–1870*. Toronto: University of Toronto Press.

Ruggles, Richard I. 1991. *A Country So Interesting*. Montreal: McGill-Queen's University Press.

Thompson, David. 1971. *Travels in Western North America, 1784–1812*. Edited by Victor G. Hopwood. Toronto: Macmillan of Canada.

Warhus, Mark. 1997. *Another America: Native American Maps and the History of Our Land*. New York: St. Martin's Press.

Weinberg, Albert K. 1935. *Manifest Destiny*. Baltimore: Johns Hopkins Press.

Williams, Robert A. 1990. *The American Indian in Western Legal Thought*. New York: Oxford University Press.

Wilson, Daniel. 1851. *The Archaeology and Prehistoric Annals of Scotland*. Edinburgh: Shetland and Knox.

3. Revisionist Anthropology
Aboriginal North America

Often, a paper is published, even in a leading journal such as the international *Current Anthropology*, without making much impact. This paper of mine is an example. Google Scholar shows it has had twenty-five citations, of which nine are by colleagues who know me. So far as I can find, they didn't use my scheme of cultural areas, or of the poleis, or revived Nuclear America. William Folan told me years ago that he was using my culture areas in his teaching, something that doesn't get in Google Scholar's citations lists.

The paper begins by establishing my standpoint critiquing standard formulations of North American First Nations, cogently labeled "the cant of conquest" by Fritz (Francis) Jennings, an ethnohistorian. In the next section, I align with the then-popular (1970s to 1980s) viewpoint of ecological determinism, without following the usual extrapolation of animal models for human food gathering. Instead, I emphasize techniques for increasing food production, ultimately adapted to ecological constraints as well as potential. Maize was America's greatest invention, the grain that cannot reproduce without human intervention, the food source that could only spread person-to-person. Our anthropological forebears recognized and labeled Nuclear America, the vast expanse across the Americas where maize was the subsistence base. Anticipating what would later be labeled the historicist approach in archaeology, this section argues for more recognition of stratified societies in North America, proposing Aristotle's concept of the *polis* (plural, *poleis*) for perhaps most of them. Both these, stratification and *poleis*, came from my experiences with First Nations in Saskatchewan and with Blackfoot: I saw that these communities recognized leading families who trained their children to be leaders, and related to this, I could perceive in historical and ethnographic descriptions that the annual rendezvous activated economic, political, judicial, and social customs constituting them as *poleis*. A *polis* does not require a stone wall;

at the Plains rendezvous, armed soldiers rode watch. Decades later, I read how the Caddo had been described in this way (Barr 2017).

Rereading this paper now makes me cringe at how crudely I squeezed in the work and thought I had put into my textbook *North American Indians*. Most of that book was researched and written during my sabbatical year, 1979, when an unexpected invitation came to write a text for anthropology courses on North American Indians, usually taught in anthropology departments at that time. Having school-aged children to care for, I could not travel for extended fieldwork or archival research, whereas an overview textbook was feasible, given university libraries in Milwaukee and my years of preparations for teaching the course. I proposed to write an ethnohistory of North America from its earliest populations to the present, 1980. All four professors who reviewed the book proposal declared it was radical, definitely not what they taught, those vignettes of each culture area drawn from mostly late nineteenth-century ethnographies. Right, said I, and high time now to teach the histories of our continent as histories—the standpoint of the then-new American Society for Ethnohistory. The publisher's editor agreed to, as he put it, "take a gamble" on my proposal. The textbook was favorably reviewed *as ethnohistory* in the *American Anthropologist*, sold well, and went into three editions, the last one published in 2006. Subsequent textbooks for that market followed my scheme. That, I believe, has been a real contribution toward rejecting colonialist presumptions.

Current Anthropology's commentators clearly were struggling, like me, to rebuild the discipline's approach to its traditional prime research field, the populations native to North America. The federal Indian Claims Commission's hearings were the arena where anthropology-trained historians such as Florence Shipek, one of the commentators for my paper (and a friend), presented detailed archival documentation combined with ethnographic fieldwork. That radically crossed disciplinary boundaries: PhD historians, such as George Stocking, Jr., told us anthropologists, including me, that we were not trained in historiography and should not attempt to breach the canon. Within anthropology, some felt compelled to testify out of concern for field collaborators or simply from a sense of justice; others felt compelled to uphold governmental actions that had built the United

States of America. Both sides amassed more data than most had expected to obtain. Having come together in testifying, realizing the multifarious field the Claims Commission had created, ethnohistory became Ethnohistory.

During the 1970s, ecology and biological evolution as explanation of observed human behavior—or should I say, of *men's* behavior, Man the Hunter—were argued to be more scientific than the "soft" practice of ethnography. Other primates could be objectively observed (unless you were a woman: Jane Goodall or Dian Fossey). They were the new primitives, fitting colonial powers' descriptions of American Natives as gatherers who did not labor, had no religion nor writing (see comment by Joan Chandler mentioning writing as essential to a *polis*). Primatology as it expanded from the 1960s proved primates are hardly simplistic, some of the animal behavior studies proved to be too narrow even for the species studied, and Man the Hunter had to admit Woman the Gatherer. In effect, the 1960s promise of fundamental understanding of humankind through simplistic ecological premises had failed by 1980.

Ecology is the basis for Kroeber's *Cultural and Natural Areas of Native North America* (1939), generally not taken seriously as the ecological study it is. Carl Sauer was Kroeber's university neighbor, working and teaching in geography, but postwar ecology had sought to look more scientific by modeling plant and animal behavior, rather than working within Sauer's historical geography (see Chapter 4). Julian Steward, a student of both Kroeber and Sauer, created a *Theory of Culture Change* in 1955, throwing the gauntlet to other anthropologists. I recall being quite excited as I read it then. My 1981 paper comes out of that, of Kroeber's *Cultural and Natural Areas*, my field experiences, and my efforts, in writing *North American Indians*, to consistently frame its chapters as history. The paper certainly is confused, yet I will stick to the importance of recognizing Nuclear America, the maize-growing polities, as one vast culture area physically linked as one person passed on kernels and the art of raising maize to another person. And I consider Aristotle's delineation of the functions of the *polis* to be an insightful analysis of the essential characteristics of human communities.

In short, I still urge archaeologists and other anthropologists to use as tools, these postulates:

- The Americas are marked by one central cultural-natural area that was termed Nuclear America up to about 1950, which remains a meaningful framework.
- Human societies, at least those of *Homo sapiens sapiens*, manage communities through these functions (delineated by Aristotle as those of the *polis*):

1. it has recognized rights to territory from which subsistence may be drawn,
2. its members engage in food production (not necessarily agriculture),
3. its members engage in arts and crafts production,
4. it uses arms, to maintain internal order and to protect against foreign aggression,
5. it sponsors public worship, and
6. "most vitally necessary, is a method of deciding what is demanded by the public interest and what is just in men's private dealings" (Aristotle 1946, 299).

The polis can entertain foreign visitors, traders, and workers, so long as their numbers do not overwhelm the citizens (Aristotle 1946, 292). See also my "Chiefdoms" paper, Chapter 7, for using *polis* for Blackfoot latent structure.

When it comes to the cant of conquest, the discipline is now "woke" to it. Not so the general public, even some of the most highly educated jurists; see Chapter 9.

Revisionist Anthropology
Aboriginal North America

Prologue

Slowly there has crept into the social sciences the realization that these disciplines, no less than religions or political philosophies, embody axioms and values which are built into ideologies. To claim that one's opinions are value-free, based upon purely objective data, is to express the ideology of

empirical positivism. Anthropology as a whole, and archaeology in particular, have lagged behind sister disciplines in becoming conscious of their
ideological biases (notable exceptions are Asad 1973; Fried 1975; Huizer
and Mannheim 1979; Hymes 1969; Polgar 1975; Tax, e.g., 1975; Trigger 1978,
1980). The time is ripe for revisionist anthropology, and an examination
of aboriginal North America can be a fruitful exercise in this mode.

Revisionism can proceed on two planes. On an obvious level is what
Jennings (1975) labels "the cant of conquest," propaganda serving the
political-economic interests of, in North America, Europeans and later
Euramericans invading aborigines' land. The cant of conquest includes
both the conscious construction of self-serving doctrine that Jennings
emphasizes and the subtler myth-making from European philosophies
described by Sheehan (1973, 1980). On a far deeper level, insidious and
pervasive, are the biases produced by the fundamental structures of languages and cultural traditions, structures inculcated so early in life that
they appear natural and inevitable. Anthropologists have talked about the
"Sapir-Whorf hypothesis" for decades with precious little effort to apply
it to their own discourse. Underlying much anthropological and archaeological analysis can be discerned both the kind of structuring that Dumézil (1968) discusses and also more particular problems in categorization
in which scholastic or colloquial conventions are naively incorporated.
Foucault (1970, 378–80) has claimed that "ethnology" has the potential
to explore the nature of humans and of societies back to their epistemological bases, in contradistinction to other sciences, which only elaborate
received epistemes, but this potential has so far been poorly realized. I
shall briefly examine some aspects of our episteme for the ethnology of
aboriginal North America and then suggest a revisionist conceptualization.

Structuring Principles in the European Tradition

Dumézil, in *Mythe et épopée* and many other works, dissects histories,
legends, tales, and societal organizations of the Indo-European peoples to
reveal two powerful structuring principles. One of these is the tripartite
schema, typified in Caesar's "Gallia est omnis divisa in partes tres." The
classically educated minds of the Enlightenment were fond of tripartite
schemata, for example, the three-branch system of government for the
United States and Adam Smith's arrangement of economic activities into

three sectors. The Indo-European tradition conceived the ideal society to be constructed of three essentially equally valuable segments: juridical-religious power (wisdom), secular authority, and material production. The Greek myth of Paris and the golden apple shows the conceptualization clearly, Athena, Hera, and Aphrodite representing the three segments and any preference shown to one over the others unleashing disaster. In addition to the tripartite predilection, Dumézil sees in the European tradition a principle of oppositional dualism derived from the Semitic tradition. Associated with the Bible, oppositional dualism tends to be applied especially to religious and moral thinking, while tripartite schemata are more often applied to secular matters (this contrast between sacred and profane itself, of course, being a product of Semitic dualism). During the eighteenth century, when the distinction between religious and secular became more clearly recognized, Hegel's brilliance was able to fuse the two structuring principles as the dialectic.

Within anthropology and archaeology, the structuring principles of the European tradition are frequently manifest. The Three Ages, whether Thomsen's of 1819 or the familiar Paleo-, Meso-, and Neolithic and its derivative Paleo-, Meso-, and Neo-Indian, blatantly illustrate the a priori Indo-European tripartite convention. It is true that any dividing of the past must be arbitrary and heuristic, but that the past, on two great continents, and Caesar's Gaul should always exhibit three parts seems to prove Dumézil's thesis more than it reflects any inherent properties of time or of Gaul. Semitic oppositional dualism is reflected in the dichotomy between primitive and civilized (or non- or preliterate/literate, or hunter-gatherer/food-producer) and in rural/urban, kin-based/ territorial, traditional/progressive, farmer/pastoralist, and the host of similar contrasting pairs that are logical but never fit well any real-life situation. Whether, as Lévi-Strauss supposes, the human mind operates, as do computers, in binary fashion or not, the premise that concepts and societies are so structured ought to be examined rather than assumed as a primitive postulate.

The Cant of Conquest

The European invasions of America commencing in the sixteenth century were a significant component of the scientific and philosophical revolutions leading to the modern world. Accretions of geographical knowledge beginning in the fifteenth century slowly forced a rejection of medieval cosmography (O'Gorman 1961). There was honest questioning of the status of the apparent hominids inhabiting the new lands and, following the consensus that they were indeed human, eager realization that observations of them might prove or disprove competing theories of human nature and social good. As Sheehan (1973, 102) summarizes, Europeans' descriptions of American Indians embodied "the paradox of realistic experience set in the mold of mythic expression." Contrary to Foucault's vision, ethnology worked from Procrustean European epistemes, stretching here, lopping off there to make the subjects fit the beds prepared.

Marshalling a substantial compendium of both primary sources and historical analyses, Sheehan (1980) argues that the dominant European view of American Indians has been based on an extrapolation of the concept of an earthly paradise. Both Biblical and Hellenistic, the notion of an earthly paradise was widely discussed in the sixteenth and seventeenth centuries. The characteristics of paradise were defined through opposition to those of familiar European societies: subsistence was gained without toil, there was no competition for resources or even women, gold was a cheap ornament, people went naked in shameless innocence, and government, laws, officials, military, writing, science, philosophy, and formal art were all absent. The savage, noble or brutish, was a *negative* construct, a creature *without* the need for toil or knowledge, one that lay passively in the garden as a *thing* of nature. The European, expecting to find the earthly paradise in this other hemisphere (since it certainly wasn't in Europe or the Levant), recognized it in the absence of familiar architecture, agriculture, clothing, and symbols of rank. Observations to the contrary were then muted. The Englishman Gabriel Archer, for example, recounting his voyage up the James River in Virginia in 1607, stated that, for the natives, "neither is there scarce that we call meum et tuum among them" but soon after noted that "kinges know their owne territoryes, & the people their severall gardens" (quoted in Sheehan 1980, 23).

Berkhofer (1978) agrees with Sheehan that European and subsequent Euramerican views of the aboriginal inhabitants of America and their descendants are first and foremost European projections. Tracing images of the American Indian beyond Sheehan's focus on the first century of contact, Berkhofer points to late-eighteenth-century French and especially Scottish philosophers' efforts to fit analyses of human nature into the increasingly impressive framework of observational science. The natural experiment that could be seen in the distribution of peoples around the world urged the comparison of peoples to discover natural law, just as Linnaean natural-history collection comparisons were revealing basic principles and types of organisms and laboratory experiments were fixing the properties of inorganic substances. This perspective could perpetuate earlier stereotypes, as is evidenced in William Robertson's influential 1777 *History of America*: "In America, man appears under the rudest form in which we can conceive him to subsist. . . . The greater part of its inhabitants were stranger to industry and labour, ignorant of arts, and almost unacquainted with property, enjoying in common the blessings which flowed spontaneously from the bounty of nature" (quoted in Berkhofer 1978, 48). Clearly, the key word in Robertson's text is *conceive*. The conceptualization of American Indians as the type specimen of primitive humans continued unabated in the nineteenth century, supported by the adherence of social scientists of the period to a model of science embodied in comparative anatomy (Ackerknecht 1954). Lorimer (1978) suggests that the linked spread of industrialism and democracy in Western nations during this century replaced an earlier evaluation of strangers based on European social-class criteria with a true racism that would ignore gentlemanly attributes. Thus the initial European postulate that American Indians lacked the characteristics of civilization because they had always lived in another ("new") world that had to be the earthly paradise, became in the eighteenth century a postulate that American Indians were a specimen of noncivilized humans such as reason demanded must exist and then in the nineteenth century a postulate that they were examples of aborted evolution. Berkhofer concludes that Boasian anthropology finally countered the long-prevailing European (-Euramerican) concept of the American Indian as a negative, passive entity, but he notes that the oppositional construct of the Noble Savage continues to have such power in Europeanist thought that it has resurged in John Collier's apprehension of American Indians and again in the 1960s counterculture movement (Berkhofer 1978, 108, 178–85).

As proper intellectual historians, Sheehan and Berkhofer do not castigate the writers whose biases they reveal. Jennings (1975) looks more sternly upon the seventeenth-century New England colonists who benefitted from, in his opinion, sometimes deliberate manipulation of records. Convinced that they were God's chosen people, these Puritans saw themselves the proper occupiers of New England, against whom the Indians must not prevail. In an appendix, Jennings compares European and American history to bring out similarities between Europe in the millennium after the disintegration of the Roman empire and post-Columbian America. In both areas, semiautonomous nobles claimed and then attempted to conquer by force lands already inhabited by farmers. Justification was often sought in an affirmation of the racial (ethnic) and/or religious superiority of the ambitious lord and his following—Norman over Saxon, English over French (reverberating in Shakespeare's lines), Protestant over Catholic or vice versa. Jennings then selects the English conquest of Ireland as a precedent for the Puritan conquest of New England. Irish resistance to England's sovereignty called up application of the term "savage" to the unhappy natives opposing alien takeover. The parallel between English denigration of the Irish and Puritan denigration of American Indians supports Jennings's contention that the Puritans' description of events involving Indians was the cant of conquest.

Although Jennings restricts the focus of his work to seventeenth-century New England, its implications are broader. His "feudal-expansion" model can be applied across the continent and carries with it the feature that the term "savage" denotes inhabitants resisting conquest. To borrow a phrase from the Vietnam War, the Irish and then the Indians were "gooks." In the Judaeo-Christian-Islamic tradition, wars require moral justification, with God's favor claimed by the victors; the losers should be gooks, savages who lack the signs of God's chosen. Semitic oppositional dualism seizes upon every contrast between the conquerors and the gooks and labels the gooks inferior. European invaders came from states with formal governments, they practiced plough agriculture, they valued cities, they recognized ordained priesthoods, professions, literati, social classes. The gooks would be assumed to lack these attributes of the Chosen People. Where a dispassionate observer would see in North America alternative modes of government, resource production, religious congregations, etc., European colonists ethnocentrically denied the authenticity of alternative modes and created a continent of savages. The frontier image of the gook was reinforced, rather than challenged, by the philosophers and scientists distant from the fray, for although the savants had less to gain materially, they derived intellectual satisfaction from reports conforming to their predictions.

The strength of the Europeanist tradition is demonstrated by the persistence of its postulates even in present-day anthropology and archaeology. Berkhofer (1978, 67) cites Leacock and Lurie's 1971 *North American Indians in Historical Perspective* as the first general study to break with the standard Europeanist image of the Indian. With few exceptions, American anthropological works continue uncritically to embed the Europeanist oppositional dualism of primitive and civilized ("advanced," "complex," "literate," "state," depending upon one's professional interests or sensitivity to racism). Anthropologists tend, further, to accept the traditional European collocation of "primitive" with kin-based, nonagricultural, nonstratified, nonliterate, nonscientific, having shamans rather than priests and lacking professions, commerce, or industry. As did sixteenth- and seventeenth-century explorers' reports, anthropological works tend to mute or disregard observations that would call into question such collocation. Where a simple oppositional dualism is felt to be too reductionist, recourse tends to be made to tripartite schemata, e.g., Morgan's (1964) triply threefold set of Lower, Middle, and Upper Savagery, Barbarism, and Civilization or Service's (1971) Egalitarian, Hierarchical, and Civilization. These stages are seen not as alternatives, but as sequent. Oppositional dualism remains, implicit, in the assumption that European and Euramerican societies have traversed the sequence from primitive egalitarian savagery to civilization. The nineteenth-century premise that there are modern societies that are fossilized examples of earlier and primitive stages of a universal human evolutionary progress has not been wholly expunged from modern anthropology, as a semiotic analysis can manifest. Nor has nineteenth-century racism ceased to taint American anthropology and archaeology (Trigger 1978, 1980).

Nearly all anthropologists and archaeologists would repudiate the cant of conquest. We accept each human as a being of inherent dignity, sharing with us a biological nature and active, *sapiens* intelligence. The task that confronts us is to reexamine the observations that have been recorded of non-Western peoples, consciously controlling, insofar as our own enculturations can be overcome, the biases of our models. There is no possibility that any of us can produce a truly value-free, objective description, but we can reject terminology that we recognize to embody principles we believe unjust.

Aboriginal North America

For me, the only tenable framework for an ordering of observations of aboriginal North America is one derived from modern evolutionary biology. American Indians are, like the rest of us, organisms whose actual and potential behaviors are, in the final analysis, governed by genetic factors. The very considerable (from our perspective) latitude in human behaviors is channeled for any one person by environmental features, natural and societal. Because *Homo sapiens* is a highly gregarious animal, it is valid for anthropologists to study societies rather than individuals and to speak of societies as adapting. My framework for viewing aboriginal North America is the principle that American Indians, like humans elsewhere in the second millennium AD, had developed sets of reasonably successful adaptations to regional environments. Each society was as evolved as any other, each in its ecological niche. Apparent resemblances between any second-millennium-AD society and what has been deduced for Pleistocene or early Holocene human societies ought to be very critically tested rather than readily accepted.

Reassessing North American Indian prehistory and ethnology with these strictures in mind, I have concluded that except in the high latitudes and perhaps in what Kroeber termed the "cultural sink" of the South Texas desert, American Indians at the time of the European invasions were living in stratified societies and manipulating subsistence resources to increase harvests beyond what their environments would have produced without such active management. Under the environmental constraints of the high latitudes, Indians do not seem to have formed class-stratified societies and seem to have adapted by developing sophisticated harvesting technologies but not means to increase the harvested populations. Comparative analyses—for purposes of inducing generalizations on *H. sapiens* behavior, generalizations which may be useful for archaeological reconstructions as well as for contemporary planning and the formulation of broad theoretical postulates—seem to me to be facilitated by conceptualizing aboriginal North America as comprising two basic ecological zones, the food-producing tropical and temperate zone and the non-food-producing north. The former zone is, I believe, usefully divisible into the eastern sector, in which Mexican domesticates (maize, amaranth, squash, beans) were produced, and the western sector, in which native plants were cultivated in preference to Mexican domesticates.

In this discussion I use the term "food production" to mean techniques that increase the harvest of preferred resources beyond their natural abundance. These techniques include regular firings of grassland or camas meadow, transplantation of roots, tubers, or bulbs, irrigation, weeding, and hoe cultivation of undomesticated plants. By "stratified societies" I mean internally and externally recognized communities or groups of communities in which certain families are acknowledged by the community to occupy a superior status carrying with it the right to power and privileges absent from commoner status. These societies should be considered to be in some degree "urbanized"; we lack a really appropriate term, though perhaps Aristotle's concept of the *polis* comes reasonably close: an association of households and villages under properly constituted authority, the association making possible a fuller development of human capabilities than can occur in small independent bands. Aristotle argued that the association of humans in a *polis* is a species-specific trait, likely to eventuate where not hindered.

In one of the first informed surveys of the prehistory of North America, Thomas (1898) suggested that the watershed between the Atlantic and Pacific drainages forms a culturally significant division between two major sectors of the continent, with the Arctic a third sector. Thomas's ordering of his data no doubt represents the effect of structuring principles as well as of insight, and his placing of Mexico in the Pacific division (on the basis of circum-Pacific traits discussed recently by Birket-Smith [1967, 1971]) is ill-advised, but a good argument can be made for a fundamental distinction between the zone in which food production is possible and that in which it is not, at least in quantities and reliability sufficient to maintain a dependent human population. Within the food-producing zone, a further distinction can be made between the regions in which cultigens of Mexican origin were major staples and those in which these domesticates never became major staples; this division is not nearly as significant as that between the tropical-temperate food-production latitudes and the high latitudes. I shall term the Mexican-cultigens sector the *continental core*, the western food-producing sector lacking these as staples the *Pacific drainage*, and the northern sector the *high latitudes*. My purpose in proposing this classification scheme is not to promote the aesthetic gratification of a tripartite frame superimposed on oppositional dualism, but to emphasize certain characteristics of aboriginal North American societies that have been obscured by the conventional Europeanist paradigm of a primitive America.

Continental Core

The continental core comprises Mexico and the lands east of the Cordillera but including the American Southwest and extending north through the Laurentian-Lakes region. The core at the time of historic contact relied on the indigenous Mexican cultigens maize, amaranth, squash, and beans, supplemented by deer and lesser game, fish, waterfowl, and various local resources. Nearly all the core societies were stratified (exceptions would be the small bands of the Texas desert and the recently immigrant Apacheans in the Southwest). All the aboriginal American cities occur in the core, the majority in Mexico but some in the United States, the most northerly being Cahokia in the central Mississippi Valley. The presence of maize, beans, and squash proves contacts within the core, although the diffusion of these plants unquestionably involved several routes and different time periods and does not in itself indicate any regular or long-continued economic intercourse throughout the core.

Presumably the early migrants into North America were hunter-gatherers in small, flexibly recruited groups. By the Terminal Pleistocene, about 12,000 BCE, some migrants may have represented Eurasian peoples that had developed the intensive symbiosis with selected resources argued by Higgs and Jarman (1969), a symbiosis in which domestication could have been taking place (see also Bahn 1978). Thus, some deliberate manipulation, or active management, of selected food resources may have been within the cultural patterns carried into North America and may have been practiced in conjunction with intensive harvesting of preferred resources.

Direct evidence for Early Holocene food production in America comes from Oaxaca, where, in a level radiocarbon-dated to about 7000 BCE, squash, beans, and maize-type pollen were discovered. None of these plants is indigenous to the locality, so the most plausible interpretation of the data is that they were planted and cultivated (Schoenwetter 1974). This trinity of cultigens, plus, probably, grain amaranths, gradually diffused during the ensuing millennia throughout North America east of the 100th meridian to the limits of maize in the Great Lakes region and St. Lawrence Valley; the trinity also diffused into the Colorado drainage to the northwest of Mexico. Progress of these cultigens into the temperate regions depended upon the development of new varieties, particularly of maize, capable of maturing under conditions inimical to the early cultigens. By the Thermal Maximum, third millennium BCE, the tropical cultigens were being grown in the American Southwest and the southern Midwest (Chomko and Crawford 1978; Kay, King, and Robinson 1980). Maize was not widely grown in the northernmost zone (northern United States), however, until after about AD 700, when the variety Northern Flint appeared. To what extent techniques of cultivation were diffused with the cultigens or independently invented is difficult to judge, but the more parsimonious explanation is that such common practices as swiddening, ditching and irrigation, hoe cultivation, and ridged fields accompanied the spread of the plants toward which the techniques were directed. Diffusion *before* the cultigens of techniques that could be employed to increase harvests of indigenous plants is also likely. An overview suggests that in America, as elsewhere, there developed during the Terminal Pleistocene and Early Holocene an intensification of human symbiosis with selected food resources as adaptation to regional environments; that aspects of this symbiosis included technologies to increase harvests, to allow storage, to extend land available for food production, and to make labor more effective; that techniques and cultigens diffused, not necessarily always together; and that as resource bases altered there were shifts in societal economies, settlement patterns, and ideologies. This powerful symbiosis was well established throughout Mexico and the American Southeast by the early second millennium BCE.

Allied with the planting and cultivation of crops in North America was the management of pasturage. In contrast to the Eurasian livestock management familiar to European observers, American Indian stock management did not usually involve bringing herd animals under direct and constant human control. Indians did not, in North America, replace the natural herd leaders of large stock with human herders, nor did they fodder herds. Instead, their techniques were based on maintaining optimum grass or browse over large areas suitably placed for hunting from settlements or for drives. Annual firing was the principal means for achieving the goal. Harvesting techniques shrewdly capitalized upon species behaviors to bring meat into traps, nets, and pounds. The American techniques for producing animal food were cost-effective, yielding relatively large quantities of meat in return for limited labor inputs, in contrast with the constantly labor-intensive Eurasian modes of stock management. In Eurasia, methods similar to the American were generally restricted to deer parks maintained by aristocracies. The major differences between Eurasian subsistence economies' livestock techniques and those of American Indians derive from the animal products obtained, which in Eurasia include traction, milk, and blood from living stock as well as meat and hides, while in America only meat, hides, and bones were sought and the daily control of living animals was unnecessary.

Active management of resources supported sedentism in America as elsewhere. By the second millennium BCE in Mexico, by the end of that millennium at Poverty Point in the lower Mississippi Valley, and by the end of the first millennium BCE throughout most of the American Midwest and Papaguería in the American Southwest, relatively large populations— thousands of persons—were organized around population centers where the functions of an urban economy were carried out. These functions are (1) extractive (Adam Smith's primary sector), including agriculture and fisheries; (2) transformative (Smith's secondary sector), including mining, manufacturing, and construction; (3) distributive, including commerce and transportation; (4) regulative, including governmental, medical, legal, and priestly activities; and (5) personal, including domestic and recreational activities (Functions 3 through 5 constitute Smith's tertiary sector) (modified from Browning 1978 and Mamalakis 1972). The centering of these functions and their elaboration into offices, roles, and statuses was frequently, but not invariably, marked by monumental structures. These organized populations frequently, but by no means invariably, lived permanently in contiguity. In America it was not unusual for the populations of polities to gather only for a limited period annually to perform the functions (3–5) that generally (following Smith) are labeled "urban." Thus the Maya, with their "ceremonial centers" and markets, and the Plains Indians, with their annual tribal rendezvous of several thousand persons, were polities, civilized in the Aristotelian sense of the *polis*. Aboriginal American forms of the polity, like aboriginal American agriculture and livestock management, sometimes but not in all cases coincided with European expressions of these culminations of human adaptation. American Indian food production tended to work through modification and extension of the preferred ecosystems, rather than through massive destruction of an indigenous ecosystem and its replacement by an artifact ecosystem as was general in historic Europe. American Indian polities could perform urban functions with only intermittent coresidence of citizens and did not confuse the city as a physical entity with the *polis* as a social-political-economic construct.

From AD 900 to the European invasions, American Indian societies displayed what are best termed their protohistoric cultural patterns. In each region, people had mastered the extractive, transformative, and social techniques observed by the invaders of the sixteenth through nineteenth century. The entire continental core, except perhaps for South Texas, was populated by communities that performed, at least to some recognizable degree, urban functions. Nearly all the core societies were stratified. All participated in wide trade networks—even the inhabitants of the Texas cultural sink (Kelley 1955). European *philosophes* were eager to find support for their theories in a virginal New World. The history of Europeanist conceptions of the peoples of the American continental core is an impressive demonstration of the force of hypothesis over observation.

Pacific Drainage

The lands west of the Cordillera, except in Mexico, from Baja California through British Columbia, and including the intermontane troughs, comprise the Pacific drainage sector. Peoples of this sector have often been cited as textbook examples of hunter-gatherers, but there is ample evidence for their active management of food resources to the point of food production. Bean is perhaps best known for arguing this position (Bean and Saubel 1972; Bean and King 1974; Bean and Blackburn 1976), although Steward (1933) had introduced the data for Owens Valley Paiute and Shipek (1977) has contributed significant ethnographic data for southernmost California. Gibson's (1978a, 1978b) recently published material on northernmost Northwest Coast food production extends the implications of Suttles's (1951) work on the Coast Salish, calling for a reevaluation of food resource management in this culture area. A revisionist view of Pacific-drainage food production fits Spencer's (1966, 170–71) discussion of swiddening on the Asian side of the Pacific, where he came to "the recognition of shifting cultivation as an early, broad and general system of crop growing, perhaps referable to the Neolithic, within which each sub-pattern constitutes an effort to match elements of culture to particular attributes of a physical environment that is ecologically different from any other environment."

Preference for the cultivation of indigenous plants rather than the Mexican cultigens maize, beans, squash, and amaranth marked off the Pacific-drainage peoples from those of the continental core. Californian and Basin peoples sowed native grains (Wissler's [1922] "wild seeds") in valley bottoms prepared by firing; they also transplanted and cultivated roots, tubers, and bulbs and planted groves of nut trees and, in southern California, fruiting cactuses. Shipek reports that in southern California maize was planted, especially in upland valleys, if the preferred crop of native grain seemed likely to fail from drought or other problems early in its growing season. Deer parks were maintained by firing along the lower valley slopes in California. In the Plateau and Northwest Coast, tubers were the principal carbohydrate staple, with camas prairies maintained by firing on the higher elevations and wapato harvested at lower ones. It seems quite possible that the true potato, which is larger, substituted for the wapato, often called "wild potato," after Europeans introduced the potato after 1820 (Gibson 1978b, 370). By 1845, Tlingit had developed commercial agriculture to the point of selling 246,450 pounds of potatoes to the Russians at New Archangel (Sitka) (Gibson 1978a, 55). Meat production was also commercialized, the Tlingit selling 903 head of sheep (presumably Dall's mountain sheep) and 138,096 pounds of halibut to New Archangel in 1851 (Gibson 1978a, 55). These figures refer to a period one to two generations after Russian attempts to exploit Tlingit territory began but a full generation before Boas's visits to the Northwest Coast; they suggest that food production on the Northwest Coast has been masked by Europeanist assumptions that agriculture involves dependence upon wholly domesticated, and usually nonindigenous, plants. It may be, also, that since cultivation and harvesting of plants were tasks of women and slaves this aspect of Northwest Coast culture was muted in the standard ethnographies.

Complex societal structures also characterized Pacific-drainage peoples, with class stratification and development of Smith's tertiary-sector functions clearly evidenced close to the ocean and weaker, but not lacking, in most of the Plateau and Basin. Again, Bean has brought together material on the social classes and the commerce, which in central California included the use of money, for the Californians. Spier and Sapir's (1930, 226) publication of observations of the Wishram town at The Dalles of the Columbia River describes what sounds like a Las Vegas, with three thousand persons trading and gambling and the Wishram hosts selling dried pounded salmon, wapato, and other staples prepackaged in standard-sized bags. Both in California and on the Northwest Coast, offices, roles, and statuses were formal and permanent, the various functions within the tertiary sector explicitly differentiated. For most of the Pacific drainage, populations were physically centered in residential contiguity only intermittently, for festivals during which the various "urban" functions were performed. In the remainder of the year, in the southern portion, or in the summer in the north, these functions were latent or performed on a minor scale while, as was common in so many regions of North America, the people resided in hamlets or camps. The antiquity of these polities is difficult to determine when their physical manifestation was ephemeral, but archaeological evidence for the establishment of protohistoric settlement and resource utilization patterns suggests that they may well date from the mid-first millennium BCE in California and the mid-first millennium AD in the Northwest.

High Latitudes

The high-latitudes zone comprises the boreal forests, the tundra barrens, and the Arctic coasts of North America. Because slow retreat of the glaciers left much of this area uninhabitable until roughly the Thermal Maximum, parts of it underwent initial human colonization as late as the third millennium BCE. These colonists' cultural pattern seems in general outline to resemble that of the Terminal Pleistocene reindeer symbiosts. Throughout the high latitudes in America, economies were based on a combination of caribou, the hides of which were essential for winter clothing, and one or more other protein source, frequently fish. Poor drainage in this relatively recently unglaciated zone hampered burning and development of grass pasturage or deer browse in many regions, so this animal-management technique for increasing food production was not widely practiced. Plant manipulation was similarly impeded by the environment, a critical factor being the brevity of the frost-free summer. In place of active management of resource populations, the high-latitudes peoples adapted by perfecting a variety of techniques to increase harvests of the natural populations. Drives and pounds were utilized, along with an ingenious diversity of snares, traps, and nets, to increase the frequency of kills per human, the devices functioning as mechanical surrogate hunters multiplying the presence of the human at game trails. Many of the hunting and fishing techniques were used in the temperate latitudes, too, but the peak of technological finesse was in the north.

Forced to live high on the food chain, humans in the high latitudes kept population densities low. Even the summer congregations at fecund fishing stations or coastal markets totaled only hundreds rather than thousands of persons. Societies were not stratified (except by sex and age), and the functions of Smith's tertiary sector were generally undeveloped or performed only informally and sporadically. Camps of a few related nuclear families seem to have been the basic organization of the high-latitude peoples, brought together in summer by desire for recreation and need to agree upon allocation of territories for the winter months (Bishop 1974, 289–96). The latter has historically included a consciousness of the advisability of avoiding overhunting, leaving a section fallow, as it were, but whether this passive management of resources is aboriginal or reflects Hudson's Bay Company conservation dictates remains debatable. Also debated is the primary social structure of high-latitude peoples. Helm has argued for years against "the existence of unilineal or unilocal organization of either persuasion" (1980, 271), while Bishop (1977) sees a definite tendency toward matrilocality. The Gordian knot may have been cut by Asch (1980a), demonstrating from his fieldwork at Fort Wrigley that the Mackenzie Dene, and very possibly other boreal-forest groups, are concerned to create the appearance of unilocality by emphasizing those among multiple kin ties that make the men in a residence group kin and the women in that group kin to each other and affines to the men; crosscutting relationships are not spoken of. Helm has emphasized the objective genealogical composition of residence groups, and Bishop and others have included statements of what Asch terms the ideology of these groups.

Trade was established in the high latitudes long before European fur markets directly impinged. Inuit traded with each other and with Chukchi across Bering Strait. Tareumiut Inuit traded with Nunamiut Inuit on the lower reaches of rivers. Northeastern Algonkians traded with the Hurons in the Laurentian-Lakes zone. Trade, for example Tareumiut-Nunamiut or Algonkian-Huron, allowed these high-latitude peoples to specialize in the production of certain regionally abundant resources and thereby increase the efficiency of their subsistence efforts, but the lack of an overarching political structure meant that the societies were at best marginally complex. Lack of consistently demarcated functions and offices is clearly correlated with population densities, the few larger groups, such as the Barrow Inuit of Alaska, exhibiting features such as rank and some specialization within the community. This correlation, and the sophistication of food-harvesting techniques, should put to rest any notion that the high-latitude peoples were in any reasonable sense "primitive."

Conclusions

Attempting to work inductively rather than within an a priori Indo-European tripartite scheme or on the premise of oppositional dualism, I have found that the prehistory of North America can be well and parsimoniously modeled as a set of adaptations of human societies to regional conditions, the set exhibiting trends toward polities with class stratification, occupational specialization, and economies built upon food production. In this, the American Indians paralleled human societies in each of the other continents. As in other continents, the adaptations of American societies were facilitated by the diffusion of techniques and of cultigens within and between regions. The various intelligent, if sometimes diverse and ideologically disparate, modes of adaptation fit the modern understanding of biological evolution, a theoretical framework that has no place for the nineteenth-century notion of "living fossils" representing in the present the bygone stages of an evolutionary sequence.

American Indians, like most of the Old World peoples, developed during the final Pleistocene and the Holocene sophisticated methods of food production. Throughout tropical and eastern temperate North America, which I have here termed the continental core, economies were based on the planting and cultivation of maize, beans, squash, amaranth, sunflowers, and lesser quantities of other plants and the maintenance of deer in deer parks. On the Plains, bison substituted for deer and the prairie turnip for other carbohydrate staples (Reid 1977, 1979). West of the Cordillera, the Pacific-drainage peoples preferred indigenous food plants to the Mexican cultigens but similarly employed a variety of management techniques to increase the harvestable populations of native grains, nuts, cactus fruits, tubers, and deer. These techniques were largely unusable in the high latitudes, so adaptation there focused more narrowly on perfecting technologies of harvest. Because American Indian food production techniques did not, as a rule, resemble the Eurasian techniques based upon massive destruction of the indigenous ecosystem and its replacement by an artifact ecosystem, the suitability and cost-effectiveness of the American techniques were seldom appreciated by European observers.

North American Indian societies tended to differ from European societies also in their settlement patterns. Permanent physical contiguity of urban populations was less common in many, though not all, American regions than periodic congregation of the population at a center where the urban functions (Adam Smith's tertiary sector) were performed, these functions remaining latent or sporadic during most of the year when the members of the population were dispersed into hamlets or nomadic bands. Only in the high latitudes, where the position of humans high on the food chain kept their populations low and requiring large territories, were complex societies generally lacking.

Doctrinaire views of North American Indian societies, particularly in Anglo America, as egalitarian hunter-gatherers or horticulturists unable to control nature seem to stem more from the cant of conquest than from reflective observation. European invaders uncritically assumed that their own cultural patterns were "natural" or "civilized" and alternative modes of life unnatural or savage. Rejection of the validity of alternative cultural patterns served the economic and political interests of many of the colonialists; other Europeans and Euramericans were inclined to accept their propaganda because it conformed to the oppositional dualism of European moral education. Although anthropologists and archaeologists should be highly distrustful of cultural conventions, most do not apply to their own tradition the analyses they have been trained to make of others. The received wisdom of the nineteenth-century social evolutionists remains embedded in anthropological terminology and theories. These have been Procrustean beds into which ethnographic and archaeological data from North America have been thrust. The time is ripe for revisionist anthropology.

Comments

by Michael I. Asch

DEPARTMENT OF ANTHROPOLOGY, UNIVERSITY OF ALBERTA,
EDMONTON, ALBERTA, CANADA T5J 2H4. 12 III 81

Kehoe's comments on the ethnocentric manner in which Westerners have viewed Native Americans are well-taken but perhaps a bit overzealous. One can, albeit with some difficulty, uncover a theme in the writings of the colonial period which is, if not more balanced, at least more realistic in its appreciation of Native American society. Such a view is exemplified in the writings of explorers such as Alexander Henry and Alexander Mackenzie and also, upon occasion, even in reports of British Parliamentary committees such as the 1837 *Report from the Select Committee on Aborigines*. Although not in vogue, it is a theme which can be applied with justice to an interpretation of the work of Locke and Hobbes. To my mind, these were scholars struggling to come to grips with the concept of polity in societies with very unfamiliar forms. That they failed to do so in a way which is acceptable to modern scientific anthropology is irrelevant, for their very struggle is part of the motivation for the invention of our discipline.

Nonetheless, I concur that it is well past time to ensure that the paradigms we anthropologists now use "reject terminology that we recognize to embody principles we believe unjust." The issue is whether a model based on evolutionary biology represents, as Kehoe asserts, "the only tenable framework" for generating the terminological neutrality necessary to enhance objectivity in our observations.

In my opinion, the answer is no. There are definitely other viable frameworks available, ones that may indeed be superior to the ecological-evolutionary approach advanced here. Elsewhere (Asch 1978, 1980b) I have detailed some of my concerns about this approach. One of these is a discomfort with the frequent uncritical acceptance as a first premise that societies can be profitably compared to organisms (a position advocated initially by Hobbes to justify his metaphysics). Another is a concern that the terminology used may convey inappropriate impressions about the nature of Native American society, in particular that of a high degree of similarity between Indian societies with a hunting-gathering mode of subsistence and animal species. For example, to describe Indians as "living high on the food chain" can convey the impression that somehow they are like animals. Thus this terminological orientation may reinforce the very ethnocentric notion of Indian hunter-gatherers as precivilized that use of the model is intended to avoid.

One alternative to this approach focuses on the mode of production (Asch 1978; Bender 1978; Friedman 1975; Legros 1977; Lee 1979). This model is useful in that it hooks ecological and economic data directly to a political-institutional framework and thus allows the reader to see the essentially human link between economy and polity. Another links ecological and economic data with a culturally derived cognitive framework (Alland 1975; Basso 1972; Tanner 1979), thus allowing the reader to focus on the cultural rationality within which decisions about resource management are taken. Kehoe alludes to both approaches; it is unfortunate that she does not choose to develop them.

by Bernard Bernier
DÉPARTMENT D'ANTHROPOLOGIE, UNIVERSITÉ DE MONTREAL, C.P.
6128 SUCCURSALE "A", MONTREAL, QUÉBEC, CANADA H3C 3J7. 26 III 81

It seems to me there are two major inconsistencies in Kehoe's article. First, she rejects bipartite and tripartite classifications as based on "Semitic oppositional dualism" and as never fitting any real-life situation. Yet she uses a bipartite/tripartite classification of North American aboriginal peoples, offering as justification the fact that she does so not for reasons of "aesthetic gratification" but because of the characteristics of the object of study. Furthermore, she uses dichotomies, such as stratified/nonstratified, hunter-gatherers/food-producers, which she has previously rejected. If these types of classifications "never fit well any real-life situation," I fail to see why they should fit the prehistoric situation of North American peoples. If they do, then Kehoe's blanket rejection of bipartite or tripartite classifications is unacceptable (and I think it is). Their usefulness must be judged through application and not as a matter of principle, all the more so because they are not at all peculiar to Western civilization.

Secondly, Kehoe rejects evolutionism, even in its modern form, because it postulates sequent stages; she prefers the analysis of alternative modes of adaptation. Yet she writes that North American aboriginal peoples exhibited a trend toward food production and stratification and that "in this, the American Indians paralleled human societies in each of the other continents." If we are to believe this last sentence, it is not so much to bipartite divisions or to sequent stages that Kehoe objects as seemingly to the characterization of aboriginal peoples as not stratified. Yet in her analysis of the high-latitudes region she writes that "societies were not stratified."

This is somewhat confusing, but it seems that what Kehoe really objects to is the characterization of North American aboriginal peoples as "primitive." Yet in discussing the peoples of the high latitudes, she uses almost all the characteristics she has subsumed under "primitive": they were "forced to live high on the food chain"; they had an undeveloped "tertiary sector"; they were not stratified, except by sex and age; the basic organization was the camp of a few related families; they lacked consistently demarcated functions and offices. The only characteristic that does not fit her definition of "primitive" is the presence of trade. This analysis clearly weakens her argument, for most of the characteristics mentioned (including trade) could, with little modification, probably be applied to hunter-gatherers of the Late Paleolithic or Mesolithic in Europe. What I mean here is not that contemporary hunter-gatherers are totally equivalent to our hunter-gatherer fairly recent ancestors, but that Kehoe's rejection of the use of contemporary societies to understand what are, in human evolutionary terms, fairly recent past societies (I am not talking here of *Homo erectus*) is much too strong. This practice, provided it is careful, should not be utterly condemned, and I think many contemporary anthropologists do use it carefully and with valuable results. There have been and still are abuses, but they should not be taken as an excuse for eliminating what is a very useful analytical tool. What is to be condemned is not the attempt to understand past societies through the careful use of data on contemporary or recently vanished ones, but rather the attachment of moral superiority to political and economic developments which are fairly recent. What is most objectionable to me in nineteenth-century evolutionism is the assumption that all societies go through the same stages and the stage Western society has attained confers on it intellectual and moral superiority. This, I think, is absent from some modern forms of evolutionism, but it seems to me that it is not totally absent from Kehoe's article. Her statement about parallel developments towards stratification seems to imply universal stages defined by the presence or absence of rank. Furthermore, her discussion of the nonprimitive character of the Barrow Inuit, based on the fact that, even though living in the high latitudes, being a larger group they exhibited such features as rank and specialization, seems to imply a definite intellectual if not moral superiority for stratification and specialization. Implicit is the fact that they—as well as their neighbors who did not exhibit these features but are saved by the fact that the Barrow Inuit did—would be primitive if they had not. Implicit also is the assumption that prehistoric *sapiens* societies were in some sense "primitive." But, in this case, would not Kehoe's statement about American Indians that "each human [is] a being of inherent dignity, sharing with us a biological nature and active, *sapiens* intelligence," apply also to *sapiens* societies of the past?

I think Kehoe's article deals with important problems, but I really do not believe it helps us much in solving them.

by George F. Carter

DEPARTMENT OF GEOGRAPHY, TEXAS A&M UNIVERSITY, COLLEGE STATION, TEXAS 77843, UNITED STATES. 32 II 81

There is no doubt that mankind is very able at rationalizing its destructive actions against "the others" and that classifications have been used as aids to such destructive acts. This seems to impel Kehoe to reduce classifications to an absolute minimum and leads to the statement that each society in North America was as evolved as any other—a statement that reduces the Mexican civilizations to the same level as the unclad and unhoused natives of southern Baja California. In pursuit of her aim of avoiding invidious comparisons, Kehoe expands the term "food production" to encompass all environmental manipulations by man that in any way improve the food supply. Thus even the most highly developed agriculture is lumped with such simple manipulations as burning. This reductionism may be useful for her purpose, but for anyone interested in food-production efficiency or the development of agriculture it is counterproductive.

One of Kehoe's aims seems to be to avoid comparisons that lead to judgments such as "higher" or "lower." She is particularly concerned with the racial overtones of this. There are, however, more and less complex economies, and they may be more or less efficient in producing food and more or less destructive of the environment. These are relatively simple facts. Anyone can force them into a physical environmental or a racial explanation, though they are probably seldom if ever so caused. It does not seem rational to throw out useful classifications because they are at times misused. One does not stop driving because some people speed.

Kehoe's other contribution is to call attention to the north-south and east-west differences in development in North America. If her proposed classification leads to inquiry into why agriculture began in tropical America and spread so unevenly to the north, then it will serve a useful purpose. There is a slight overtone of physical environmentalism in the use of an ecological niche into which all societies are supposed to have fitted themselves equally well. The inference here seems to be that there is a best use of a given environment, and this is obviously not true. There are many uses, and this actually fits with Kehoe's concept of alternatives. Judgment of better or worse has to be on some basis. The Mediterranean was destructively used by the agriculturalists that occupied it; it was magnificently used in terms of cultural productivity.

There is also some slight bias against the sequence of cultures from early and simple to late and complex. One can, of course, argue whether the Mexican civilizations were better than the simple cultures of the Great Basin, though one has to define the "good" being discussed. They most certainly were different. Also, it is quite clear that Mexico was once on much the same cultural-economic level as the Great Basin and that it became complex through a series of stages. It is becoming apparent that all of the ecological niches in North America were once filled with people in the hunting-and-gathering stage and that greater changes occurred in some areas than in others. Some people have remained closer to the ancient simple way of life; others have changed to a vastly more complex one. In my view the causative factors are cultural-historical and not at all racial or even to any great extent physical-environmental. There is no reason in physical geography that Alaska could not have been a Finland, but neither is there any racial reason. The discrepancy is a fact calling for explanation.

by Joan Chandler

UNIVERSITY OF TEXAS AT DALLAS, BOX 688, RICHARDSON,

TEXAS 75080, UNITED STATES. 22 III 81

This article is thought-provoking, and Kehoe is undoubtedly right in supposing that anthropologists have been too ready to assume that their work is by definition free of cultural bias. But how are we in fact to escape from our own cultural swaddling clothes? It appears to me that, despite her best efforts, even Kehoe has not done so.

She accepts, for instance, Jennings's idea of the "cant of conquest." It seems extraordinarily difficult for scholars who do not believe in a *dies irae* to comprehend the aspirations of those who do. Actions may speak louder than words; but to read Cromwell's correspondence (Carlyle n.d.) or John Winthrop's diary is to enter a world in which men are justifying their acts not to each other, but to God, before Whom each of them will ultimately stand alone. By the mid-nineteenth century, most Americans who fought, defrauded, or tried to help Indians were much less conscious of their final destiny, and to many of them Indians were almost certainly "gooks" (Horsman 1968). To dismiss this as "cant," however, and to congratulate ourselves because we "repudiate" it is to miss the point. In the twenty-first century, a desire to embrace "modern evolutionary biology" may be regarded as a similar sign of unfitness to organize theoretical schemas; our successors may castigate us for having bowed down to the god of scientism as Kehoe castigates twentieth-century anthropologists for their devotion to nineteenth-century idols. It seems, therefore, important to reject terminology not so much because it is "unjust" as because it is inaccurate.

Similarly, Kehoe tries to stretch the concept of the *polis*. The Greek *polis* was indeed a "physical entity" in which collective human memory was systematized in writing. Why reduce the term to a "social-political-economic construct" unless one is seeking to demonstrate that Indian societies were actually more stratified and institutionalized (and therefore in some sense more "civilized") than anthropologists have hitherto been disposed to believe?

I am not qualified to assess Kehoe's cogent reordering of archeological data, but it appears almost as if she fears her system of classification will not get a proper hearing unless she can demonstrate that the accepted categories are ideologically, not just conceptually, inadequate. Her own case does not rest on the accuracy of her analysis of European structuring principles (and given the continuous trouble the concept of the Trinity has occasioned in Christian thought, I must question her notion of religious dualism). If her fears are justified, anthropologists are even more hidebound than she suggests—in which case a "revisionist anthropology" won't help much, as we shall simply move from one Procrustean bed to another. If Kehoe's reinterpretation is correct, then we ought to be investigating, not general nineteenth-century intellectual baggage, but the actual training of those who have been too long satisfied with inadequate models of Indian societies (see, for instance, Crane 1972). Perhaps what we need is not a revisionist anthropology, but more historical scholarship?

by Don E. Dumond

DEPARTMENT OF ANTHROPOLOGY, UNIVERSITY OF OREGON,
EUGENE, OREGON 97403, UNITED STATES. 25 III 81

Kehoe's argument is the logical extension of a trend toward reevaluation of conceptions of American Indian society that perhaps first became visible when the value-laden notions of pre-Columbian Mexico espoused by Bandelier (1880; see also Vaillant 1941)—who saw the Aztecs as southern reflections of the Iroquois—were revised in the middle of this century (e.g., Soustelle 1955 and later authors) to provide the picture of a truly large, urban, class-structured, politically centralized society. The argument must contribute to improvement of our overall view, but it goes too far. Perhaps it would not had Kehoe included Mexico—a part of North America—in her careful examination.

The briefest glance at what is known of the Indians of central Mexico in 1519 shows clearly that these people and their immediate predecessors had, like Eurasians, based their subsistence upon "massive destruction of the indigenous ecosystem and its replacement by an artifact ecosystem" to the point that the "indigenous" ecosystem is often all but impossible to recover. A less hasty glance raises the suspicion that several prehistoric Mexican societies even engineered their own disruption through mismanagement and overuse of these same artifact ecosystems—as, for instance, the Teotihuacanos, with massive deforestation and imperfect soil management, or those lowland Maya who allowed their population mass to outreach the resource-intensification measures available within their delicately balanced economy. These situations are entirely parallel to some of those of the Old World—for example, the fatal salinization of lands through continued irrigation—or to that which may shortly face us all. The superficially different position of people north of Mexico, with their seemingly variant strategy of ecosystem management, is a correlate not of a unique approach to the world, but of a lower population density just as is, according to Kehoe, the relative lack of internal functional differentiation among societies of the high latitudes when compared with their southern neighbors. Among organisms the biomass supported (in human terms, the population density) is after all a measure of evolutionary success.

Thus, if one's view includes all of America north of Panama, one must see that societies very much like those of Eurasia—dense, internally differentiated, urban, so extractive that they consume capital resources—were located in the south and that in a synchronic traverse to the north these gave way steadily to societies less dense, less differentiated internally, less urban, and less dangerously extractive until an opposite extreme was reached on the Arctic coast. Like Redfield (e.g., 1941, 349), one suspects that this spatial line of continuous variation must be the analog, if never the completely accurate representation, of a temporal and developmental pathway. That the societies of the areas discussed by Kehoe were not simply "fossils" of bygone times is made clear by archaeology, which (as she demonstrates) shows that virtually all had been caught by the European invasion mid-stride in a dynamic history of development. Development toward what? Why, toward ever more differentiated forms. Although peoples north of Mexico in their various regions had not yet worked out means to support such a mass of their own species as was found farther south, they could be expected in the course of time to approach ever more closely the condition of the densely settled and internally differentiated societies of central Mexico—or of Eurasia.

What this says is that Old World and New were not so different. Indeed, much of the difference seeming to remain between them may well be attributed to the relative newness of the New, for whereas in all Old World regions of internally very differentiated societies hominids can be shown to have been present since the Middle Pleistocene and plentiful thereafter, in the New World no widespread human presence can be documented before the very end of the Pleistocene. And do we really know when human environmental management began?

Kehoe's argument is stimulating and welcome in that it replaces invidious comparisons with relativist ones. It is also humane. But one must suspect that if it had included a careful examination of Mesoamerican societies it would have been directed toward a somewhat different conclusion.

by Knut R. Fladmark

DEPARTMENT OF ARCHAEOLOGY, SIMON FRASER UNIVERSITY,

BURNABY, BRITISH COLUMBIA, CANADA V5A 1S6. 19 II 81

Kehoe's article is a breath of fresh air in the stagnant halls of American ethnology. Whether one agrees with all the specifics of the "revisionist" perspective or not, Kehoe's arguments represent sweeping new insights into New World anthropology which should prove valuable foci of research and discussion for years to come.

There is little doubt that the politics of conquest have distorted perceptions of American Indian culture. However, some current heuristic models may be more serious sources of misconception than the naive biases of early European observers. The culture-area concept imposes static, standardized trait lists over vast regions, obscuring real cultural diversity. Normative attributes of culture areas are quoted by successive generations of students and textbooks without critical testing of fundamental premises. It is indicative that the culture-area concept has never been successfully applied in the Old World, where anthropologists of European heritage recognize a diversity of cultures defying simplistic categorization, while American Indians are still routinely forced into a few unyielding molds. Sharp taxonomic dichotomies such as "hunter-gatherers" vs. "horticulturalists" hamper understanding of the real range and overlap of economic patterns, just as rigid tripartite systems (e.g., Paleo-Indian, Archaic, Sedentary) can often create formidable barriers to recognition of continuity and variability in prehistory.

Such taxonomies are cemented into the "grammar" of anthropology, just as shelves full of ethnographies represent its basic lexicon. This impressive academic baggage makes it easy to assume that American Indian cultures are well known. Yet, with the possible exception of a few east-coast and Mexican groups recorded at the moment of earliest contact, we really have very little reliable information about the genuine aboriginal lifeways of North America prior to direct or indirect European influences. The bulk of the ethnographic edifice is based on data collected long after Indian cultures had been profoundly disturbed by the effects of contact. Even so, when statements by early observers such as the various chroniclers of the de Soto expedition imply a more complex Native culture than that perpetuated in the accepted ethnographic reconstruction, it is the primary historical sources, not the constructs of contemporary ethnology, that are usually accused of inaccuracy. In parts of North America late prehistoric cultures do appear to be more complex, involving larger populations than suggested by ethnography. Perhaps existing ethnographic models of aboriginal North America should be seriously reevaluated on the basis of archaeology, rather than archaeological interpretation always bent to fit the ethnographic analogue.

Kehoe states that aboriginal American game-management strategies made "daily control of living animals unnecessary." I would like to suggest that we really do not know what forms precontact man-animal interdependence may have taken. Given the widespread use of empoundments and surrounds as hunting methods in North America, it becomes conceptually a simple step to the live maintenance of animals in corrals or managed herds. Some Great Basin groups did keep antelope alive in pounds after a drive, killing only five or six a day as needed (cited in Steward 1938, 35), and Lowie (1935, 37) reports that the Crow sometimes kept live bison calves which were ridden and play-hunted by young boys.

My initial reaction to Kehoe's claim for swidden horticulture on the Northwest Coast was shocked disagreement—this was going too far! However, there is no doubt that some Northwest Coast groups were aware of the basic principles of horticulture. The Haida, for instance, apparently aboriginally planted and managed tobacco gardens (Dawson 1880, 114), while virtually all groups owned, cleared, cultivated, and conserved extensive "wild" edible root crops, including camas and clover (Turner 1975, 79, 164). Nevertheless, vegetable foods and land mammals did not constitute the major food resources for most of this area. Instead, a more intriguing question is to what extent four to five thousand years of intensive managed exploitation of salmon and shellfish might result in a system of "food production" approximating domestication.

Finally, it is worth noting that the "high latitudes" were not immune to management. Environmental modification through controlled burning was widespread through at least the southern margins of the boreal forest (e.g., Lewis 1977).

by David H. French

DEPARTMENT OF ANTHROPOLOGY, REED COLLEGE,

PORTLAND, OREGON 97202, UNITED STATES. 18 III 81

Kehoe argues well that anthropologists have been slow to realize that their opinions are not value-free and are not based on purely objective data. This is analogous to the historical relativist position that histories always have a bias and must regularly be rewritten.

I want to consider Kehoe's article within a broad framework which can be called "the anthropology of knowledge" (cf. French n.d.). This framework includes the study of the knowledge, information, or "beliefs" possessed by various kinds of persons in various parts of the world; thus, it is like a broader version of the sociology of knowledge and includes "folk knowledge." Here, we are first concerned with which writers, mainly of European ancestry, have held which biased views needing to be amended by revisionist anthropologists. A problem in reading the article, however, is identifying the current "bad guys" and bad positions within anthropology and outside of it. Are any of them straw men? (Kehoe does name some diverse good people whose knowledge includes insight as to biases.)

Her interesting section on "the cant of conquest" identifies various culture-bound views of Indians, e.g., as savages, frequently noble. Such views are still held by some Americans and others, but attacks on them are not as new as she implies. Attacks constituted a major thrust in the writings of Boas (e.g., 1911) and many of his students, among them Radin (1927) and Sapir. Were not they often writing as revisionists? Is not such writing an old and major function of various kinds of anthropology? Other types of early revisionists could include certain synchronically oriented European social anthropologists, often with a debt to Durkheim.

It is Kehoe's view that we should review not only our assumptions but also our phrasings, including linguistic subtleties. An example might be her phrase "the Indian" (without quotation marks). One hopes she was thinking about this as a stereotypic phrase; the irony would have been made obvious by using quotation marks. In other contexts, "the anthropologist" can replace the words "the Jew" or "the Indian" with simple plurals, e.g., "Indians."

She correctly relates the term "gook" to the Vietnam War. It does not weaken her point that "gook" was by then an old pejorative term, having been applied to various Asiatics, e.g., Filipinos, Japanese, and Koreans (Burchfield 1972, 1265–66).

Her bold division of North America into three areas, each adapted to its environment(s), has much to recommend it. Yet, when she adopts the framework of evolutionary biology, should she not have made even more provision for environmental (and cultural) variability? Her Pacific-drainage section includes the Great Basin, which doesn't so drain and which is significantly arid; the Owens Valley Paiutes, cited by Kehoe, are not typical, for example, in the management of food resources. Despite her qualifying words indicating awareness of such problems, she should not have included the Basin in an area she characterizes as societally complex, e.g., with class stratification. With more attention to ecological considerations (e.g., maize does not flourish without irrigation in the dry summers of the Far West), she would not have needed to say that Pacific-drainage peoples "preferred" local plants. There are better explanations than preference.

Her finding of *polis* to be widespread on the continent is excellent, and she makes clear that the Pacific-drainage area had a range from temporary settlements (summer camps) to true towns; mentioned is a Wishram trade center (Nixluidix) near The Dalles (see also French 1961, 341–49). *Villages* were more typical of the area, some being occupied in the summer, some in the winter, others throughout the year.

Anthropological knowledge can be skewed by simple errors. Kehoe exaggerates the importance of wapato and camas as staples in the Northwest; here she has been misled by poor ethnographic research (e.g., by Ray) in the past. On the Plateau, carrot-related plants were much more important than the above as carbohydrate sources (Hunn and French n.d.).

What one writes is partly a function of sociocultural biases: I applaud Kehoe's stress on biases and her insistence that we all have them. Despite the problematic nature of "facts" and "objectivity," it is somehow also possible to identify errors and poor theory without being an "empirical positivist." Revisionism did not begin just yesterday, and we may hope that tomorrow will continue to produce articles like this one.

by Paul F. Healy

DEPARTMENT OF ANTHROPOLOGY, TRENT UNIVERSITY,

PETERBOROUGH, ONTARIO, CANADA. 2 IV 81

Kehoe's paper appropriately raises questions about implicit values and ideologies and how these can affect our anthropological and archaeological interpretations. It is hardly surprising, however, that the model and stereotypes developed with the arrival of the Europeans are "first and foremost European projections." What else could be expected? On the other hand, Kehoe is right in arguing for some "consciousness raising" on the subject, since it would appear that some of the more traditional stereotypes continue to crop up in anthropological writings, despite the fact that it is now quite clear that they are distortions of reality.

My concerns are primarily archaeological, and I consider Kehoe's paper, like several others recently published (Trigger 1978, 1980), useful in making us more conscious of the way such traditional biases color our modern interpretations of prehistory. In my own area of interest, Mesoamerican and Lower Central American archaeology, it is possible to see what Kehoe labels as European structuring principles clearly at work in the standard tripartite chronological scheme (Preclassic, Classic, and Postclassic periods). This system is entrenched in the literature and preserved despite the growing awareness that it is no longer suitable for dividing all Middle American prehistory and that the burgeoning number of radiocarbon dates make such a three-part schema virtually an anachronism (Webb 1978, 156–60; Sanders, Parsons, and Santley 1979). Nevertheless, it is maintained, and it shows the grip such traditional biases have on us. What is worse, of course, is the effort of some to maintain the schema by forcing archaeological data into its "value-charged" framework.

Regarding Kehoe's "cant of conquest," one has only to examine early Spanish accounts of the *entradas* into this area of the New World to see the validity of the "feudal-expansion" model, with the Spanish being God's chosen victors. And although the pre-Columbian Native societies of Mesoamerica were perhaps closer to the level and style of social organization that the Spanish were accustomed to than some North American groups, they were definitely viewed not as alternative modes of life, but as works of the devil. Even today writings often discriminate between Native groups in Middle America on the basis of how closely they fit traditional definitions of "civilized" and "noncivilized." The "civilized" Olmecs, Maya, Toltecs, and Aztecs, for example, are viewed as somehow better than their neighbors in, say, Lower Central America (Honduras to Panama), where the achievements were equally remarkable but where social organization fails to fit our traditional stereotype of "civilized" or "advanced." Consequently, these latter areas have failed to attract the level of archaeological interest characteristic of the Mesoamerican heartland (Mexico-Guatemala-Belize); the discrepancy is based on a value judgment rooted in the traditional European mentality.

Kehoe's model for North American prehistory as a "set of adaptations of human societies to regional conditions" is equally valid for Middle and Central America and could be usefully applied there. A key issue raised recently at a School of American Research advanced seminar in Santa Fe on Lower Central American archaeology was whether bigger is always better. One can certainly think of many modern examples to the contrary, and we (as anthropologists) have to struggle with this Western notion of superiority.

Since it is easy to fall into the trap of traditional stereotypical thinking, we need reminders like Kehoe's paper to jar our thoughts and coax us to higher levels of critical, and more objective, evaluation. I look forward to seeing if in her new book *North American Indians* (Kehoe 1981) she has been able to practice what she preaches.

by Robert Jarvenpa

DEPARTMENT OF ANTHROPOLOGY, STATE UNIVERSITY OF NEW YORK AT ALBANY, ALBANY, NEW YORK 12222, UNITED STATES. 20 III 81

Kehoe's revisionist view of aboriginal North America is an impressive essay. It synthesizes a diverse and increasingly specialized literature in a macrogeographic model of cultural-ecological adaptations and challenges archaeologists, ethnohistorians, and ethnographers to make explicit the epistemological assumptions of the Western intellectual tradition that bias their portrayals of Native American society and culture change. Clearly, there is a need to correct simplistic applications of evolutionary thought. The idea that sophisticated social forms and rather complex regulation of environmental resources can occur without cultivation of domesticates and in the absence of residential-settlement arrangements conventionally viewed as "urban" deserves consideration.

Kehoe's definition of a Pacific-drainage region based upon "food production" without cultigens is particularly thought-provoking. The widespread instances of management of indigenous plant species and manipulation of cervid populations by the burning of vegetation are noteworthy, and more attention to the data from western North America may prove important in modeling the process of change from food gathering to the highly mutualistic relationships involved in domestication. While it is generally recognized that food production develops along a *continuum* of symbioses between humans and other organisms (Brisbin 1971, 243–45; Smith 1976, 7–18), anthropologists rarely focus upon behaviors that represent intermediate stages on this continuum. As systems of management to increase production of naturally occurring plant and animal populations, the adaptations of *some* western Indian groups were, I would agree, qualitatively different from those in the high latitudes.

However, it remains an empirical matter whether or not all systems of management were energetically more productive or cost-effective than procurement systems based upon harvesting "unmanaged" populations. For example, can we assume that the limited sowing of native grains by Great Basin Shoshoneans, albeit a form of food production, resulted in general subsistence economies that were more productive or efficient than the hunting and fishing activity of northern Athapaskans, northeastern Algonkians, and Inuit? Meaningful comparisons of productivity require systematic measurement of the unit costs and marginal costs of alternative subsistence strategies, in the manner suggested by Earle (1980). Until this kind of analysis is performed, I see little heuristic value in lumping the Great Basin groups with the Californian and Northwest Coast societies, where productive capacities, population sizes, differentiation of social groups horizontally and hierarchically, and the formality of social controls are often pronounced.

On the other hand, there is a marked similarity in organization among many of the historically known groups in the subarctic-arctic regions, the Great Basin, and parts of the Plateau if such basic dimensions as low population size and density, seasonal concentration-dispersion cycles of nomadic settlement, and the egalitarian structure of social life are considered. In this regard, it is difficult to appreciate how the annual social-recreational gatherings of Great Basin Indians manifest the urban functions of the *polis*, as Kehoe implies, any more than do the annual aggregations of many northern Indian and Inuit groups. It would appear that the organizational similarities between these groups are more important than the differences and that these organizations reflect fundamentally the same kind of ecological adaptation, one first recognized by Steward (1936).

To the extent that constructs like "band" (or "tribe" and "chiefdom") mask variability and satisfy preconceived notions of evolutionary advancement, they are, perhaps, projections of the European conception of the "primitive." Evolutionary schemas cannot be condemned, however, simply because they exhibit tripartite structuring. A typology with thirty categories may be no more informative if it remains a rigid yardstick of change rather than a means for explaining the process underlying changes (Leacock 1963).

No doubt, the ability to perceive Indian America as a continent of savages, lacking the characteristics of "civilized" Europeans, serves the needs of colonial expansion, conquest, and exploitation. Kehoe's explanation of the development and persistence of such ethnocentrism in terms of oppositional dualism is enlightening and convincing. If there is a need to purge the "primitive" archetype from academic discourse, there certainly is equal merit in correcting the neo-Rousseauian vision of Indian America in the recent popular media. The appealing image of Native Americans as inherently noble, natural conservationists living in idyllic harmony with their surroundings serves a positive function as an aesthetic and emotional rallying point for political action and the enhancement of a collective identity. Yet this construct is as far removed from reality as any other imagery and promises little in the way of educating the public and government policy makers on the nature of cultural variation and change and the complex history of Indian/European relations.

by Henry T. Lewis

DEPARTMENT OF ANTHROPOLOGY, UNIVERSITY OF ALBERTA,

EDMONTON, ALBERTA, CANADA T6G 2H4. 5 III 81

"Procrustean beds," to be sure! However, simply turning the mattress upside down hardly represents a solution to the problem. If only it *were* possible to achieve the outdated, Boasian ideal of pure induction and free ourselves of our primitive triadic and dyadic preconceptions! (Are there any other sciences out there that still invoke the myth of induction?) Kehoe's own admittedly trinary division is interesting and suggestive for certain kinds of broad, regional questions on Indian adaptations (though any serious discussion of the importance of trichotomies in Western science should surely acknowledge Dundes [1968]). However, employing but another variant of the kind of preconception she claims to eschew, her polemics are laden with Rousseauian, very Euro-American ethnocentrisms and overstatements. There are also clear omissions.

Without going into examples of her biases and exaggerations, I would comment only on some materials which she might have used to greater purpose. Work which would buttress her position relates to the uses of fire by Plains Indians in her continental core (Arthur 1954) and by California Indians in her Pacific drainage (Bean and Lawton 1973; Lewis 1973). These uses of fire were much more complex than her comments suggest. On the other hand, studies on the indigenous uses of fire in the high latitudes—at least in the parklands and boreal forests of Alaska and Canada—contradict her argument that there was little or no resource management there (Lewis 1977, 1978, 1980, 1981). Contrary to her contention that "poor drainage" hampered habitat manipulation, Indians used fire extensively throughout selected areas of the northern forest: parklands, meadows, lakeshores, streamsides, river terraces, sloughs, brush stands, and deadfall forests.

The ways in which these data might strengthen or weaken her argument are, however, beside the point in terms of the central questions that she raises regarding anthropological perspectives, her own cant included. There is no question that ethnographic and archaeological interpretations about any people must be reevaluated in terms of new (deductive-intuitive) perspectives, but this is exactly what has been happening, albeit often slowly and unevenly, throughout the history of the discipline. Like history, anthropology is bound to be rewritten, and it will continue to be reformulated in the years ahead, when much of what we write in the 1980s will undoubtedly be viewed with some revisionist dismay. But this process is what science is all about. Suggesting that we alter or give up our preconceptual biases (e.g., the hoary evolutionary canon that hunter-gatherers do not manipulate their environments) is reasonable enough, but proposing that we institute the kind of inverted ethnocentrism represented in Kehoe's polemic is no solution to the problem at all.

by Florence Shipek

DIVISION OF BEHAVIORAL SCIENCES, UNIVERSITY OF WISCONSIN

PARKSIDE, KENOSHA, WISCONSIN 53140, UNITED STATES. 17 III 81

Since Kehoe has referred to my work, it is obvious that I have been a revisionist for some time, and I would suggest that she not except the high-latitude forest and South Texas desert peoples from revision. Lewis's (1977) work on northern Cree demonstrates creative use of fire to increase food and shelter for desired fur and food animals. This is production at a different level, but definitely production, much like the management of pasture by herders. At the other extreme, Cabeza de Vaca's (Nuñez 1905) description of South Texas suggests conscious environmental manipulation for food production and fire-herding of game. Careful ecological research may thus include these people as food producers.

Perhaps the most effective conversion to revisionism results from long-term applied research undertaken *for* Indian groups. I began working for Southern California Indians, at their request, in 1954. I had read all the standard anthropological and historical works on California and felt that I "knew" the culture and had the necessary background. In less than a year, I had thrown out most that I had read, since the egalitarian hunter-gatherer concepts of these works did not accord with my observations and experiences among Kumeyaay (Diegueño-Kamia), San Luiseño, Cupeño, and Cahuilla. Rather than egalitarian societies, these were hierarchical societies with inherited leadership positions at the supposedly nonexistent national level as well as at the band or reservation level. Later, White (1957) correctly analzyed the Luiseño theory of knowledge, presenting the hierarchical system in which I functioned, and Luomala (1963) recognized the flexibility of the Kumeyaay (Diegueño). When Bean (1972) began his Cahuilla research, I pointed out the hierarchical structure and suggested he explore it—which he successfully did.

By 1959, working on a number of legal cases (see Shipek 1972), I had commenced ethnobotanical and land use and tenure studies and reexamination of contact-period records. I discovered that Boscana (1933) and Sales (Rudkin 1956) had recorded the hierarchical systems of the Luiseño and Kumeyaay specialists (shamans) responsible for the increase and production of food plants but felt that the people were deluded by these "crafty old men." In my land-use research, I was taken by the national sociopolitical leaders to surviving plant specialists in families which had avoided both mission and American contact until after 1900—some until 1930 (Shipek 1968). These specialists described planting seeds and vegetative cuttings and transplanting to increase food-plant stands and locations. This and a rereading of explorers' descriptions from an environmental-ecological viewpoint brought the realization that, in this erratic climate, the landscape had been managed by all the agricultural techniques, including fire, for the long-term production of interplanted species and hybrids with various moisture and temperature requirements. This provided a more certain supply of food than could the genetically stabilized high-yield corn-beans-squash triumvirate, which had one set of moisture-temperature requirements (Shipek 1977).

Examination of Baja California records indicates that the same type of hierarchical structure existed there, undoubtedly for the same purpose; Aschmann (1967) has estimated one person per square mile as the contact-period population density for the driest, least populated part, and creative management of the environment must have been required to provide food for such a population. Further, the attitude of the Spanish was often that these "pagans" scarcely needed the chiefs who served as headmen (see Wilbur 1967, 38), in spite of elsewhere describing leaders with control over people and even complex coordinated military maneuvers by three bands speaking different languages (Burrus 1971, 114–23).

The contact-period literature on California confirms Kehoe's observations on conquest-justification concepts and the misunderstanding of any system of land use or social stratification that did not fit European patterns. Building on that ethnocentric bias of contact and conquest, most historical, geographic, and sociological as well as anthropological literature perpetuated these same myths—that populations were small, that the people were simple, egalitarian, noneconomic creatures with no understanding of land tenure or ownership, and that they did nothing to the environment except exist upon nature's bounty in a rich, stable land. All such myths need reexamination. We must learn to specify our own assumptions and to recognize that our concepts, definitions, and hypotheses control what we see, our interpretation of it, and even the questions we ask.[1] We must be open to all possibilities even to ask the right questions.

NOTES

1. Elsewhere (Shipek n.d.) I discuss how the one-tribe/one-culture concept long prevented recognition of the identity of the Kamia as Kumeyaay (Diegueño).

by Theodore Stern

DEPARTMENT OF ANTHROPOLOGY, UNIVERSITY OF OREGON, EUGENE, OREGON 97403, UNITED STATES. 30 III 81

In her new text (1981) Kehoe has given us a responsible survey of the continent, with a sympathetic presentation of its peoples, given particular interest by vignettes and by provocative ideas. She is less well served by the overbrief paper under review here. Her discussion of the "cant of conquest" and of the hobbling effect of dualism and what Sapir once termed the "triune formula" is intended only obliquely, if at all, as a stricture upon her fellow anthropologists. Indeed, she herself lumps the culture areas meticulously drawn by her predecessors into exactly three major regions: apparently, the habit is difficult to suppress.

Kehoe does well to call attention to techniques for the management and encouragement of plants and of animal domains and to compare them to farming and animal husbandry. This is a view in part adumbrated in earlier work by Kroeber (1941) and by Leeds and Vayda (1965), to mention but two examples. One might recall as a supplementary observation the extent to which such a farming people as the Pima relied upon wild plants. However, in this brief space, Kehoe cannot adequately assess the degree to which some of the instances of what Bean terms "proto-agricultural" practices in southern California were modeled upon those of neighboring farming peoples. There seems to be an oversystematization in the presentation of such practices for the Pacific region. To say for the peoples residing there that they "preferred indigenous food plants to the Mexican cultigens" is to endow them with a choice most of them (save those living near farmers) never had.

Why a revisionist anthropology requires a change in definitions seems problematical. Kehoe seems to be of the opinion that "stratification" and "urbanism" as currently used are shaped too closely to Western European standards. Still, they have proved useful in treating Asian societies, and much is lost in comparability when new definitions are invoked here. When it can be said that the peoples of the continental core and Pacific regions dwelt in "stratified" societies, the term has lost much of its power to differentiate among a wide range of social structures. Similar criticisms can be leveled at the standard that would array the Plains camp circle with Tenochtitlan as "urban." Finally, there are no functions that are distinctive of an urban economy: what instead is distinctive is the existence of complex and permanent institutions for discharging those functions.

Reply

by Alice B. Kehoe

MILWAUKEE, WISCONSIN, UNITED STATES. 15 V 81

Bernier's comment seems to me to highlight a difficulty several readers encountered in assessing my paper. Bernier castigates me for labeling high-latitude societies "primitive" when what I attempted was to divorce certain attributes of low-population-density societies from the value-laden term "primitive." My understanding of evolutionary biology is that every successfully reproducing species (or society) is at the moment at the end of its evolutionary pathway and in this comparable to any other successfully reproducing species (or society); conversely, no species (or society) can be considered to be a truly final product until it has become extinct. While biomass may be one measure of successful adaptation, as Dumond states, another and sometimes conflicting measure must be long-term viability (e.g., mammoths of the Late Pleistocene achieved considerable biomass but did not persist as long as humans). This type of discussion in biological terms does not, as Asch suggests, demean Indians: all members of the genus *Homo*, whether the Sun King or Ishi the Yana, are biological organisms and subject to the principles governing life on earth. The denigration in the colloquial epithet "animal" must not blind us to the fact that we are animals.

Shipek's comment answers several of the others. She explains, as French himself does, the California peoples' preference for indigenous rather than alien food resources, and she implies that Steward (1936), cited by Jarvenpa, is not the best guide to Basin ethnography. She specifically mentions the organization of the Baja California peoples that, in answer to Carter's comment, makes them comparable to their distant neighbors in better-watered regions of Mexico. In answer to Stern, who implies that only the Southern California groups studied by Shipek and her immediate colleagues had any choice on cultigens, I can point out that some acquaintance with the maize-growing Southwest extended at least into Pomo territory north of San Francisco Bay; the existence of a major trade route between these two areas is attested by archaeological finds. Shipek's comment may also answer Chandler: the traditions of knowledge that Shipek refers to seem to me to be functionally equivalent to writing in maintaining a *polis*. Aristotle considered writing useful but stressed the crucial importance of the gathering of citizens for political deliberation, fostered by education; education may be facilitated by writing, but we have numerous examples of highly formalized, extensive bodies of knowledge passed down by oral instruction—-e.g., the Rg Veda—to demonstrate that not even formal education need depend upon writing. In reply to Stern, I must ask him whether "complex and permanent" institutions are necessarily *continuously* functioning. The more theoretical urban sociologists (e.g., in Pickvance 1976) disclose the shaky foundations of much current thinking on urbanism.

Carter brings up another angle in reminding us that one's research interests will be ground for evaluating the categories and criteria to be employed. A geographer concerned with food production efficiency certainly has a clear "good" to compare against data. My paper sought to differentiate between a heuristic "good" and the extension of such a delimited "good" to general rankings. As for why Alaska wasn't a Finland, aside from the obvious lack of contacts with Europe resulting in the Finnish cultural content, we can consider whether sites such as Ipiutak and the early historic cross-Bering trade and raids tying Alaska into the Northern Pacific sphere may not have functioned to make Alaska more comparable to pre-twentieth-century Finland than a superficial glance might suggest.

Dumond's thoughtful comment emphasizes a south-north cline more than I wanted to (I did very briefly include Mexico in my continental core—I felt it unnecessary to argue that Mexico was "civilized"). It appears to me that more attention to Dumond's points constitutes a perspective different from, but not inherently contradictory to, mine. Where I emphasized inter-American similarities and contrasted them to Eurasian modes, Dumond suggests a contrary emphasis; neither emphasis is wrong. Dumond's final remarks fit with Fladmark's intriguing comment on the possible comparability of managed herds and self-managed schools of fish intensively exploited as food staples by human societies.

Several commentators criticize my presentation of classes similar, in their opinions, to those I critiqued. The crux, I believe, is whether one proposes a schema without reflection upon its epistemology or carefully derives one from specified data and delimits it accordingly. As with the culture-area concept mentioned by Fladmark, concepts or frameworks may have been misused but are not therefore to be discarded with the bathwater. The culture-area concept has been successfully applied to Europe by Arensberg and remains, I think, valid as a rough approximation to important ecological-cultural configurations. It simply should not be used as if normative or all-or-none.

Healy's comment very nicely points up the biasing effect of preconceptions on the direction of archaeological research.

Finally, I am familiar with Lewis's and Arthur's work but have the impression it has not been demonstrated to apply to the Shield or the northern (tundra-edge) boreal forest. Arthur studied the Northern Plains, which I don't consider "high-latitude." Lewis and his students, so far as I have read, have been researching northernmost Alberta, the southern boreal-forest-parkland-Plains borderland, and while their work is highly instructive I am unsure how widely it can be generalized north or east. A paper by him on this issue would be welcome indeed.

REFERENCES

Ackerknecht, Erwin H. 1954. "On the comparative method in anthropology." In *Method and perspective in anthropology*, edited by R. F. Spencer. Minneapolis: University of Minnesota Press.

Alland, Alexander. 1975. Adaptation. *Annual Review of Anthropology* 4:59–73. [MIA]

Arthur, George W. 1975. *An introduction to the ecology of early historic communal bison hunting among the northern Plains Indians.* Mercury Series, Archaeological Survey of Canada, Paper 37. [HTL]

Asad, Talal, ed. 1973. *Anthropology and the colonial encounter.* New York: Humanities Press.

Asch, Michael I. 1978. "The ecological-evolutionary model and the concept of mode of production." In *Challenging anthropology,* edited by D. Turner and G. Smith, 81–99. Toronto: McGraw-Hill Ryerson. [MIA]

———. 1980a. "Steps toward the analysis of aboriginal Athapaskan social organization." *Arctic Anthropology* 17 (2): 46–51. [MIA]

———. 1980b. Comment on: Quantum adjustment, macroevolution, and the social field, by P. Diener. *Current Anthropology* 21:432. [MIA]

Aschmann, Homer. 1967. *The central desert of Baja California: Demography and ecology.* Riverside: Manessier. [FS]

Bahn, Paul G. 1978. "The 'unacceptable face' of the West European Upper Palaeolithic." *Antiquity* 52:183–92.

Bandelier, Adolph F. 1880. "On the social organization and mode of government of the ancient Mexicans." *12th Annual Report of the Peabody Museum of American Archaeology and Ethnology,* vol. 2, 557–699. [DED]

Basso, Keith. 1972. "Ice and travel among the Fort Norman Slave: Folk taxonomies and cultural rules." *Language in Society* 1:31–49. [MIA]

Bean, Lowell J. 1972. *Mukat's people.* Berkeley: University of California Press. [FS]

Bean, Lowell J., and Thomas C. Blackburn, eds. 1976. *Native Californians: A theoretical retrospective.* Ramona: Ballena Press.

Bean, Lowell J., and Thomas F. King, eds. 1974. *'Antap: California Indian political and economic organization.* Ramona: Ballena Press.

Bean, Lowell J., and Harry W. Lawton. 1974. "Some explanation for the rise of cultural complexity in native California, with comments on proto-agriculture and agriculture." In *Patterns of Indian burning in California: Ecology and ethnohistory,* by Henry T. Lewis, v-xlvii. Ramona: Ballena Press. [HTL]

Bean, Lowell J., and Katherine Siva Saubel. 1972. *Temalpakh.* Morongo Indian Reservation, CA: Malki Museum Press.

Bender, Barbara. 1978. "Hunter-gatherer to farmer: A social perspective." *World Archaeology* 10:204–22. [MIA]

Berkhofer, Robert F., Jr. 1978. *The white man's Indian.* New York: Knopf.

Birket-Smith, Kaj. [1967] 1971. *Studies in circumpacific culture relations.* Kongelige Danske Videnskabernes Selskab Historisk-Filosofiske Meddelelser 42(3), 45(2).

Bishop, Charles A. 1974. *The Northern Ojibwa and the fur trade.* Toronto: Holt, Rinehart and Winston of Canada.

————. 1977. "Aboriginal Cree social organization." Paper presented to the 9th Algonquian Conference, Worcester, MA.

Boas, Franz. 1911. *The mind of primitive man.* New York: Macmillan. [DHF]

Boscana, Fr. Geronimo. 1933. "Chinigchinich." In *Chinigchinich: A revised and annotated version of Alfred Robinson's translation of Father Geronimo Boscana's "Historical account of the beliefs, usages, customs and extravagancies of the Indians of the Mission of San Juan Capistrano called the Acagchemen tribe,"* edited by P. T. Hanna. Santa Ana: Fine Arts Press. [FS]

Brisbin, I. Lehr. 1971. "Artificial selection: Domestication." In *Fundamentals of ecology,* edited by Eugene P. Odum, 243–45. Philadelphia: Saunders. [RTI]

Browning, Harley L. 1978. "Some problematics of the tertiarization process in Latin America." In *Urbanization in the Americas from its beginnings to the present,* edited by Richard P. Schaedel, Jorge E. Hardoy, and Nora Scott Kinzer. The Hague: Mouton.

Burchfield, R. W., ed. 1972. *A supplement to the Oxford English dictionary.* Vol. 1. Oxford: Clarendon Press. [DHF]

Burrus, Ernest J., S.J., trans. 1971. *Juan Maria de Salvatierra, S.J.: Selected letters about Lower California.* Los Angeles: Dawson's Book Shop. [FS]

Carlyle, Thomas. n.d. *Oliver Cromwell's letters and speeches with elucidations.* Boston: Dana Estes. [JC]

Chomko, Stephen A., and Gary W. Crawford. 1978. "Plant husbandry in prehistoric Eastern North America: New evidence for its development." *American Antiquity* 43:405–8.

Crane, Diana. 1972. *Invisible colleges: Diffusion of knowledge in scientific communities.* Chicago: University of Chicago Press. [JC]

Dawson, George M. 1880. "Report on the Queen Charlotte Islands." In *Geological Survey of Canada, Report of progress for 1878–79.* Montreal: Dawson Brothers. [KRF]

Dumézil, Georges. 1968. *Mythe et épopée.* Paris: Editions Gallimard.

Dundes, Alan. 1968. "The number three in American culture." In *Every man his way,* edited by Alan Dundes, 401–24. Englewood Cliffs: Prentice-Hall. [HTL]

Earle, Timothy K. 1980. "A model of subsistence change." In *Modeling change in prehistoric subsistence systems,* edited by Timothy K. Earle and Andrew L. Christenson, 1–29. New York: Academic Press. [RTI]

Foucault, Michel. 1970. *The order of things (Les mots et les choses).* New York: Random House.

French, David H. 1961. "Wasco-Wishram." In *Perspectives in American Indian culture change,* edited by Edward H. Spicer, 337–430. Chicago: University of Chicago Press. [DHF]

————. n.d. "Neglected aspects of North American ethnobotany." *Canadian Journal of Botany.* [DHF]

Fried, Morton H. 1975. *The notion of tribe.* Menlo Park, CA: Cummings.

Friedman, Jonathan. 1975. "Tribes, states, and transformations." In *Marxist analyses and social anthropology*, edited by M. Bloch, 161–202. London: Malaby. [MIA]

Gibson, James R. 1978a. "Old Russia in the New World." In *European settlement and development in North America*, edited by James R. Gibson. Toronto: University of Toronto Press.

———. 1978b. "European dependence upon American natives: The case of Russian America." *Ethnohistory* 25:359–85.

Helm, June. 1980. "Female infanticide, European diseases, and population levels among the Mackenzie Dene." *American Ethnologist* 7:259–85.

Higgs, E. S., and M. R. Jarman. 1969. "The origins of agriculture: A reconsideration." *Antiquity* 43:31–41.

Horsman, Reginald. 1968. "American Indian policy and the origins of manifest destiny." *University of Birmingham Historical Journal* 11:128–40. [JC]

Huizer, Gerrit, and Bruce Mannheim, eds. 1979. *The politics of anthropology*. The Hague: Mouton.

Hunn, Eugene S., and David H. French. n.d. "*Lomatium*: A key resource for Columbia Plateau native subsistence." *Northwest Science*. [DHF]

Hymes, Dell, ed. 1969. *Reinventing anthropology*. New York: Random House.

Jennings, Francis. 1975. *The invasion of America*. Chapel Hill: University of North Carolina Press.

Kay, Marvin, Francis B. King, and Christine K. Robinson. 1980. "Cucurbits from Phillips Spring: New evidence and interpretations." *American Antiquity* 45:806–22.

Kehoe, Alice Beck. 1981. *North American Indians: A comprehensive account*. Englewood Cliffs: Prentice-Hall.

Kelley, J. Charles. 1955. "Juan Sabeata and diffusion in aboriginal Texas." *American Anthropologist* 57:981–95.

Kroeber, A. L. 1941. *Salt, dogs, tobacco. Anthropological Records* 6 (1). [TS]

Leacock, Eleanor, ed. 1963. "Introduction." In *Ancient society* by Lewis Henry Morgan. New York: Meridian Books. [RJ]

Lee, Richard. 1979. *The !Kung San: Men, women, and work in a foraging society*. London: Cambridge University Press. [MIA]

Leeds, Anthony, and A. P. Vayda, eds. 1965. *Man, culture, and animals: The role of animals in human ecological adjustments*. American Association for the Advancement of Science 78. [TS]

Legros, Dominique. 1977. "Chance, necessity, and mode of production: A Marxist critique of cultural evolutionism." *American Anthropologist* 79:26–41. [MIA]

Lewis, Henry T. 1973. *Patterns of Indian burning in California: Ecology and ethnohistory*. Ramona: Ballena Press. [HTL]

———. 1977. "Maskuta: The ecology of Indian fires in northern Alberta." *Western Canadian Journal of Anthropology* 7:15–52. [KRF, HTL, FS]

————. 1978. "Traditional uses of fire by Indians in northern Alberta." *Current Anthropology* 19:401–2. [HTL]

————. 1980. "Indian fires of spring." *Natural History* 89:76–83. [HTL]

————. 1981. "Hunter-gatherers and problems for fire history." In *Proceedings, Fire History Workshop, October 20–24, 1980*, 115–19. Rocky Mountain Forest and Range Experiment Station Forest Service, U.S. Department of Agriculture, General Technical Report RM-81. [HTL]

Lorimer, Douglas A. 1978. *Colour, class, and the Victorians.* Leicester: Leicester University Press/Holmes and Meier.

Lowie, Robert H. [1935] 1956. *The Crow Indians.* New York: Holt, Rinehart and Winston. [KRF]

Luomala, Katherine. 1963. "Flexibility in sib affiliation among the Diegueño." *Ethnology* 2:282–301. [FS]

Mamalakis, Markos. 1972. "Urbanization and sectoral transformation in Latin America, 1950–65." In *Actas y memorias del XXXIX Congreso internacional de Americanistas,* vol. 2. Lima: Instituto de Estudios Peruanos.

Morgan, Lewis Henry. [1877] 1964. *Ancient society.* Cambridge: Harvard University Press.

Núñez Cabeza de Vaca, Álvar. 1905. *Journey of Álvar Núñez Cabeza de Vaca.* Translated by Fanny Bandelier. New York. [FS]

O'Gorman, Edmundo. 1961. *The invention of America.* Bloomington: Indiana University Press.

Pickvance, C. G. 1976. *Urban sociology: Critical essays.* London: Tavistock.

Polgar, Steven, ed. 1975. *Population, ecology, and social evolution.* The Hague: Mouton.

Radin, Paul. 1927. *Primitive man as philosopher.* New York: Appleton. [DHF]

Redfield, Robert. 1941. *The folk culture of Yucatan.* Chicago: University of Chicago Press. [DED]

Reid, Kenneth C. 1977. "*Psoralea esculenta* as a prairie resource: An ethnographic appraisal." *Plains Anthropologist* 22:321–27.

————. 1979. "Getting to the root of the problem: A rejoinder to Kaye and Moodie." *Plains Anthropologist* 24:339–40.

Rudkin, Charles, ed. and trans. 1956. *Observations on California 1772–1790 by Father Luis Sales, O.P.* Los Angeles: Dawson's Book Shop. [FS]

Sanders, W. T., J. R. Parsons, and R. S. Santley. 1979. *The Basin of Mexico: Ecological processes in the evolution of a civilization.* New York: Academic Press. [PH]

Schoenwetter, James. 1974. "Pollen records of Guila Naquitz cave." *American Antiquity* 39:292–303.

Service, Elman R. 1971. *Cultural evolutionism.* New York: Holt, Rinehart, and Winston.

Sheehan, Bernard W. 1973. *Seeds of extinction.* Chapel Hill: University of North Carolina Press.

————. 1980. *Savagism and civility*. Cambridge: Cambridge University Press.

Shipek, Florence C. 1968. *The autobiography of Delfina Cuero, a Diegueño woman, as told to Florence C. Shipek*. Los Angeles: Dawson's Book Shop. [FS]

————. 1972. "Prepared direct testimony of Florence C. Shipek." Federal Power Commission Project 176, San Diego County California, Exhibit B-50. [FS]

————. 1977. "A strategy for change: The Luiseño of southern California." Unpublished Ph.D. dissertation. University of Hawaii Honolulu, Hawaii.

————. n.d. "Indians of California claims cases." *Journal of California and Great Basin Anthropology.* [FS]

Smith, Philip E. L. 1976. *Food production and its consequences*. Menlo Park: Cummings. [RJ]

Soustelle, Jacques. 1955. *La vie quotidienne des Azteques*. Paris: Librairie Hachette. [DED]

Spencer, J. E. 1966. *Shifting cultivation in southeastern Asia*. University of California Publications in Geography 19.

Spier, Leslie, and Edward Sapir. 1930. "Wishram ethnography." *University of Washington Publications in Anthropology* 3:151–300.

Steward, Julian H. 1933. "Ethnography of the Owens Valley Paiute." *University of California Publications in American Archaeology and Ethnology* 33:233–350.

————. 1936. "The economic and social basis of primitive bands." In *Essays in honor of A. L. Kroeber*, edited by Robert H. Lowie, 331–50. Berkeley: University of California Press. [RJ]

————. 1938. *Basin-Plateau aboriginal sociopolitical groups*. Bureau of American Ethnology Bulletin 120. [KRF]

Suttles, Wayne. 1951. "The early diffusion of the potato among the Coast Salish." *Southwestern Journal of Anthropology* 7:272–88.

Tanner, Adrian. 1979. *Bringing home animals: Religious ideology and mode of production of the Mistassini Cree hunters*. New York: St. Martin's Press. [MIA]

Tax, Sol. 1975. "General editor's preface." In *Population, ecology and social evolution*, edited by Steven Polgar. The Hague: Mouton.

Thomas, Cyrus. 1898. *Introduction to the study of North American archaeology*. Cincinnati: Robert Clarke.

Trigger, Bruce G. 1978. *Time and traditions*. New York: Columbia University Press.

————. 1980. "Archaeology and image of the American Indian." *American Antiquity* 45:662–76.

Turner, Nancy J. 1975. *Food plants of British Columbia Indians. Pt. 1. Coastal peoples*. British Columbia Provincial Museum Handbook 34. [KRF]

Vaillant, George C. 1941. *The Aztecs of Mexico*. Garden City: Doubleday, Doran. [DED]

Webb, M. C. 1978. "The significance of the 'Epi-Classic' period in Mesoamerican prehistory." In *Cultural continuity in Mesoamerica*, edited by D. L. Browman, 155–78. The Hague: Mouton. [PH]

White, Raymond C. 1957. "The Luiseño theory of knowledge." *American Anthropologist* 59:1–19. [FS]

Wilbur, Marguerite Eyer, ed. and trans. 1931. *The Indian uprising in Lower California 1734–1737 as described by Father Sigismundo Taraval*. Los Angeles: Quivira Society. [FS]

Wissler, Clark. 1922. *The American Indian*. New York: Oxford University Press.

Interpolation

Metis and Rationality, a Classical Class Struggle

At this point, we should consider whether rational thinking could be sufficient to understand American archaeology. Archaeology involves physical activity, moving muscles and coordinating them neurologically. Kneeling, troweling, critically eyeing a tip of something touched . . . sweating under the sun or shivering from wind, flare far from stately libraries' cerebral ambience. Ideally, we balance fieldwork with archival searches. Actually, each of us squirms as writing and reading contest time for hands-on field and lab work. Brain work versus muscle, words versus sensual knowledge. The Classical Greeks saw not only difference but also conflict between these powers with very real consequences.

Deep, deep in deepest time, the time of the Titans, Tethy, the Ocean's sister-wife, had a daughter, Metis. She appeared as the cosmic egg. Zeus tried to free his siblings from their father, Cronus, and was able to do so by Metis's aid. He and Metis then married, and she conceived. Zeus was very upset because it was prophesied that he would be killed by his son. To avert that, Zeus swallowed Metis. She lived, inside him, and bore and raised their daughter, Athena. In time, Athena determined to free herself from her father. Given shield and spear, she broke full-grown through Zeus's forehead. Her mother, Metis, continued to live within Zeus, whispering advice to him from within his head.

Metis was—is—wise and smart. She was patron of craftworkers and those cunning enough to obtain their goals without brutal force. In this, she contrasted with Zeus, the masculine ideal. Her daughter Athena had wisdom but was also *parthenos*, virgin, formal wisdom without experience. Plato saw *metis* as the opposite of rational thinking, the work of philosophers. The Athenians, true to their name, celebrated the mighty daughter armed with spear and shield, letting her eclipse her hidden mother. Classical education teaches rational thinking to be ideal, while craftworkers' embodied skills and how-to thinking are said to be limiting, unworthy of intelligent men.

Kent Flannery's khaki-clad field archaeologist, helplessly eyeing his blunted golden trowel, listened to Metis. His companions were both rational men, one already famous and empowered, the younger man aiming to get by using words, not a trowel. In my following chapters, Metis will be whispering.

Acknowledgment: I am deeply grateful to Elisabetta Cova for introducing me to Metis. Cova quickly grasped, from her own field experience, how *metis* fit my struggles to elucidate how archaeology is a craft as well as a discipline.

PART 2. Archaeology Is a Historical Science

Archaeology makes histories. How? Contrary to a catchy book title in the 1960s, the mute stones do not speak. They stand, or lie fallen, in landscapes. We archaeologists are ventriloquists, projecting voices as if from the past. Since the mid-nineteenth century, we present ourselves as scientists, organizing empirical data to point to probable pictures of past situations. What should that entail?

My research in Edinburgh in 1989 turned up a fascinating web of connections around the rise of a middle class and its desire for a meritocracy in place of feudal classes (Kehoe 1998). At issue in the 1840s was the Society of Antiquaries, an elite group fixated on the Roman presence in Scotland, versus the reform group interested in Scotland's independent past. Taking note of Thomsen's work in Denmark displaying, in literal terms, that nation's roots deep in the past, evidenced by excavations, the Edinburgh reform group invited Thomsen's protégé Jens Worsaae to come to advise the Scots on using the Danes' methods and three-age framework of Stone, Bronze, and Iron Ages. Active in geology as well as collecting artifacts and skulls, the reform group adopted stratigraphy in the ground as key to relative ages of strata and artifacts found within them. It was a golden age for Scottish geology, with native son Charles Lyell earning a dominant position with Darwin's cohort in the Royal Society, and James Hutton identifying a volcanic intrusion in an older rock along the Radical Road up Arthur's Seat in the middle of Edinburgh, proving the long durée of the earth. (A small marker is beside the rock, under the gorse, if you look for it.)

Daniel Wilson, a protégé of the reformers, reorganized artifacts in the Society of Antiquaries collection to show Scotland's deep-time history, publishing the material in 1851 as *The Archaeology and Prehistoric Annals of Scotland*—the first use of the term "prehistory" in English. Reflecting Lyell's point of view, the book oriented readers to landscapes as clues to the past. Artifacts are, as it were, keywords in stories of the past. Artifacts and stratigraphic series in the earth should be archaeologists' studies, not classical literature and previously-documented Roman ruins. Archaeology is sister science to geology. Archaeology should be pursued through the canons of field science.

George Gaylord Simpson laid down those canons a century after Wilson's book, in publications and by mentoring paleontologists. In a magisterial essay late in his career, he outlined the method of historical science as:

(1) obtaining and studying the historical data . . . ;
(2) determination of present processes . . . ;
    confrontation of (1) and (2) with a view to ordering, filling in, and explaining history. (Simpson 1970, 84–85)

For archaeologists, the second step is usually and properly done by means of careful ethnographic analogies (Currie 2016). Simpson additionally stated that historical sciences are built upon the principle of actualism, observing "present configurations . . . [to] infer configurations that preceded them" (Simpson 1970, 81).[1] "Actualism claims that our knowledge of the past needs to be grounded in examinations of processes acting today: it is about how to get knowledge" (Currie 2019, 5).

Paleontologists infer from living organisms that can be matched more or less closely to earlier ones. Genetics may be available to display biological relationships between the excavated specimen and postulated exemplars. Structural and physiological constraints as well as genealogical links focus comparisons. Archaeologists have fewer constraints on interpretation[2] because humans broke through physical limitations some two million years ago by extrasomatic technologies and practices. That makes ethnographic analogies less controlled than biological comparisons. Nonetheless, the principles of historical sciences hold: we infer from *actual* observed similarities in the present, reasonable interpretations of human activities in the past.

Straightforward, yet involving multiple choices with branching logical pathways. Too seldom can archaeologists be their own ethnographers. Most archaeologists are employed not to observe living makers of artifacts, but to survey, excavate, and analyze data. Ethnoarchaeology is a subfield that may describe practices continuing from the time of excavated sites, as in the work of Dorothy Keur (1941), Sue Kent (1993), and Kathryn Arthur

(2019), or observations of particular crafts as in Longacre's study of Philippine village pottery (2007). Tom Kehoe and I lived in First Nations territories where we could inquire of descendants of the sites' creators and sometimes do ethnoarchaeology, as we described in the paper, reprinted here, on the "direct ethnographic approach." Any contemporary ethnoarchaeology is disturbed, insofar as we are inferring past practices, by intrusions that may affect practices being studied, for example in Longacre's study of ceramics use-lives when plastic buckets are available and used. Lewis Binford's famous ethnography of Nunamiut hunting and butchering visited a community using metal tools and rifles, no longer camping in the bush—to what degree could they represent precontact, much less Paleolithic, reindeer hunters? His thick tome, full of his own direct questions and insistence on direct answers (Schmidt and Kehoe 2019, 6–8, 19n1) substituted graphs and tables for patient observation.

Ethnographic comparisons being the "present processes" Simpson required, it would be wise to understand what they should be and how to use them in "ordering, filling in, and explaining history." For a start, Matei Candea's 2019 *Comparison in Anthropology* sorts out a variety of stances of us vs. them, of which analogies are only one form. In archaeology, analogies often have one discrete component: the site and its contents and features, to be compared for similarities with a range of observed behaviors apparently sharing features with one or more of those of the site. Candea points out that "[within] each 'us' there are multiple others, and within each 'them' also" (2019, 316), as well as many choices of ethnographic or historical comparisons. We can frame questions such as how an artifact could be used, or whether reddened soil means fire, and look for similar artifacts or descriptions of reddened soil in ethnographic studies. Another approach is to seek ethnographies of communities living in similar landscapes or settlements. Simply taking an identification out of a much-cited standard book is not wise; it may perpetuate an error, perhaps one rooted in politically charged prejudices. See my 1991 "No possible, probable shadow of doubt" for an unambiguous carving of the male genitals insistently described as women's breasts by analogy to contemporary Western fascination with breasts.

Alison Wylie, the only philosopher of science to focus on archaeology, formally discussed analogy in several papers collected in her 2002 *Thinking from Things,* particularly the essay "The Reaction Against Analogy" (136–53). She later collaborated with Robert Chapman to collect essays from experienced archaeologists critically reflecting on choices of practice that frame interpretations (Chapman and Wylie 2015). Overall, that volume's excellent, thoughtful contributions make it clear that, first, archaeological practices are historically situated in regard to techniques, goals, and ideological premises, not to mention sources of funds and the related factor of social class. Richard Bradley's opening chapter (Chapman and Wiley 2015, 23–41) contrasting Lane-Fox Pitt-Rivers's work at the end of the nineteenth century, Piggott's excavation of a Scottish stone circle in the 1950s, and re-excavations of both sites by Bradley and collaborators decades later, sensitively touches upon these factors. His choice of key figures brings out the factor, also, of personalities, General Pitt-Rivers's military career (Bradley makes sure we notice his rank) versus Stuart Piggott's cultivated intellect drawing upon Collingwood's explications of historical practices (Colllingwood 1939, 1946).[3] The volume as a whole forcefully foregrounds the power of archaeological work itself to subordinate principles to the exigencies of the field.

Fieldwork; it revolutionized antiquarianism in the mid-nineteenth century. Geology, not art history, is our parent. We observe directly the syntagm of data as they are excavated. All that we can recognize are relevant, should be accounted for, remembering that an excavated site no longer exists. At the point of recognizing data, trained cognition becomes crucial. Without field experience and its follow-ups in the lab, we would be like the rancher surprised when I told him he was holding sherds, "I thought them was dried up orange peels! Just wondered who the hell was eating oranges out here." Sequence of work from survey to excavation to lab to report is a series of re-cognitions, mental identifications from trained brains. In this sense, archaeology is natural history: observing, collecting, classifying, the classifications keys to larger pictures. We can't manipulate variables, only note them, as our philosophers of historical sciences remind us (Turner 2007, 24). In the sequence from recognizing data to identifying them, comes,

the paramount importance of contextual background knowledge. When archaeologists are investigating a particular question about a particular site, they do so in a rich informational context that includes established investigative practices and lots of relevant background knowledge, as well as multiple lines of evidence. This is a way of leveraging previous epistemic successes. (Turner and Turner 2021, 10)

Established investigative practices, ever increasing, yield data that, to a mind furnished with a broad range of experiential and scholarly knowledge, can pursue logical chains to best interpretations—always provisional, always reflecting the researcher's own time and social experiences.

Three Examples of Doing Historical Science

In this and the next two chapters, I offer three of my efforts to contribute to archaeology as a historical science. "Relevant background knowledge" is why archaeologists should be familiar with Carl Sauer's work; "multiple lines of evidence" can include the use of direct ethnographic experience and listening; critiquing Lewis Binford's innovation of saying "foragers" instead of "hunter-gatherers" attempted to purge archaeology of a grossly inappropriate analogy.

Overall, these three papers argue that historical sciences study situations strongly affected by *contingencies*. For archaeologists, these are particulars of innumerable personal contacts and acts that may be customary or unique, *multiplicities* not "regularities." They may persist for millennia, as management of fescue pasture has on the Prairies, or only for a few centuries, like Cahokia. Our ethnographic analogies come from experiences within historical particularities, to use the term for Franz Boas's understanding of communities' histories. Stephen Jay Gould explained,

[I]n contingency lies the power of each person, no matter how apparently insignificant he may seem, to make a difference in an unconstrained world bristly with possibilities, and nudgeable by the smallest of unpredictable inputs into markedly different channels. (Gould 2002, 1141)[4]

Notes

1. Relevant to my paper on Cahokia in this volume, a full discussion of the principle of actualism in the Stanford online encyclopedia of philosophy rejects "haecceitism" as incompatible with actualism (Menzel 2023, 4.2, 4.3; https://plato.stanford.edu/entries/possibilism-actualism/#PossNeceLogiTrut).

2. During May 2021, Currie and I corresponded about issues in historical sciences, and I asked him why he and Derek Turner worked primarily with paleontology rather than archaeology. He responded that "anthropological theory is scary" and paleontology under-analyzed and simpler (personal correspondence, May 2021). When I noted that his emphasis on "multiplicities" of differing situations resembled Franz Boas's historical particularism, Currie agreed, emphasizing that humans' overcoming of geographical and ecological constraints, as well as technologies, gave such daunting multiplicities of multiplicities that archaeology complicated philosophical analysis.

3. Robin Collingwood was literally born to archaeology: his parents were employed to carry out archaeology for John Ruskin, his mother brought him as a baby in a basket to their site, and his adult fieldwork on Roman sites in Britain made him an authority on the period (D'Oro and Connelly 2020 for biography and extensive discussion of his philosophical works and biography).

4. Gould defined "contingency, or the tendency of complex systems with substantial stochastic components, and intricate nonlinear interactions among components, to be *unpredictable* in principle from *full knowledge of antecedent conditions*, but fully explainable after time's actual unfolding" (Gould 2002, 46; my italics) *if* one could see the *actual* unfolding. Archaeology can reveal only remnants of the actual unfolding.

4. Looking at Landscapes
Disciplinary Boundaries and Unrecognized Precursors

Landscapes are Telling

"Cultural landscape" as a viewpoint for archaeology hit the profession as a new concept in the surge of "more scientific" archaeology from the late 1960s through the 1980s. It coincided, although not limited to, the advent of Geographical Information Systems (GIS) (Hu 2011, 80). Such a trigger fits the mindset, all too prevalent, that new publications are all one needs for research. If the shoe fits, wear it, walk on without paying the price of discovering its material, construction, wearability, or style. One shoemaker whose boots have proved sturdy and longwearing for archaeologists' paths is Carl O. Sauer. His students George F. Carter and Carl Johannessen collected reams of data relevant to transmissions of cultural and biological phenomena, and in the next generation, William Denevan trained archaeologists Carole Crumley, Clark Erickson, and William Gartner to see landscapes. They also have all been truly collegial; it seems part of the Sauer heritage.

Sauer's field was geography, obviously—one would suppose—closely interdigitating with archaeology? No. Archaeologists seldom cite geographers or include them in projects. When it comes to Carl Sauer's work, this neglect is crippling. The crux of Sauer's work is a premise that we could call oecological, in the original sense that organisms live in *oikos*, "houses": the etymology conveys the meaning of *constructed* homes. For humans, that includes cultural landscapes. The concept is in opposition to Enlightenment science of discovering things, the *ding-an-sich*, out there in the Book of Nature waiting to be classified. Sauer was a field man, physically immersed in landscapes, recalling them when he read histories. His *The Early Spanish Main* (1966) is a masterpiece of embedded history, understood through firsthand knowledge of terrains, weather, technologies of food production, so much that was not known to the early Spanish invaders nor to academic historians using their documents. Sauer was postcolonial to his core, ground-truthing, respecting local farmers at least as much as archived documents.

George Carter said to me once, at a Chacmool conference in Calgary, "In science, we have to test alternative hypotheses." These could be the "present processes" that Simpson requires for historical sciences. At the time we were speaking, Binford's formula of Hypothetical-Deductive procedure was the proclaimed only way to work scientifically (Kehoe 1998, 134, 137). H-D began with *a* hypothesis that begot one logical chain toward validation, something you could do with laboratory physical sciences but solipsistic if working with field situations. When I asked new archaeologists from whence came their hypotheses, they looked blank. What a tautology, hypothesizing de nuevo out of one's Western-cultured mind and then selecting purportedly validating data! In contrast, the Sauerians were not dinosaurs but highly observant humans "scaffolding" interpretations (Chapman and Wylie 2015, 12–14).

Looking at Landscapes
Disciplinary Boundaries and Unrecognized Precursors

Introduction

Since the 1990s, "cultural landscape" has become a recognized focal term in archaeology and cultural anthropology. Eric Hirsch claimed at that time, that "landscape has received little overt anthropological treatment," merely describing how the ethnographer and the natives perceive a place (Hirsch 1995, 1). Hirsch and the contributors to his edited volume, all prominent British cultural anthropologists, wanted to use "landscape" as "foreground" and "background" in individuals' and communities' processes of building identities. Archaeologists appropriated "cultural landscape" as a "paradigm" to bring together "settlement ecology, ritual landscapes, and ethnic landscapes" (Anschuetz, Wilshusen, and Scheick 2001, 157), or "to link methods with theories in the scientific way associated with the [aspirations] of processual archaeology" (Rossignol 1992, 3).

Remarkably, the surge in cultural landscape discussions remains within strict disciplinary boundaries, citing legions of archaeologists without mentioning the great geographer Carl Sauer who formulated the field of cultural geography in the 1920s, or his legacy of three generations of significant researchers in geography.[1] In this paper, I introduce Sauer and the Sauerian lineage,[2] provide a case study central to Sauer's interests, and outline the ideological burden weighting conventional rejection of Sauer's position. Sauer's global standpoint is at odds with mainstream American archaeology's commitment to the paradigm based on the Doctrine of Discovery. Excluding Sauer and his students from archaeological discourse not only falsely attributes the concept of "cultural landscape" to archaeologists decades later than its academic introduction, it also dismisses data and argument supporting Sauer's recognition of the probabilities of pre-Columbian contacts between Eurasia and the Americas. To put it simply, failure to cite Sauer on "cultural geography" is poor scholarship, failure to evaluate data on pre-Columbian contacts is poor science, and failure to perceive ideological bias in archaeological interpretations is dangerously naive.[3]

Carl Sauer

Waldo Wedel recalled that in his graduate student days at UC Berkeley, 1932–1936, he found "all but total neglect of archeological research and teaching" in the Department of Anthropology. When he outlined to A. L. Kroeber his proposed doctoral research on Nebraska archaeology, the great man told him he was wrong to hypothesize environmental influences on culture history. Fortunately, Wedel had already met "Kroeber's counterpart and, at that time, political ally . . . Carl Sauer, chairman of the Department of Geography. . . . Thereafter, it was Sauer to whom I went, and whose lectures and teachings were of prime significance in formulating my own later approaches to Plains human ecology" (Wedel 1982, 154–59).

Carl Sauer (1889–1975), like Kroeber, combined a strong humanities education with an understanding of scientific method honed by pioneering fieldwork (Williams 2015). Both scholars grasped the importance of historical trajectories (Hornbeck, Earle, and Rodrigue 1996). Both built leading departments in their disciplines, producing lineages of noted figures. Their common interest, along with Robert Lowie's, in "Anthropogeographie," led to sending students to each other, to Sauer being appointed a member of many anthropological dissertation committees, and to Kroeber and Sauer jointly teaching seminars (Kerns 2003, 88). Sauer contributed a landmark paper in landscape studies, "Morphology" (1925) early in his Berkeley career, and much richer and more sophisticated treatments later, climaxing in his "The Agency of Man on the Earth," keynote for the 1955 conference he shaped, "Man's Role in Changing the Face of the Earth" (Rowntree 1996, 132–33). Sauer is credited with "moving American human geography beyond environmental determinism in favor of an emphasis on humans as active agents in environmental change and, equally important, of an articulation of explicit and rigorous method" (Rowntree 1996, 133).

"Cultural landscape." "Humans as active agents." "Explicit and rigorous method." Phrases resonating in so many archaeological studies today (e.g., Ashmore 2002; Ashmore and Knapp 1999; Crumley 1994; David and Thomas 2008; Hoffecker 2002, 2004; Johnson 2007; Van Dyke 2008), yet Sauer and his students are not acknowledged. Carl Sauer's powerfully framed concept of cultural landscape has been foundational in cultural geography. It merits recognition by archaeologists and other anthropologists interpreting landscapes (Mathewson 2011, 59).

Carl Sauer's Integration of Cultural and Historical Geography

Carl Sauer's vision of landscape was above all dynamic. People moved about the land, doing things, and the land responded. Climate, soils, rock, water had *potential*; social practices realized the potential. Agency inheres in cultural materiality. As Waldo Wedel learned, Kroeber's focus on "cultures" tended to attribute social developments to a "superorganic" power (Kroeber 1917). Sauer's sensitivity to landscape and practical experience with regional studies kept him aware of historical events and movements—real people and their capabilities. His was always a historical as well as cultural geography, and the link lay in a processual perspective (Mathewson 1987, 99).

"Ecological reasoning enabled the Sauerians to appraise the historical impact of human activities on cultural landscapes," suggesting the most appropriate term for Sauer's work is "cultural-historical ecology" (Zimmerer 1996, 168). Sauer and his students took it as a premise that landscapes they observed are anthropogenic, a major move forward from Sauer's (and Boas's) foundation in nineteenth-century anthropogeographie. They eschewed explicit theorizing, considering it premature so long as their databases were, in their estimation, inadequate to support inductive generalizations (again, like Boas [Lowie 1937, 151–52]).[4] Therefore, "Sauerians" worked long and hard to gather detailed, well-documented data. Their avoidance of published theorizing rendered them unfashionable when theorizing became the vogue in the 1960s. Enthusiasm first for establishing analytical closed systems, and then, a couple decades later, for "agency," seemed to leave Sauerians in the dust. Advocates of the former claimed to be more scientific, because it employed more statistics and abstract models; with the latter they claimed to factor in individual decisions rather than project generalized "societies" (Zimmerer 1996, 171–76). Few, if any, following either of the two approaches took time to map distributions as did Sauer, V. Gordon Childe, Grahame Clark, and in his final work, James A. Ford (e.g., Childe's series of editions of *Dawn of European Civilization*; Clark 1952; Ford 1969).

Plant geography became Sauer's focus in the latter part of his career. His *Agricultural Origins and Dispersals*, 1952, is a landmark. Archaeological data were utilized, along with contemporary distributions and historical documents, to elucidate not just the development of specific agricultural regimes but also human agency in plant dispersals: plants became proxies for human movements and contacts. In collating masses of reports of plant occurrences with paleontologists' reconstructions of original habitats, Sauer and his students encountered numerous anomalies, animal as well as botanical. When ancient distributions before the present continents separated, and possibilities of dispersal by floating on the sea or carried by birds had been ruled out as an explanation, the parsimonious hypothesis would be dispersal by human carriers (e.g., Sauer 1962). The prime case is maize, an artifact of human cultivation that cannot go feral. Kroeber (1939, 221, citing Sauer) and his generation mapped the distribution of maize cultivation in the Americas, identifying "Nuclear America" as a huge zone in which agricultural knowledge and often rituals had been spread along with maize seed (Brown 2006, 656–60). Donald Lathrap said (Benz and Staller 2006, 669) that his provocative studies of agriculture in South America were stimulated by Sauer's work, especially Sauer's magisterial chapter in the *Handbook of South American Indians* edited by Julian Steward (Sauer 1950).

Boundaries of Discourse

Archaeological folk wisdom conventionally rejects hypotheses of trans-oceanic voyages before 1492 CE. The foolishness of such a stance is overwhelmingly evidenced. Already in the Pleistocene, humans traveled over the open ocean to Australia and western Pacific islands (Bednarik 1997, 2000, 2014; McGrail 2001). Carole Mandryk cogently exposed the folk belief opposing the coastal migration hypothesis for Paleoamericans (Mandryk 2004), in spite of strong arguments for it by, e.g., Schurr and Sherry (2004), and Goebel, Waters, and O'Rourke (2008). American archaeologists' "horror aquae" encompasses even crossings of the Gulf of Mexico in the Postclassic/Mississippian period, the feasibility of which is well attested by Columbus's sighting of substantial Mayan trading vessels in the Caribbean (Sauer 1987, 167). A list of authenticated transoceanic crossings by an astounding variety of small boats amply attests the feasibility of ocean crossings on anything that floats (Kehoe [1971] 2003, 1998, 199–200; see also Doran 1973 on boat traditions).

Jane Holden Kelley presented a model of American archaeology as a core set of beliefs and practitioners, ringed by a series of circles of less-accepted postulates and scholars (Kelley and Hanen 1988; Shapin 1994, 413–15). Dena Dincauze implicitly used this model of a core-set when she showed that claims to pre-Clovis sites in the Americas are subject to more stringent demands for validation than are those assigned to the conventional schema (Dincauze 1984). The case for pre-Columbian transoceanic contacts, like that for trans-Gulf contacts, has corollaries embedded in colonialist discourse (Trigger 2006, 114) and in debates about science itself (e.g., Turner 2007). Neglect of Carl Sauer's priority and work establishing a domain of cultural landscape research becomes a clue to fundamental premises in archaeological models that seriously undermine its efforts toward scientific practice.

Going back to the Enlightenment, Western anthropology constructed an "evolutionary" Great Chain of Being for humans, assigning the peoples of modern colonies to savage or barbarian classes (Powell 1881; Kehoe 1998, 58–59). Even students of Boas, as late as the mid-twentieth century, parroted the conventional myth. Alexander Goldenweiser on "Our primitive contemporaries":

The primary local unit of culture is numerically small . . . isolated geo-graphically . . . patterns set in a rigid frame. . . . cut off from its own past . . . tradition soon passes into myth . . . the elders are in the saddle. . . . They stand for established routine, a fearful avoidance of the new. . . . The individual here is but a miniature reproduction of the group culture. . . . Nor does this exhaust the factors which stand for conservatism. . . . Here every breath of cultural life is dominated by natural things and events. . . . Under such conditions the economic adjustment is taken almost as a fact of nature. It may be sorely inadequate, but it works after a fashion and is accepted as final. (Goldenweiser [1937] 1946, 407–10).

And Paul Radin explained the colonized in this way:

One of the fundamental traits of these major civilizations [Egyptian, Sumerian-Babylonian, Hebrew, India, Christianity and Mohammedan-ism] was their essential instability, the frequent socio-economic crises through which they passed. . . . Contrasted with these major civiliza-tions, there have always existed other civilizations, those of aboriginal peoples, where societies were fundamentally stable, where no basic internal social-economic crises occurred. . . . Here we have an amazing antithesis which it is of fundamental importance to remember if we wish to understand the civilizations of aboriginal peoples and to see them in their proper perspective. (Radin 1953, 7–8)

Repudiating such blatantly racist and untrue characterizations of people not organized into state polities demands reconsideration of the paradigm they embodied. "Isolated geographically" is one of its untenable premises.

Colonialist discourse went hand-in-hand with positivist science. From the seventeenth-century subculture of gentlemen scientists described by Shapin (1994) there developed the usually unspoken assumption that science is the domain exclusively of educated white men. Indigenous knowledge was scorned. The praxis of the educated class constituted "the reasonable." Alexander von Humboldt's 1814 list of intriguing par-allels between indigenous American and Asian cultures fell outside the boundaries of "reasonable" discourse, based on educated white men's tenets. Although increasingly during the nineteenth and into the twentieth century, scientific method was promoted to be the means of discovering valid knowledge; method alone could not cut through tacit conventions of acceptability (Barnes, Bloor, and Henry 1996, 140–41).

Carl Sauer practiced inductive science. He, like Boas and Kroeber, was rooted in German historicism, fundamentally opposed to Enlightenment rationalism and its universalist orientation (Speth 1996). Not "natural laws" but actual histories, rife with contingencies, were Sauer's goal. Although Sauer personally wasn't interested in nautical matters, he did not presume that "primitive" people could not cross water; he and his students saw plants in places they could not have reached on their own, so particularly for cultivars, he inferred humans had transported them. If a large body of water intervened, *ergo*, those humans used boats. Inductive empiricism does not reject data a priori.[5]

Sauer's approach collided head-on with core American archaeology's paradigm when, in 1991, *Antiquity* published a report of sweet potatoes dated to 1100 CE in the central Polynesian island of Mangaia (Hather and Kirch 1991). Both authors and the journal of publication are highly respected; their work is considered valid. If so, it indisputably proves pre-Columbian voyaging between the island and South America (Rouillier et al. 2013). Nevertheless, a 2007 publication, again in a highly respected journal, disputes reports of the presence of Polynesian chicken bones in a pre-Columbian site in Chile (Storey et al., 2007; cf. Gongora et al. 2008; Thomson et al. 2014; but see Storey and Matisoo-Smith 2014). This is a classic set of examples of Dincauze's recognition of higher standards of proof for interpretations outside core beliefs.

The Doctrine of Discovery Paradigm

"Every historical change creates its mythology but indirectly related to historical fact, . . . a constant by-product of . . . of sociological status, which demands precedent; of moral rule, which requires sanction" (Malinowski [1926] 1954, 146). To legitimate their invasions and conquests of the Americas, European powers agreed on a Doctrine of Discovery articulated by Pope Alexander VI in May, 1493, in the papal bull *Inter Caetera*. Purporting to address the need to bring Christian salvation to all peoples, the bull gave "Christian princes" jurisdiction over all lands and peoples not already ruled by a Christian. Conquest and domination were morally justified as means to teach Christianity and impose Christian ways of life upon the heathen (Miller 2006; Miller et al. 2010; Robertson 2005). Implicit in the doctrine is the inferiority of non-Christians, "waiting in darkness" until Europeans discover them—they languish in "prehistory." Anglo colonizations were further legitimated by John Locke (1689), writing to justify his patron's Carolina Colony takeover of Indian land and the English Board of Trade encouragement of mercantile ventures in colonies (Kehoe 2009; Tully 1995, 70–89).

The myth of Columbus discovering a wholly unknown New World covered with wilderness inhabited by savages is so palpably erroneous that its persistence displays the enormous power of social chartering myth (Meek 1976). Chartering colonial policies underlying First Nations' present disastrous poverty, it undergirds white privilege (Jungkunz 2011, 9–11). Unilinear cultural evolution ("evolution" in a pre-Darwinian sense) is the model generated by the Doctrine of Discovery's characterization of non-Christian nations as lacking essential knowledge. A governing class of white, educated, Western European men form the apex of cultural evolution, defining what it is to be "civilized." Anglo Whig history continues to dominate school curricula, inculcating the idea that North America's history began in 1607 (Kehoe 1990). Such early socialization, constantly reinforced by civil religion rituals as well as in schools and popular books, has prepared American archaeologists to accept the concept of "prehistory" and its concomitant recourse to postulated academic models of cultural evolution, rather than a more strictly empirical, inductive science utilizing a range of historical forms of societies for interpretive models. In effect, with notable exceptions, the dominant paradigm renders American First Nations "peoples without history" (Wolf 1982).

Beginning this century, James Whitley (2002) bemoaned that,

> Ancestors were to the 1990s what chiefdoms (Yoffee 1993) were to the 1970s—the explanation of choice for a whole range of archaeological phenomena . . . [it] has gone from being a suggestion to becoming an orthodoxy without ever having had to suffer the indignity of being treated as a mere hypothesis. (Whitley 2002, 119)

Such cavalier treatment of data from "prehistory" is tolerated because, following the Doctrine of Discovery, the colonized were de facto different from their conquerors, the "civilized." North American First Nations are said to have lived in "tribes," "chiefdoms," many of them "foragers" (a word that applies technically only to grazing herbivores). Pictured clothed in hides, their fabrics impressed on millions of sherds are ignored by mainstream archaeologists (Kehoe 2001). "Emergent complexity" is preferred, rather than hypothesizing achieved kingdoms, states (in the case of Cahokia), or sophisticated sustainable economies such as that of the Blackfoot (Zedeño et al. 2014; Kehoe 1993, 2014).

A formally postcolonial world with a glaringly global economy clashes with the racist Eurocentric paradigm built from the Doctrine of Discovery. During Pope Francis's visit to the United States, a number of Catholic organizations as well as spokespeople for First Nations called upon the pontiff to rescind the papal bulls that the Doctrine is founded upon (Noisecat 2015). Multilinear evolution was proposed by Julian Steward in 1955, and briefly stimulated comparative studies, but was eclipsed by 1960s New Archaeology promotion of statistics and "hypothetico-deductive" tautologies. At a time when the thrust in Anglo American politics was to terminate Indian communities, no significance was accorded to First Nations' own histories and methods of organization. Instead, the academic formulations decried by Whitley were taken to be real. Robert Merton described such practice as the

> fallacy of the latest word . . . the tacit assumption that the latest word is the best word. . . . the Phoenix phenomenon . . . the continuing resiliency of theories or theoretically derived hypotheses . . . even though they have been periodically subjected to much and allegedly conclusive demolition ("falsification"). (Merton 1968, 1092)

Jane Kelley's core set is relevant here: demolitions of the reigning colonialist paradigms have fallen outside core praxis even when published by faculty in elite universities, e.g., Fried's (1975) denunciation of "tribes" and Yoffee's (1993) denunciation of "chiefdoms." To resort to historical particularism would demolish not only cherished academic terms, it would topple the legitimating story of European discovery of a wilderness without civilization.

Integrative Research

While most archaeologists have been digging in their trenches, fallaciously accepting the latest word of theorists, scientists working with organisms have been rallied to look beyond their subfields, both toward integrated research and toward "understanding that science and scientists must address societal needs and questions in new, wide-ranging, and synthetic ways" (Wake 2008, 352). Aside from supplying heritage management (Kehoe 2007), addressing societal needs has only slowly advanced in archaeological discourse. A number of First Nations now employ archaeologists to research their histories and identify sites to protect, while Section 101(d)(2) of the National Historic Preservation Act, enacted in 1996, enables tribes to appoint and maintain their own THPOS (Tribal Historic Preservation Office and Officers). As these grow, they erode the hegemonic colonialist paradigm.

Integrative research could be archaeology's twenty-first century program, as it is advocated for biologists (Wake 2008). One of Sauer's progeny in geography, Kent Mathewson, argues that broad, integrated research has been characteristic of Sauer and his legacy (Mathewson 2011). In these studies, cultural landscapes are dynamic; there are no peoples without history, no restrictively totalizing recourse to abstract academic terms. Part of the research agenda is historical particularism, the Boasian position that details of actual local history, so far as they are recounted or documented materially, are integral to any understanding of landscapes. "Multilineal evolution" is congruent with Sauerian geography and historical particularism.

Returning to Sauer's interest in dealing forthrightly with anomalous occurrences of organisms associated with humans, the case of the American sweet potatoes in a Polynesian site dated before Columbus calls for an integrative approach. Beyond the collaboration of experienced oceanic archaeologist Patrick Kirch and archaeobotanist Jon Hather, the independent genetic analyses of the team led by Caroline Roullier (2013), and high-precision radiocarbon dating (Wilmshurst et al. 2011), interpreting the discovery requires knowledge of Polynesian histories and seafaring (Anderson, Barrett, and Boyle 2010). These several independent analyses both support and nuance the archaeologically revealed cultural landscape of Mangaia a thousand years ago. Their concurrence overturns the Doctrine of Discovery paradigm of American isolation.

In spite of the onslaught of attacks upon identification of a pre-Columbian Polynesian landfall in Chile, the probability of such landfalls is high, given the Mangaia evidence for an earlier landfall with a return voyage. Ocean currents and Polynesian history make other claims of landfalls reasonable inferences (Jones et al. 2011). Beyond Polynesia, it is plausible that other seafaring societies may have touched the Americas, not to found civilizations but to seek valuables to trade or opportunities for settlement (Kehoe 2015). Historical particularism points to the medieval spice trade, when strong competition for Island Southeast Asian spices and woods launched hundreds of large seaworthy Asian merchant ships upon eastward explorations. Private ventures, their records were seldom archived (the same situation affects knowledge of Atlantic European deep-sea fishing). Such enterprises may have brought the very anomalous wheeled animal figurines to Mesoamerica, where in one site they co-occur with large animal figurines remarkably like Asian lion-dog temple guardians, and are apparently associated with a temple in the American site. Like lion-dogs, the Mesoamerican figurine wears a collar of little bells (Kehoe 2015). This is not diffusion, which means an innovation permeates a community; the data instead indicate contacts and limited intercourse such as occurred millions of times in the last 100,000 years, at least.

Conclusion

Archaeologists have been using concepts of landscape without recognizing Carl Sauer's foundational work. The apparent ignorance of his and his students' large body of research may reflect only a narrow purview, the assumption that only one's own discipline will have relevant material for one's projects. Or, it may testify to scientists' anxiety over achieving and keeping a credible reputation among peers (Barnes, Bloor, and Henry 1996, 155). Or it may indicate a recalcitrance in turning away from Western Enlightenment culture.

We need more than a sociology of science to understand the dismaying refusal of most American archaeologists to consider both probabilities and evidence of pre-Columbian transoceanic contacts. It has been more than two decades since Hather and Kirch published their evidence for sweet potatoes in central Polynesia a thousand years ago. The probability that Polynesian explorers made landfalls on the American continents as they worked eastward from Hawai'i and Rapa Nui has been obvious since the nineteenth century, strengthened during the twentieth century by experiments and analyses of Polynesian ships and navigation (e.g., Doran 1973; Feinberg 1993; Finney 1994). Only an anthropological appreciation of the power of early-socialized "common sense" can explain rejection of sound observational data.

American archaeology developed through the nineteenth century in an era celebrating Manifest Destiny (Weinberg 1935). Superiority of the white race was fundamental to legitimating European conquests and displacements of American First Nations. Columbus discovering a totally isolated New World that, lacking white men, had never evolved civilizations, supported the ideology of Manifest Destiny. Debates over whether American Indians were truly human began soon after Columbus's landing, famously among Spanish theologians (Lyman 1990, 47–52). Secularization and the rise of science as authority in the nineteenth century moved the issue into questions over races' capabilities. Daniel Brinton, an American anthropologist writing after the Civil War, used the concept of psychic unity of humans to argue that whatever progress Indians may have made toward civilization indicated their human innate capacity for culture, while their failure to achieve civilizations comparable to those of the Old World (in his estimation) was due to their isolation since initial migrations over Bering Strait (Lyman 1990, 54–58). Fitting (and reflecting) the dominant ideology so well, Brinton's authoritative pronouncements reinforced dichotomization of "prehistory" and ethnography from "history," economics, sociology, and political science. American archaeology and anthropology became *sui generis*, a body of material about primitives from which to build an assertion of unilinear cultural evolution.

Postwar New Archaeology continued the Enlightenment science search for universal laws of human behavior, somewhat more restrained in that "cultural processes" were the goal of "middle-range theory" (e.g., Binford 1965). Mere culture histories were eschewed as, literally, too provincial. Landscape archaeology was expected to deduce general cultural processes. Sauer and his students' strongly-inductive empirical studies did not fit the reigning paradigm. We should see evidence-based practice, to borrow a term from medical practice, take precedence over theory pronouncements. It's time for nineteenth-century ideology to be retired and empirical data privileged.

Acknowledgments. I thank Alison Rautman for suggesting I collaborate with Carl Johannessen on developing a geographer's paper into a format suited to an anthropological journal, Carl for agreeing to the trial, and Jim Weil for critically reading the result and suggesting our intent would be better served by my focusing on the archaeological perspective. Rautman decided that the paper would not be of sufficient interest to *American Antiquity* readers to justify publishing it in that journal. The editor of *American Anthropologist* had a similar opinion. Uploading online seems the best way to make this work available.

NOTES

1. A few American archaeologists are exceptions, having studied with William Denevan, who was Carl O. Sauer Professor of Geography at the University of Wisconsin–Madison, and a student of Sauer's student James Parsons. These include Carole Crumley, who works in historical ecology, and Clark Erickson, who continues the Sauer-Denevan research into South American cultural landscapes.

2. "Mechtild Rössler, who has just been appointed Director of the UNESCO Heritage Division and Director of the World Heritage Centre, was a key presence at the meeting. A long-time UNESCO heritage official, Rössler is a geographer schooled in the German cultural landscapes tradition that was transplanted so successfully to the U.S. by Cal-Berkeley's Carl Sauer. Rössler has been highly influential in UNESCO's efforts to integrate nature and culture . . ." (Meeting on "archaeological parks" convened in Salalah, Oman, by ICOMOS Oman, 2015. SSAA Government Affairs and International Government Affairs Update, October 2015, online).

3. *Delgamuukw v. Regina*, 1987–1997, is a prime examplar of the human consequences of a judicial decision derived from colonialist cultural evolution. It is particularly striking because it is so recent. See McCreary 2014 for description and analysis of the case, and Schmidt and Mrozowski 2013 for more cases.

4. Robert Lowie explained Boas's position by a quote from Ernst Mach: "To the scientist who always detects new features in every major solution of a problem systematizing and schematizing always appear premature, and he gladly leaves it to the more practised philosophers" (Lowie 1937, 152).

5. Bruce D. Smith and co-authors reporting on genetic evidence for an Asian origin of bottle gourds, in tropical America stated that,

> Paleoindian groups could have carried bottle gourds and still-viable seeds through the northern noncultivation zone along the south coast of Beringia, either on foot or in near-shore water craft, rapidly enough to have introduced domesticated *L. siceraria* to the New World along with the dog ... In contrast, any scenarios involving straight line, long-distance trans-Pacific transport of domesticated bottle gourds from Asia to the Americas by open-ocean seafaring vessels can be considered as having a close-to-zero probability, given the absence of evidence for watercraft capable of making such a voyage in the Late Pleistocene time frame required for bottle gourd to have reached the interior southern highlands of Mexico by 10,000 B.P. ... we favor a Paleoindian near-coast (land and/or water) introduction as representing the most plausible alternative. (Erickson et al. 2005, 18319)

In other words, Smith believed tropical gourd seeds could have been carried north along and completely around the North Pacific Rim by paddlers in small boats who needed to fish, hunt, and camp daily. Reference handbooks on bottle gourd seed viability agree that these seeds ordinarily remain viable only for months (Doijode 2001, 302–3). Several years later, Smith and others published a revision based on additional genetic data for gourds, now finding American gourds derived from African species, and postulating they floated across the Atlantic, taking root on American shores (Kistler et al. 2014).

REFERENCES

Ames, Oakes. 1939. *Economic Annuals and Human Cultures*. Cambridge MA: Botanical Museum of Harvard University.

Anderson, Atholl, James H. Barrett, and Katherine V. Boyle, eds. 2010. *The Global Origins and Development of Seafaring*. Cambridge: McDonald Institute for Archaeological Research.

Anschuetz, Kurt F., Richard H. Wilshusen, and Cherie L. Scheick. 2001. "An Archaeology of Landscapes: Perspectives and Directions." *Journal of Archaeological Research* 9 (2): 157–211.

Ashmore, Wendy. 2002. "'Decisions and Dispositions': Socializing Spatial Archaeology." *American Anthropologist* 104 (4): 1172–83.

Ashmore, Wendy, and A. Bernard Knapp. 1999. *Archaeologies of Landscape: Contemporary Perspectives*. Malden MA: Blackwell.

Balabanova, Svetlana, Boyuan Wei, and M. Krämer. 1995. "First Detection of Nicotine in Ancient Population of Southern China." *Homo* 46:68–75.

Balabanova, Svetlana, Franz Parsche, and Wolfgang Pirsig. 1992. "First Report of Drugs in Egyptian Mummies." *Naturwissenschaften* 79:358.

Barnes, Barry, David Bloor, and John Henry. 1996. *Scientific Knowledge*. Chicago: University of Chicago Press.

Bednarik, Robert G. 1997. "The Earliest Evidence of Ocean Navigation." *International Journal of Nautical Archaeology* 26 (3): 183–91.

———. 2000. "Crossing the Timor Sea by Middle Palaeolithic Raft." *Anthropos* 95 (1): 37–47.

———. 2014. "The Beginnings of Maritime Travel." *Advances in Anthropology* 4:209–21.

Benz, Bruce F., and John E. Staller. 2006. "The Antiquity, Biogeography, and Culture History of Maize in the Americas." In *Histories of Maize*, edited by J. E. Staller, R. H. Tykot, and B. F. Benz, 665–73. Amsterdam: Elsevier Academic Press.

Binford, Lewis R. 1965. "Archaeological Systematics and the Study of Culture Process." *American Antiquity* 31 (2): 203–10.

Bretschneider, E. 1882. *Botanicon Sinicum. Notes on Chinese Botany From Native and Western Sources*. London: Trübner.

———. 1896. "Botanicon Sinicum. Part III: Botanical Investigations into the Materia Medica of the Ancient Chinese." *Journal of the Royal Asiatic Society*, Chinese Branch 29:1–623.

Brown, Cecil H. 2006. "Glottochronology and the Chronology of Maize in the Americas." In *Histories of Maize*, edited by J. E. Staller, R. H. Tykot, and B. F. Benz, 647–63. Amsterdam: Elsevier Academic Press.

Chang, Kwang-Chih. 1977. *The Archaeology of Ancient China*. New Haven CT: Yale University Press.

Childe, V. Gordon. [1925] 1957. *The Dawn of European Civilisation*, sixth edition. London: Routledge and Kegan Paul.

China Heritage Project. 2007. "China's Oldest Peanuts." http://www.chinaheritage quarterly.org/briefs.php?searchterm=012_HAM_Briefs.inc&issue=012.

Clark, J. Grahame. 1952. *Prehistoric Europe: The Economic Basis*. London: Methuen.

Crumley, Carol, ed. 1994. *Historical Ecology: Cultural Knowledge and Changing Landscapes*. Santa Fe: SAR Press.

David, Bruno, and Julian Thomas, eds. 2008. *Handbook of Landscape Archaeology*. Walnut Cree CA: Left Coast Press.

Desmond, Ray. 1992. *The European Discovery of Indian Flora*. New York: Oxford University Press.

Dincauze, Dena F. 1984. "An Archaeological Evaluation of the Case for Pre-Clovis Occupations." *Advances in World Archaeology* 3:275–323.

Doijode, S. D. 2001. *Seed Storage of Horticultural Crops*. Boca Raton FL: CRC Press.

Doran, Edwin, Jr. 1973. *Nao, Junk, and Vaka: Boats and Culture History*. College Station TX: University Lecture Series, Texas A&M University.

Erickson, David L., Bruce D. Smith, Andrew C. Clarke, Daniel H. Sandweiss, and Noreen Tuross. 2005. "An Asian Origin for a 10,000-year-old Domesticated Plant in the Americas." *Proceedings of the National Academy of Sciences* 102 (51): 18315–20.

Feinberg, Richard. [1988] 1993. *Polynesian Seafaring and Navigation.* Kent OH: Kent State University Press.

Finney, Ben. 1994. "Polynesian-South America Round Trip Canoe Voyages." *Rapa Nui Journal* 8 (2): 33–35.

Ford, James A. 1969. *"A Comparison of Formative Cultures in the Americas: Diffusion or the Psychic Unity of Man."* In *Smithsonian Contributions to Anthropology*, vol. 11. Washington DC: Smithsonian Institution Press.

Fried, Morton. 1975. *The Notion of the Tribe.* Menlo Park, CA: Cummings.

Goebel, Theodore, Michael R. Waters, and D. H. O'Rourke. 2008. "The Late Pleistocene Dispersal of Modern Humans in the Americas." *Science* 319 (5869): 1497–502.

Goldenweiser, Alexander. [1937] 1946. *Anthropology: An Introduction to Primitive Culture.* New York: F. S. Crofts.

Gongora, Jaime, Nicolas J. Rawlence, Victor A. Mobegi, Han Jianlin, Jose A. Alcalde, Jose T. Matus, Olivier Hanotte, Chris Moran, Jeremy J. Austin, Sean Ulm, Atholl J. Anderson, Greger Larson, and Alan Cooper. 2008. "Indo-European and Asian origins for Chilean and Pacific chickens revealed by mtDNA." *Proceedings of the National Academy of Sciences* 105 (30): 10308–13.

Hather, Jon G., and Patrick V. Kirch. 1991. "Prehistoric Sweet Potato (*Ipomoea batatas*) from Mangaia Island, Central Polynesia." *Antiquity* 65:887–93.

Hirsch, Eric. 1995. "Landscape: Between Place and Space." In *The Anthropology of Landscape*, edited by Eric Hirsch and Michael O'Hanlon, 1–30. Oxford: Clarendon Press.

Hoffecker, John F. 2002. *Desolate Landscapes: Ice-Age Settlement in Eastern Europe.* New Brunswick NJ: Rutgers University Press.

———. 2004. *A Prehistory of the North: Human Settlement of the Higher Latitudes.* New Brunswick NJ: Rutgers University Press.

Hornbeck, David, Carville Earle, and Christine M. Rodrigue. 1996. "The Way We Were: Deployments (and Redeployments) of Time in Human Geography." In *Concepts in Human Geography*, edited by C. Earle, K. Mathewson, and M. S. Kenzer, 33–61. Lanham MD: Rowman and Littlefield.

Humboldt, Alexander von. 1814. *Researches Concerning the Institutions and Monuments of the Ancient Inhabitants of America, with Descriptions and Views of Some of the Most Striking Scenes in the Cordillera!* Translated by H. M. Williams. London: Longman, Hurst, Rees, Orme, Brown, Murray & Colburn.

Johannessen, Carl L. 1989a. "Maize Ears Sculpted in 12th and 13th Century A.D. India as Indicators of Pre-Columbian Diffusion." *Economic Botany* 43:164–80.

————. 1989b. "American Crop Plants in Asia Prior to European Contact." *Proceedings of the Conference of Latin Americanist Geographers* 13:14–19.

————. 1997. "Des epis de mais en Inde sur des sculptures des XII–XIIIeme siecles?" *Kadath: Chroniques des Civilisations Disparues* (Fall/Winter) 4–31.

————. 1998. "Maize Difused to India before Columbus." In *Across Before Columbus,* edited by Don Y. Gilmore and Linda S. McElroy, 111–24. Edgecomb, ME: New England Antiquities Research Association, NEARA Publications.

————. 2000. "Three-Dimensional Corn representations from India in Pre-Columbian Times." *Epigraphical Society Occasional Papers* 24.

Johannessen, Carl, and Ann Z. Parker. 1989a. "Maize Ears Sculpted in 12th and 13th Century A.D. India as Indicators of Pre-Columbian Diffusion." *Economic Botany* 43:164–80.

————. 1989b. American Crop Plants in Asia Prior to European Contact. Year Book 1988, *Proceedings of the Conference of Latin Americanist Geographers* 13:14–19.

Johnson, Matthew. 2007. *Ideas of Landscape.* Malden MA: Blackwell.

Jones, Terry L., Alice A. Storey, Elizabeth A. Matisoo-Smith, and José Miguel Ramírez-Aliaga, eds. 2011. *Polynesians in America: Pre-Columbian Contacts with the New World.* Lanham MD: AltaMira.

Jungkunz, Vincent. 2011. "Dismantling Whiteness: Silent Yielding and the Potentiality of Political Suicide." *Contemporary Political Theory* 10:3–20.

Kehoe, Alice Beck. 1971. "Small Boats Upon the North Atlantic." In *Man Across the Sea,* edited by C. Riley et al., 275–92. Austin: University of Texas Press.

————. 1978. "Early Civilizations in Asia and Mesoamerica. (Report of 1977 Wenner-Gren conference organized by Kehoe and David H. Kelley)." *Current Anthropology* 19 (1): 204–5.

————. 1990. "'In Fourteen Hundred and Ninety-two, Columbus Sailed . . .': The Primacy of the National Myth in American Schools." In *The Excluded Past,* edited by Peter Stone and Robert MacKenzie, 201–16. London: Unwin Hyman.

————. 1993. "How the Ancient Peigans Lived." In *Research in Economic Anthropology* 14, edited by Barry Isaac, 87–105. Greenwich CT: JAI Press.

————. 1998. *The Land of Prehistory: A Critical History of American Archaeology.* New York: Routledge.

————. 2001. "From Spirit Cave to the Blackfoot Rez: The Importance of Twined Fabric in North American Indian Societies." In *Fleeting Identities,* edited by Penelope Drooker, 210–25. Carbondale: Southern Illinois University Press.

————. 2003. "The Fringe of American Archaeology: Trans-oceanic and Trans-continental Contacts in Prehistoric America." *Journal of Scientific Exploration* 17 (1): 19–36.

————. 2007. "Archaeology within Marketing Capitalism." In *Archaeology and Cap-*

italism: From Ethics to Politics, edited by Yannis Hamilakis and Philip Duke, 169–78. Walnut Creek CA: Left Coast Press.

———. 2009. "Deconstructing John Locke." In *Postcolonial Perspectives in Archaeology*, edited by Peter Bikouis, Dominic Lacroix, and Meaghan M. Peuramaki-Brown, 125–32. Calgary: University of Calgary Archaeological Association.

———. 2014. "A Comment on Zedeño et al." *Current Anthropology* 55 (6): 813.

———. 2015. *Traveling Prehistoric Seas: Critical Thinking on Ancient Transoceanic Voyages*. Walnut Creek CA: Left Coast Press.

Kelley, Jane Holden and Marcia P. Hanen. 1988. *Archaeology and the Methodology of Science*. Albuquerque: University of New Mexico Press.

Kerns, Virginia. 2003. *Scenes from the High Desert: Julian Steward's Life and Theory*. Champaign: University of Illinois Press.

Kistler, Logan, Álvaro Montenegro, Bruce D. Smith, John A. Gifford, Richard E. Green, Lee A. Newsom, and Beth Shapiro. 2014. "Transoceanic Drift and the Domestication of African Bottle Gourds in the Americas." *Proceedings of the National Academy of Sciences* 111 (8): 2937–41.

Kroeber, A. L. [1917] 1952. "The Superorganic." *American Anthropologist* 19:163–213.

———. 1939. *Cultural and Natural Areas of North America*. Berkeley: University of California Press.

Ladefoged, Thegn N., Michael W. Graves, and James H. Coil. 2005. "The Introduction of Sweet Potato in Polynesia: Early Remains in Hawai'i." *Journal of the Polynesian Society* 114 (4): 359–73.

Lowie, Robert H. 1937. *History of Ethnological Thought*. New York: Holt, Rinehart and Winston.

Luna-Cavazos, Mario, Robert Bye, and Meijun Jiao. 2009. "The origin of Datura metel (Solanaceae): genetic and phylogenetic evidence." *Genetic Resources and Crop Evolution* 56:2.

Lyman, Stanford M. 1990. *Civilization: Contents, Discontents, Malcontents, and Other Essays in Social Theory*. Fayetteville: University of Arkansas Press.

Mandryk, Carole A. S. 2004. "Invented Traditions and the Ultimate American Origin Myth: In the Beginning . . . There Was an Ice-Free Corridor." In *The Settlement of the American Continent*, edited by C. M. Barton, G. A. Clark, D. R. Yesner, and G. A. Pearson, 113–20. Tucson: University of Arizona Press.

Mathewson, Kent. 1987. "Sauer South by Southwest: Antimodernism and the Austral Impulse." In *Carl O. Sauer: A Tribute*, edited by M. S. Kenzer, 90–111. Corvallis: Oregon State University Press.

———. 2011. "Sauer's Berkeley School Legacy: Foundation for an Emergent Environmental Geography?" In *Geografía y Ambiente en América Latina*, edited by Gerardo Bocco, Pedro S. Urquijo, and Antonio Vieyra, 51–81. Mexico City: Universidad Nacional Autónoma de México.

McCreary, Tyler. 2014. "The Burden of Sovereignty: Court Configurations of Indigenous and State Authority in Aboriginal Title Litigation in Canada." *North American Dialogue* 17 (2): 78–81.

McGrail, Seán. 2001. *Boats of the World: From the Stone Age to Medieval Times*. Oxford: Oxford University Press.

Meek, Ronald L. 1976. *Social Science and the Ignoble Savage*. Cambridge: Cambridge University Press.

Merton, Robert K. 1968. "The Fallacy of the Latest Word: The Case of 'Pietism and Science.'" *American Journal of Sociology* 89 (5): 1091–121.

Miller, Robert J. 2006. *Native America, Discovered and Conquered: Thomas Jefferson, Lewis and Clark, and Manifest Destiny*. New York: Praeger.

Miller, Robert J., Jacinta Ruru, Larissa Behrendt, and Tracey Lindberg. 2010. *Discovering Indigenous Lands: The Doctrine of Discovery in the English Colonies*. Oxford: Oxford University Press.

Nault, Dr. Lowell R., Dr. Richard C. Pratt, Dr. Patrick Finney, and Dr. Christine J. Bergman. 1995. "Four Letters to Carl Johannessen." Manuscripts on file from Seminar at Ohio Agricultural Research and Development Center, Ohio State University.

Noisecat, Julian Brave. 2015. "Indigenous Leaders Want Pope Francis To Rescind Bull Justifying Imperialism." *Huffington Post*. http://www.huffingtonpost.com/entry/pope-francis-doctrine-of-discovery_56058eb9e4b0dd8503076c17.

Parsche, Franz, Svetlana Balabanova, and Wolfgang Pirsig. 1993. "Drugs in ancient population." *The Lancet* 341:503.

Pokharia, A.K., and K. S. Saraswat. 1999. "Plant Economy during Kushana period (100–300 A.D.) at Ancient Sanghol, Punjab." *Pragdhara: Journal of the U.P. State Archeology Department* 9:75–104.

Powell, John W. 1881. "Report of the Director." In *First Annual Report, Bureau of Ethnology*, 1879–80, xi–xxxiii. Washington DC: Government Printing Office.

Radin, Paul. 1953. *The World of Primitive Man*. London: Abelard-Schuman.

Robertson, Lindsay G. 2005. *Conquest by Law: How the Discovery of America Dispossessed Indigenous Peoples of Their Lands*. Oxford: Oxford University Press.

Rossignol, Jacqueline. 1992. "Concepts, Methods, and Theory Building." In *Space, Time, and Archaeological Landscapes*, edited by Jacqueline Rossignol and Luann Wandsnider, 3–16. London: Plenum.

Roullier, Caroline, Laure Benoit, Doyle B. McKey, and Vincent Lebot. 2013. "Historical collections reveal patterns of diffusion of sweet potato in Oceania obscured by modern plant movements and recombination." *Proceedings of the National Academy of Sciences* 110 (6): 2205–10.

Rowntree, Lester B. 1996. "The Cultural Landscape Concept in American Human Geography." In *Concepts in Human Geography*, edited by C. Earle, K. Mathewson, and M. S. Kenzer, 127–59. Lanham MD: Rowman and Littlefield.

Saraswat, K. S., N. K. Sharma, and D. C. Saini. 1994. "Plant economy at ancient Narhan (ca. 1300 B.C–300/400 A.D)," In *Excavations at Narhan (1984–1989)*, edited by Purushottam Singh, 225–337. Varanasi: Department of Ancient Indian History, Culture and Archaeology, Banaras Hindu University.

Sauer, Carl O. 1950. "Cultivated Plants of South and Central America." In *Handbook of South American Indians*, volume 6, edited by J. H. Steward, 487–543. Washington DC: Smithsonian Institution, Bureau of American Ethnology Bulletin 143, Government Printing Office.

———. [1952] 1969. *Agricultural Origins and Dispersals*. New York: American Geographical Society. Reprint, Cambridge MA: MIT Press.

———. 1962. "Maize into Europe." *Proceedings of the 34th International Congress of Americanists* (Vienna, 1960), 777–88. Horn-Vienna, Austria: Verlag Ferdinand Berger.

———. 1987. "Observations on Trade and Gold in the Early Spanish Main." In *Carl O. Sauer: A Tribute*, edited by M. S. Kenzer, 164–74. Corvallis: Oregon State University Press.

Sauer, Jonathan D. 1950. "The grain amaranths: a survey of their history and classification." *Annals of the Missouri Botanical Garden* 37:561–632.

Schurr, Theodore G., and S. T. Sherry. 2004. "Mitochondrial DNA and Y Chromosome Diversity and the Peopling of the Americas: Evolutionary and Demographic Evidence." *American Journal of Human Biology* 16 (4): 420–39.

Schmidt, Peter R., and Stephen A. Mrozowski, eds. 2013. *The Death of Prehistory*. Oxford: Oxford University Press.

Shapin, Steven. 1994. *A Social History of Truth*. Chicago: University of Chicago Press.

Sorenson, John L., and Carl L. Johannessen. 2006. "Biological Evidence for Pre-Columbian Transoceanic Voyages." In *Contact and Exchange in the Ancient World*, edited by Victor H. Mair, 238–97. Honolulu: University of Hawai'i Press.

———. 2013. *World Trade and Biological Exchanges Before 1492 C.E*, revised and expanded edition. Scotts Valley CA: CreateSpace Independent Publishing Platform.

Speth, William W. 1987. "Historicism: The Disciplinary World View of Carl O. Sauer." In *Carl O. Sauer: A Tribute*, edited by M. S. Kenzer, 11–39. Corvallis: Oregon State University Press.

Steward, Julian H. 1955. *Theory of Culture Change: The Methodology of Multilinear Evolution*. Urbana: University of Illinois Press.

Stonor, C. E., and Edgar Anderson. 1949. "Maize Among the Hill Peoples of Assam." *Annals of the Missouri Botanical Garden* 36:355–404.

Storey, Alice A., Jose Miguel Ramirez, Daniel Quiroz, David V. Burley, David J. Addison, Richard Walter, Atholl J. Anderson, Terry L. Hunt, J. Stephen Athens, Leon Huynens, Elizabeth Matisoo-Smith. 2007. "Diocarbon and DNA Evidence for Pre-Columbian Introduction of Polynesian Chickens to Chile." *Proceedings of the National Academy of Sciences* 104 (25): 10335–39.

Storey, Alice A., and Elizabeth A. Matisoo-Smith. 2014. "No evidence against Polynesian dispersal of chickens to pre-Columbian South America." *Proceedings of the National Academy of Sciences* 111 (35): E3583.

Thomson, Vicki A., Ophélie Lebrasseur, Jeremy J. Austin, Terry L. Hunt, David A. Burney, Tim Denham, Nicolas J. Rawlence, Jamie R. Wood, Jaime Gongora, Linus Girdland Flink, Anna Linderholm, Keith Dobney, Greger Larson, and Alan Cooper. 2014. "Reply to Beavan, Bryant, and Storey and Matisoo-Smith: Ancestral Polynesian 'D' haplotypes reflect authentic Pacific chicken lineages." *Proceedings of the National Academy of Sciences* 111 (35): E3585–86.

Trigger, Bruce G. 2006. *A History of Archaeological Thought*, 2nd edition. Cambridge: Cambridge University Press.

Tully, James. 1995. *Strange Multiplicity: Constitutionalism in an Age of Diversity*. Cambridge: Cambridge University Press.

Turner, Derek. 2007. *Making Prehistory: Historical Science and the Scientific Realism Debate*. Cambridge: Cambridge University Press.

Van Dyke, Ruth. 2008. *The Chaco Experience: Landscape and Ideology at the Center Place*. Santa Fe: School for Advanced Research Press.

Vishnu-Mittre, Aruna, and Sharma Chanchala. 1986. "Ancient plant economy at Daimabad." In *Daimabad 1976–79*, edited by S. A. Dali. Calcutta: Government of India Central Publication Branch.

Wake, Marvalee H. 2008. "Integrative Biology: Science for the 21st Century." *Bioscience* 58 (4): 349–53.

Wedel, Waldo R. 1982. "The Education of a Plains Archeologist." *Reprints in Anthropology* 24:150–73.

Weinberg, Albert K. 1935. *Manifest Destiny: a Study of Nationalist Expansionism in American History*. Baltimore: Johns Hopkins Press.

Whitley, James. 2002. "Too Many Ancestors." *Antiquity* 76:119–26.

Williams, Michael. 2015. *To Pass On a Good Earth: The Life and Work of Carl O. Sauer*. Charlottesville: University of Virginia Press.

Wilmshurst, Janet M., Terry L. Hunt, Carl P. Lipo, and Atholl J. Anderson. 2011. "High-precision Radiocarbon Dating Shows Recent and Rapid Initial Human Colonization of East Polynesia." *Proceedings of the National Academy of Sciences* 108 (5): 1815–20.

Wolf, Eric R. 1982. *Europe and the People without History*. Berkeley: University of California Press.

Yoffee, Norman. 1993. "Too Many Chiefs? (or, Safe Texts for the '90s)." In *Archaeological Theory: Who Sets the Agenda?*, edited by Norman Yoffee and Andrew Sherratt, 60–78. Cambridge: Cambridge University Press.

Zedeño, Maria Nieves, Jesse A. M. Ballenger, and John R. Murray. 2014. "Landscape Engineering and Organizational Complexity among Late Prehistoric Bison Hunters of the Northwestern Plains." *Current Anthropology* 55 (1): 23–42, 51–54.

Zimmerer, Karl S. 1996. "Ecology as Cornerstone and Chimera in Human Geography." In *Concepts in Human Geography*, edited by C. Earle, K. Mathewson, and M. S. Kenzer, 161–88. Lanham MD: Rowman and Littlefield.

5. How the Ancient Peigans Lived

"How the Ancient Peigans Lived" was solicited by Barry Isaac, editor of the annual volume *Research in Economic Anthropology*. Barry was one of the stalwarts of Central States Anthropological Society, attending each year its spring meeting, serving in office, and compiling a history of the Society. Our collegial friendship extended to seeing each other at the American Anthropological Association meetings as well. Once, when AAA met in Mexico City in 1974, Barry and I planned to go to Patzcuaro afterward, he bringing a male friend and I my friend Patricia O'Brien. Both our friends canceled. We went on together, our expertise complementing each other and Barry's pleasant companionship enhancing the beauty of the Lake and valley. Platonic, satisfying.

Some of our conversations were outlets for complaints about distressing turns in our discipline. Barry's interest as an economic anthropologist in subsistence patterns made him a good listener to my strong feelings against labeling hunter-gatherers as "foragers." Lewis Binford had introduced that as a better scientific term than "hunter-gatherers," spelling out in stultifying logic the difference between "foraging" and "collector" strategies of food procurement: foragers roam about hoping to "encounter" food in an "extended foraging radius," while "collectors" send out "task groups" to obtain or cache food at known localities (Binford 1980). Of the former, "the most exclusive foragers are best known from equatorial forests" (7). Of course Binford writing for 1980 publication could not know Gustavo Politis's (2007) detailed firsthand ethnography of one equatorial society, the Nukak, whose encyclopedic knowledge of every dimension guides their sophisticated shifting seasonal harvesting subsistence. Even granted that, overall, Binford's paper reeks of white supremacy colonialism, viewing small societies harvesting native resources as so many deer browsing *apparently* randomly—although deer, too, know their territories.

Practicing historically-informed ethnography with colleagues in Mexico, Barry shared my disgust at the pseudoscience of looking at people as if they are molecules in a gas. When he suggested I write up a counter paper for his annual volume, I happily accepted, Uhlenbeck's transcription of Kánaikoan's information dancing in my head (A. B. Kehoe 1993). Years later, my colleague Gerry Oetelaar in Calgary published a summary of interpretations of bison hunting by northwestern Plains First nations, particularly Blackfoot, and by Western observers and archaeologists (Oetelaar 2014). Opening with reference to Robert Kelly's 1995 *The Foraging Spectrum: Diversity in Hunter-Gatherer Lifeways* and Binford's 1980 paper, Oetelaar sums up their "ecological approaches . . . allowing researchers to construct models where systemic change is predictable" (Oetelaar 2014, 10).

"Predicting systemic change" was the goal of fashionable 1960s science, rooted in expectation of an elite controlling the public. As I explained in my 2012 *Militant Christianity* (86), the Rockefeller "foundations ensured that a cadre of WASP men would dominate the United States, masking their capitalist agenda as enlightened science. They took it for granted that America was, and should be, a Protestant Christian nation." Noted sociologist Bernard Barber wrote in his *Science and the Social Order*, "The social sciences, *like all science*, are primarily concerned for analysis, prediction, and control of behavior and values" (Barber 1952, 259; my italics). Blatant fascism! Indeed, fascism appealed to many Americans in the 1930s, up until the 1960s counterculture movements.

Oetelaar does not oppose "science" to First Nations alleged mysticism. Instead, he explains "different perceptions of the systemic relationships between humans and the world around them. . . . humans play an essential and reciprocal role in helping to maintain an orderly balance in nature through their proper conduct in daily practice, rituals, and ceremonies" (Oetelaar 2014, 11). He then builds the case for Blackfoot *creation* of the fescue prairie and its groves of tree shelter, arguing that the *Niitsitapi* worldview has been an effective agent. In the very *longue durée* of their occupation of the land below the Backbone of the World (Front Range of the Rockies), they constructed not only the sites that archaeologists see, but aspects of the landscape, a *cultural* landscape. As Amskapi Pikuni (Blackfeet) scholar Darrell Robes Kipp told his community in 2010, the reality that abides in their languages is that living beings leave their mark on the land (see Howe 2019). I made much the same argument that Oetelaar does in my "Ancient Piegans" paper.

Archaeology is a historical science. Its practitioners are humans seeking knowledge of humans in the past. In this chapter, I've emphasized that our sites lie in cultural landscapes. Simplistic models of resource procurement coded for few data are bad science. They disrespect nearly all humans of the past, and they ignore the significance of the extraordinary *Homo* brain. Proponents of the label "forager" naively perpetuate the imperialist view of "others" as "savages." They unthinkingly accept the fascist[1] goal of controlling others through predictive "laws" of behavior. Hewing to that elitist assumption, their careers are more successful than mine (A. B. Kehoe 2022).

How the Ancient Peigans Lived

Introduction

From *Grasses and Forage Plants*, published in 1859, through 1967's *Challenges in Forage and Range Research*, from the U.S. Agricultural Research Service's Forage and Range Research Branch, to *Forages: The Science of Grassland Agriculture*, a definitive manual today, "forage" continues its primary meaning of "food for horses and cattle, esp. for horses in army" (Oxford Concise English Dictionary). Cognate with "fodder," "forage" is normally used as in this description of the prelude to the Battle of Lookout Mountain, "Forty thousand rations and 39,000 pounds of forage were landed in the morning, to provide for an army" (Kennedy 1985, 482).

What are we to make of this, from a recent book?

> After enjoying some 3 to 4 million years of success through foraging, the human species adopted a radically different adaptive strategy that within the last 10,000 years has replaced foraging in virtually every part of the world . . . the shift to producing food. (Henry 1989, 3)

A John Wayne Paleolithic, populated exclusively by cavalrymen? And why are taxpayers supporting a Forage and Range Research Service if forage ceased to be an adaptive strategy ten thousand years ago?

In this essay, I employ the Peigan Blackfoot to attack a bandwagon of mud-eyed anthropologists who want to reduce these Injuns, and all our ancestors, to the condition of desperate soldiers in enemy lands (cf. Jones

1987, 216–19). The popular term "forager" is not only etymologically inappropriate, it calls up a model inconsistent with ethnographic data (Martin 1983), malapropos to a historical science of human behavior (Keene 1991, 137), and inadequate even to describe the deer for which it was originally developed. A description of the nineteenth-century Southern Peigan illuminates the flaws of the forager model and advances an interpretation far more consistent with both evolutionary biology and historical perspective.

How the Ancient Peigans Lived

Thirty years after the establishment of the Southern Peigan Blackfeet Reservation, the Dutch linguist C. C. Uhlenbeck (1912) recorded a series of texts in Blackfoot, with facing close translations in English. The first text is a lengthy recounting of the typical annual round of a Peigan band, as recalled by the elderly Káinaikoan. I've summarized Káinaikoan's narrative in Table 1, adding a few details from John C. Ewers's (1958) ethnography prepared forty years later. It should be obvious from this account that a Southern Peigan band did not forage, though the bison, elk, deer, antelope, and moose they hunted did so: there is a radical difference between the ungulates' daily grazing on forage and the humans' planned economy. Indians modified the land by burning, to maintain prairie and maximize succulent young growth for bison pasture (Duke 1991, 62), in a livestock production strategy minimizing labor input.

Archaeological research (e.g., T. F. Kehoe 1967, 1973; Davis and Wilson 1978; Duke 1991) demonstrates that, for at least two thousand years, Northwest Plains Indians depended upon large-scale impoundment of bison herds. (This in itself invalidates applying optimal foraging theory to these peoples, for the model was developed premising the pursuit of single organisms [Martin 1983, 617].) Great skill in managing the herds was developed (Verbicky-Todd 1984), and both community structure and settlements were adapted to their exploitation (Epp 1988). Káinaikoan's account and much other ethnographic data indicate the complementary importance of vegetable foods, especially camas, prairie turnips, and berries. These foods were the domain of women, as among the neighboring Nez Perce (Marshall n.d., 11, 19). The third principal component in Northern Plains economy was trade, not only in the historic period but in the Late Prehistoric as well; although trade in bison products can only be inferred from the archaeological data, the evidence for it is persuasive (T. F. Kehoe 1973, 195–97; Brink n.d.; O'Brien n.d. b, 3).

Table 1. "How the Ancient Peigans Lived": A Peigan Band's Annual Round, Mid-Nineteenth Century, Told by Káinaikoan ("Blood," a Peigan), 1911, to C.C. Uhlenbeck (John Tatsey, interpreter)

SEASON	ACTIVITIES
Spring	Stayed on Marias River—until bison shed their hair.
Late Spring	Upstream to get lodge-pins.
	Overtook bison in Sweetgrass or Cypress Hills.
	After processing kill ("when slices of meat are dry"), moved down to Milk River "where are the better buffalo" (Uhlenbeck 1912, 3).
	[Ewers (1958): bitterroot, dug & boiled.]
Summer	Young man reported berries are ripe, camp moved to Many-berries. Women picked berries and also prepared hides for lodge covers.
	Moved to Buffalo-head for the chokecherries and other berries.
	Moved to Seven-person for elk hunting.
	Moved to Cypress Hills to cut lodge poles.
	Moved to Long-lakes.
	Moved to Where-Women-Society-Left-Their-Lodgepole.
	Moved "back to prairie" to Green lake to hunt bison for parfleches & ropes.
	Moved to Writing-on-Stone, for chokecherries and other berries to dry.
	Moved up Milk River to Women's-point.
	Moved away from river to hunt bison and antelope and to get wolf, badger, skunk pelts "to buy tobacco with" (Uhlenbeck 1912, 7); might move to six places before they found a herd to hunt (14–15).
	Went to trading post to sell bison robes (20 to 40) for powder, cartridges, tobacco, blankets, gunflints, and gun springs (Uhlenbeck 1912, 14).

June-July	[Ewers (1958): Turnips—eaten raw, roasted, boiled, and dried for winter; camas ("near the mountains"), roasted in earth baking ovens.]
Midsummer	[Ewers (1958): Sarvis berries, eaten raw, cooked, and dried.]
Fall	Moved to Cut Bank River to cut lodge poles. Hunted deer, elk, moose near the mountains.
September-October	[Ewers (1958): Chokecherries, especially in stream valleys of foothills: dried.]
Late September-October (after first frost)	[Ewers (1958): Buffalo-berries, eaten fresh or dried.]
Late Fall	Moved down from the mountains to where bison would come, and decided where they would camp for the winter, along the river; prepared robes for bedding.
Mid-winter	Moved onto the prairie away from river to hunt bison.
	"When the places where they camped a long time about became to be bad [dirty], then they moved notwithstanding [the cold]" (Uhlenbeck 1912, 12–13).
Spring	Men and their younger wives would go on hunt, but senior wives stayed in main camp.
TOTAL:	17–23 moves of main camp.

It is intriguing to see how the bison hunters' societies paralleled those of the bison. Bison are gregarious animals whose primary group is the herd of about twenty cows, to which bulls are followers (McHugh 1972, 157). Although the most dominant animal is usually a bull, cows are the most common leaders and lead by modeling advantageous behavior, for example, moving a short distance in a desired direction and waiting for followers, if any, to imitate (McHugh 1972, 155). The animals monitor each other through what McHugh (1972, 151) calls "a constant chatter," with about ten different vocalizations recognized by McHugh (1972, 152). Vocalizations are supplemented by body postures (152). McHugh (1972, 154) observed a tendency for bison to space themselves out, keeping a small but discernible and defended personal space for each adult except under adversity, when the herd clusters tightly. Bison use a K reproductive strategy (although McDonald [1981, 241, 258] makes the point that, *comparing Bison species*, the historic plains *Bison bison* had a *relatively* r strategy).

A human community wanting to efficiently hunt bison must deal with the animals' normal response to danger of bunching closely together and running off after the cow that first senses and reacts to danger (McHugh 1972, 155). (We need not discuss hunting using high-powered rifles or shooting from trains.) Stalking a herd from downwind and propelling a spear, javelin, or arrow when within range will net only one or a couple of animals before the herd takes off. Such stalking would require daily hunting because not every day's stalking would succeed in downing a bison before the herd sensed the danger. Whereas, in boreal forest, minimal human groups of two or three nuclear families are adapted to hunting solitary forest game, on grasslands the cluster-and-run response of bison calls for hunting strategy that takes advantage of this response. The alternative, on grasslands, of stalking individual animals is maladaptive in terms of potential energy gain. Corralling required only one man to expend energy in scouting and stalking, and brought in enough animals to provide for a human community for up to a month. The energy expended in constructing the corral and drive lanes, manning the lanes during the drive, and killing the impounded animals would have more amply and, through storage of dried surplus meat, consistently supported the human community than would daily stalking.

This cost-efficient and reliable (when skilled and experienced in driving [Verbicky-Todd 1984]) method is associated with a human community that, among the Blackfoot, numbered 10–20 lodges or 80–160 persons,[2] with about 20–40 vigorous adult men and a somewhat greater number of vigorous adult women (Ewers 1958, 39, 37). We can note that the human community parallels the bison community in its core of roughly 20–70 adult females. Further parallels can be noted in that, in both bison and human "herds," adult males lived auxiliary to these females, the bison bulls peripheral to the cow herd and the men in tipis owned by women (cf. "The First Marriage," Wissler and Duvall 1908, 21–22). During the summer, when food was abundant and travel easy, both bison and humans rendezvoused into groups of thousands. Leadership in both bison and Blackfoot communities was by example and demonstrated wisdom, with adults in both species expecting and insisting on personal autonomy and a degree of personal space (A. B. Kehoe 1991a, n.d. a; cf. Gardner 1991). These parallels were seen by the Blackfoot and expressed in myth (Wissler and Duvall 1908, 123; Verbicky-Todd 1984, 210–18).

The standard method of obtaining bison was by constructing a corral of poles and brush against the foot of a bluff or end of a ravine. Particularly if the corral was below the edge of a bluff, stone, stick, or brush-pile markers were set up to outline a funnel approach to the corral. While ritual leaders prayed in camp, a young man went out searching for a herd. When he found one, he approached from downwind, hid, and sang a magical song that sounds like the bleating of a calf. The cows would move toward him, looking for the calf they heard. He moved singing toward the corral, the herd following, until the animals were within the drive lane, when most of the rest of the band jumped up from hiding along the lane and stampeded the herd into the corral. Armed men stationed around the corral speared, shot, and clubbed the bison milling within. Then the entire band trooped into the corral and processed the carcasses. Organs and other delicacies were eaten raw or quickly cooked, backfat and sinews stripped off, marrow extracted, and lean meat cut into thin strips and dried on racks. (McHugh [1972, 84–94] has a good summary on processing meat.) Dried meat lasts for months, even years, cushioning the community against periods without fresh meat caused by bad weather, erratic herd movements, or plain bad luck.

Group effort was required to impound the herd. All hands were needed to butcher the carcasses; often, tough bulls were left untouched, or there were simply too many animals to process (articulated skeletons being common in the pounds we have excavated in the Northwestern Plains), although even prehistorically so many could be processed that a marketable surplus was produced (T. F. Kehoe 1973, 195–97). One Blackfoot informant claimed six persons regularly shared in butchering one bison, and a carcass was routinely divided into six portions, one for each butcher (Verbicky-Todd 1984, 53). There is a general agreement among Northwestern Plains sources that the tongue was the most prestigious portion of the bison and that tongues were presented to ritual leaders or elders, or set aside for formal feasts. (For example, the Blackfoot Sun Dance includes a ceremony, "Coming Forward to the Tongues," in which the most respected women stand forward to slice the tongues to be shared in communion by the community.)

Sources differ on the degree to which distribution of the carcasses or products was taken by leaders, but it is clear that none of the Northwestern Plains peoples considered any individual to own the pound or its contents. The general principle was that each person owned what they had produced (Wissler 1911, 27). Because anybody (except captives) had the right to leave a band and move elsewhere, no one could dictate to another; people remained in a community only so long as they enjoyed tolerable relations with the others in it. The ideal was that everyone freely cooperated for mutual benefit. Leadership was gained by publicly evincing this ideal through acts of generosity (Wissler 1911, 23).

The necessity of pooling labor to carry off bison drives selected for Northwestern Plains human communities of around one hundred or so persons, that is, twenty to forty active men and a similar number of active women. This size reflects the number of adults required to construct and man the corral and process sufficient of the slaughtered herd to support the community for a few weeks. It is not directly tied to a species herd size, because more than a few hundred animals would overwhelm a corral and fewer than twenty animals would make the labor cost of a corral too high. The *raison d'être* for the community is the operation of the drive; in a sense, the band is a task group.

Powerful as the adaptation was in molding the community, it did not preclude other forms of organization, so long as they did not conflict with the normal operation of pounds. The political economy of the Northern Plains peoples went beyond the pound-based subsistence community to include the summer rendezvous camps and trading enterprises. Each of these greatly increased the resources of the basic community, raising the survival probability of its members.

The summer rendezvous looked like a combination of fair and pilgrimage sites. Gambling, racing, singing, flirting, and exchanges went on day and night. Ceremonies were conducted, adjudication of disputes performed, and alliances negotiated. I believe the summer rendezvous should be interpreted as a form of the *polis* (A. B. Kehoe 1981, 507, 508). Aristotle listed the necessary and sufficient aspects or functions of a *polis* to be (1) territory from which subsistence may be drawn, (2) food production, (3) arts and crafts production, (4) arms, to maintain internal order and to protect against foreign aggression, (5) public worship, and (6) "most vitally necessary, is a method of deciding what is demanded by the public interest and what is just in men's private dealings" (Aristotle 1946, 299). The *polis* can entertain foreign visitors, traders, and workers, so long as their numbers do not overwhelm the citizens (Aristotle 1946, 292).

The Northwestern Plains summer rendezvous fulfills the political functions Aristotle identified and therefore can be seen to be a *polis* with one significant difference from Aristotle's Greek examples: the Northwestern Plains polities existed only in latent form for most of the year. Each of the functions existed in partial, minor, or occasional form in the communities that operated bison drives, but the full deployment of the functions occurred only in the summer during the rendezvous. Through the rendezvous, the Plains communities enjoyed that full exercise of the human capacity for complex and formalized social relations that Aristotle believed to be the true nature of our species. It was because a *polis* can remain latent for part of a year, then be activated, that the agricultural peoples such as the Cheyenne who moved onto the Plains after European invasions did not lose their culture. The traditionally nomadic hunters such as the Blackfoot, conversely, could include "urban" functions in their culture, internally developed or transmitted from neighbors such as the Mandan and Hidatsa (e.g., A. B. Kehoe 1970).

It is clear from historical and archaeological data that Northern Plains societies participated in a market system comparable to the Wallerstein world system model (O'Brien n.d. a, n.d. b). Definitely during the Mississippian (Late Prehistoric) period and probably during the Hopewell (Middle Woodland) period, trade connected the Northern Plains to the Midwest. Gregg and Picha (n.d., 3) summarize archaeological evidence for Middle Woodland trade involving the Northern Plains—listing "obsidian, Knife River flint, grizzly bear claws and canines, bison bones, and fossil shells" as Northern Plains materials discovered in Hopewellian sites in the Midwest—and note that Early Woodland (Pelican Lake) Northern Plains burials of the first millennium BCE already contain these materials plus copper and marine shell beads, proving trade from the Midwest.

Blakeslee (1975, 200–5; see also Wood 1980) described the plains trading networks as reticular, comprising both permanent trading towns along the Missouri system and periodic rendezvous. He was puzzled by the apparent lack of a market economy composed of highly specialized producers, with instead only a relative difference in production of animal derivatives among the nomadic nations and of agricultural crops among the town-based nations. Blakeslee's focus on the Plains left out the importance of the Cahokian, and possibly the earlier Hopewellian, states in the mid-continental international economy; extending his network to include the Mississippian states, as O'Brien (n.d. a, b) has done, clarifies the transition westward along the Missouri system from provincial to frontier and transfrontier polities. The Missouri towns were entrepôts as well as regional markets, and nomadic communities produced for the system, not just for the Plains towns. It is, of course, important to remember that many trade items, probably including slaves, are not represented in the archaeological record.

That the continental system was conceptualized by the Indians themselves is shown by maps drawn in February 1801 and 1802 by a Blackfoot leader, Ac ko mok ki, "The Feathers," for Peter Fidler. Fidler transcribed nine maps from Indian consultants. The most important, one used by Lewis and Clark among others, was based on two cartograms drawn by Ac ko mok ki. Two Blackfoot leaders gave Fidler two cartograms each in 1802, and an unidentified Indian gave him one (Ruggles 1991, 63). Fidler's composites of these cartograms cover most of Alberta and Montana, both the High Plains and the Rockies, although Fidler himself remained in the area near the confluence of the South Saskatchewan with the Red Deer River (Moodie and Kaye 1977, 12; Ruggles 1991, 63) We can see that the Blackfoot knew their territory thoroughly, including the western half of the Missouri River system, and also knew the Columbia and Snake systems as rivers from the Rockies to the Pacific, though not in any detail. Fidler's map, probably summing up Blackfoot knowledge of their world, encompasses more than 200,000 square miles from latitude 49° 15' N to 42° 45' N in central Wyoming (Moodie and Kaye 1977, 12). Fidler said of Ac ko mok ki that

> This Chief has seen the greater part of the different Tribes he has marked down & has heard of the rest when in company with other nations who live nearer those distant tribes . . . . Of all those different Tribes in the Indian map only the Tattood & Cottonashow [Arapaho and Kootenay] Indians have been at any of our houses to trade. (quoted in Moodie and Kaye 1977, 13)

Parenthetically, Allan Taylor (1992) has identified Crow visiting York Factory a century before Fidler, presumably stimulated by Kelsey's 1690–1691 incursion into Archithinue country.

The Blackfoot knowledge encoded in Fidler's map appears a century later in McClintock's recording of Brings-Down-the-Sun's 1905 description of the Old North Trail:

> It runs north and south along the Rocky Mountains . . . . It forked where the city of Calgary now stands. The right fork ran north into the Barren Lands as far as people live. The main trail ran south along the eastern side of the Rockies, at a uniform distance from the mountains, keeping clear of the forest, and outside of the foothills. It ran close to where the city of Helena now stands, and extended south into the country inhabited by a people with dark skins, and long hair falling over their faces (Mexico). My father once told me of an expedition from the Blackfeet, that went south by the Old Trail, to visit the people with dark skins. Elk Tongue and his wife, Natoya, were of this expedition, also Arrow Top and Pemmican, who was a boy of twelve at that time. He died only a few years ago at the age of ninety-five. They were absent four years. It took them twelve moons of steady travelling to reach the country of the dark skinned people, and eighteen moons to come north again. They returned by a longer route through the 'High Trees' or Bitter Root country . . . . Elk Tongue brought back the Dancing Pipe. He bought it nearly one hundred years ago and it was then very old . . . . I have followed the Old North Trail so often, that I know every mountain stream and river far to the south, as well as towards the distant north. (McClintock 1910, 434–37)

The Northern Plains comprised a nested set of markets, with the bulk goods market centered along the Missouri-Mississippi river routes and luxury goods following transcontinental systems. The historic pemmican trade shifted Northern Plains Indian commercial production from Indian to European buyers. The Late Prehistoric trade in fact seems basically similar to the internal trade of the United States from 1815 to 1840, as analyzed by Douglass North and his students (Mercer 1982, 80).[3] In this period, the American Old West specialized in the production of meat, shipping it via rivers to the agribusiness-dominated South. St. Louis/Cahokia has served as hub for a thousand or two thousand years. By the mid-nineteenth century, Plains Indians hide production was a substantial profit generator in the United States economy (Moore 1989). Mercer (1982, 81) notes that meat represents plant carbohydrates processed into a highly cost-efficient form in terms of transportation costs. He (1982, 80) emphasizes that the gross total of exported products, such as meat, is not so significant as the importance of the product in the regional economy: the economy is structured so that commercial production is a regularly calculated activity.

The Northern Plains was a frontier of the midcontinental region, a territory where the Late Prehistoric midcontinental economic base of maize-beans-squash-sunflower agriculture was possible only in the restricted linear zones of the river valleys that were extensions of, and gave access to, the markets of the central region. Boat transport on no-maintenance rivers was the most cost-efficient means of conveying goods (Tanner 1989, 16). This created a curvilinear series of markets—the "beads on a string" model of the Indian cartograms. Such an orientation to rivers and streams appears also in Káinaikoan's account of his Peigan band's annual round. The riverine system of movement and markets is not primitive but alternate, a sustainable adaptation to the region, as is and has been its commercial production of meat rather than grain. Like the Peigan Blackfeet today, the prehistoric and historic Northern Plains Indians appropriated (Ingold 1980, 222) the surplus of the bovine herds and processed it into marketable products, retaining some of the products for domestic use. Their careful scheduling of the seasonal round to integrate resource appropriation, processing, and marketing (Table 1) demonstrates that Northern Plains Indians were assuredly not foragers.

The Forager Bandwagon

It seems to me that the term "hunting-gathering society" and particularly its variant "forager" are tied to a conceptual model that suffers from the problems Wimsatt (1982, 190–93) identified as plaguing many heuristic models in ecology: inertia, the "time-honored status" of certain assumptions; perceptual focus, or "model-building activity . . . performed against a background of presumed mechanisms operating in the interaction of presumed units"; and perceptual reinforcement, the "cumulative effect [of] several biases [which] can be mutually supportive."

The fundamental time-honored model of hunting-gathering societies goes back to the sixteenth century (Ferguson 1979, 346, 356–81; Furet 1984, 80–81). Eighteenth-century European universal histories accepted the model of human developmental progress from a primitive early bestial state, that of "Men-Brutes of the Forrest" (Meek 1976, 137). The nineteenth-century inauguration of a science of prehistory (A. B. Kehoe 1991b) sought archaeological evidence for the stage of human existence characterized by hunters pursuing "enormous beasts of prey" (A. B. Kehoe 1990, 24–26). Mode of subsistence had been selected, in the eighteenth-century histories, as the principal and critical criterion for classifying human societies, and similarities were to be attributed to similar economies—to, as Meek emphasizes, "*environmental* causes" (Meek 1976, 64–65, his italics).

The primitive postulates that have persisted in anthropology through inertia, perceptual focus, and perceptual reinforcement are: (1) that Man the Hunter (Haraway 1989, 187), plus or containing Woman the Gatherer (Haraway 1989, 345), is the primitive human condition; and (2) that the principle of actualism allows us to discover that primitive condition by studying contemporary hunter-gatherers.

The reductionist strategy, fostered by U.S. anthropology's dependence upon National Science Foundation funding for nearly a generation (A. B. Kehoe 1989; Winterhalder 1981, 13), fits human data into ecological models (Smith and Winterhalder 1981; Winterhalder 1981). Optimal foraging theory attracted Smith and Winterhalder for its "emphasis on individual-level selection[4] and adaptation" and "analysis of the mechanisms and conditions which interact to produce adaptive processes" (Winterhalder 1981, 15). Foraging, in this theoretical model, "is usually considered in terms of four overlapping sets of questions: diet breadth and choice of items, foraging space, feeding period, and foraging group size" (Winterhalder 1981, 14).

Note that the term "foraging" is appropriate to these four questions dealing with herbivores' feeding. Winterhalder applied optimal foraging theory to analogous questions of "limited . . . cost-benefit comparison . . . in commensurate ecological units (primarily calories)," focusing on subsistence obtained from "nonproduced foodstuffs" without "the need to consider money" (Winterhalder 1981, 16–17; but cf. Haraway 1989, 213–15 to Winterhalder 1981, 20–22, for the remarkable capitalist economics embedded in foraging theory; also, Shott 1991, 6). In the 1981 Winterhalder and Smith volume, contributors seemed to distinguish between applying optimal foraging theory to the subsistence practices of human hunting-gathering groups, and to the groups themselves.

Then, in 1980, Lewis Binford conducted a formal exercise in logic wherein he created a distinction between "foragers," epitomized by the San, and "collectors," practitioners of "logistical strategies," such as the Nunamiut. With Binford, the terms "foraging strategy," "foraging system," and "foragers" are confused—not to mention the confusion (8, 10) arising from describing, as an alternative used by foragers, an "encounter of strategy" that seems identical to "collector" strategy. Although he (1980, 10) cites his friend Frison to include bison drives as "collector locations," Binford's discussion leaves no place for Northern Plains bison hunters, for these groups had no "residential bases," only "field camps" (Uhlenbeck 1912, 1–38), so far as I can interpret Binford's terms. Their entire communities certainly "mapped on" to their resources. Ten years later, Binford (1990, 136) may have given himself an out by claiming that "fully nomadic peoples (read *foragers*) are very rare in temperate and high-latitude settings. In turn seminomadic peoples are most common" (his italics). He specifies the Ona and Tasmanians as the exceptional true foragers, thereby implying that the Peigans, who are included in an adjacent table, are "seminomadic" and presumably not really foragers.

Rather than quibble over these restrictions, suffice it to state that Binford nullifies his conclusions by completely ignoring surplus production for trade. He draws upon the Mbuti, Ingalik, Slave, Copper Eskimo, Yukaghir, Cree, Micmac, and the Northwest Coast nations to construct tables for "hunter-gatherer subsistence" strategies, though all are known only from ethnographic observations, when their socioeconomic structures included regular, important production for trade. The Ona and Tasmanians did not, on present evidence, produce for trade, but observations on both groups followed severe depletion of their resource base through Western commercial exploitations;[5] furthermore, Bowdler (1980, 339) argues that the apparent Late Prehistoric impoverishment of Tasmanian technology was a shift in production techniques making the archaeologically-preserved earlier technology obsolete. Binford is caught in a tautology, abstracting a postulated closed subsistence system out of data from open, multicomponent systems, then presenting his alleged ethnographic models as bases for constructing archaeological models. What was abstracted was what had already been constructed from the archaeological data. In sum, the popular forager model propounded by Binford well illustrates the perceptual focus and reinforcements decried by Wimsatt (discussed above).

Meanwhile, in the 1960s, certain British anthropologists presented cogent arguments that perhaps no historic or contemporary human societies have lived in the pristine situations assumed for the Paleolithic and early Holocene. Higgs and Jarman (1969) demanded a rethinking of the idea of "nonproduced" food, and Allchin (1966) called into question the presumption that known tropical forest hunter-gatherers represent subsistence economies isolated from money-using societies. Allchin seems to be ignored in contemporary discussions of the question—her personal focus being the integration of archaeological and ethnographic data, not foraging models transliterated from deer to humans—and Higgs seems cited, if at all, only when the focus is on origin of agriculture. What we may call the European line of thought continues with Ingold's statement: "The contrast between food-gathering and food-production, though deeply engrained in archaeological and anthropological orthodoxy, cannot readily be sustained" (1980, 83; see also Feit 1990, 953); and with Frank's: "There is even reason to doubt the verity and utility of the supposed distinctions between 'nomad' and 'sedentary' peoples" (1991, 8).

For the Northern Plains Indians, analyzing their economies without a Eurocentric bias (A. B. Kehoe 1981) warrants the statement that they produced their food. "Money," i.e., mediating instruments of exchange in market economies, was not in general use, but Dalton (1965) emphasized years ago that the ruling factor is market exchange, especially as an integrating mechanism for the economy, not "money" per se. Granting this emphasis, it is clear from historical and archaeological data that Northern Plains societies participated in market systems. Winterhalder's criteria for "forager" thus fail to fit Northern Plains Indians such as the Peigan.

Conclusion

The term "forager" has been enthusiastically and uncritically espoused in anthropology as shorthand for "hunter-gatherer." Difference in historical meanings and contemporary perspective militates against using the terms as synonyms. We should take care that we do not ignore historical meanings of terms, lest our discourse be occulted by jargon. Equally consequential, the source of the bandwagon use of "forager," optimal foraging theory, is so limited in regard to analyses of human behavior that careless reference to it must be avoided.

Perhaps the fundamental issue is our orientation: do we seek analytical models for human behavior in natural-history studies, or through cross-cultural comparisons? The former sees humans subservient to natural forces, the latter sees humans a unique yet varied species. The issue was powerful in the nineteenth century, posing anthropologists who believed in unilinear Progress against the few, such as Boas and Mooney, whose extended field experience, heightened by personal marginality in a WASP-dominated society, led them to respect non-Western people. Standard histories of anthropology say that Boas prevailed over the nineteenth-century position, but analysis does not bear this out (Pinsky 1992,164; Barrett 1989).

The multitudinous recent debate over the nature of human foragers, summarized by Kent (1992) as "real versus ideal views," veers off the basic question by arguing over the minutiae of Basarwa history or the alleged lack of necessary nutrients in tropical forests. The broad question framed in the 1960s by Higgs and by Allchin, is whether *any Homo sapiens sapiens* society would live like animals foraging for subsistence. History and ethnography give us no untarnished examples of such humans; noble savages such as Peigan turn out to be citizens of complex, if nomadic and nonliterate, polities. It takes eight more keystrokes to write "hunter-gatherer" instead of "forager," and the power of the Principle of Least Effort may not be negated by increased caloric harvest from a heightened scholarly reputation, but the recognition that hunter-gatherers have been far more than foragers does induce a satisfying tingle from a sense of shared humanity.

Ki ánetoyi imitáiks, Káinaikoan would say to conclude his tale, "And the dogs have separated."

Acknowledgements

Portions of this paper were read before the 1990 Plains Conference, Oklahoma City, the 1991 American Anthropological Association, Chicago, and the 1992 Society for American Archaeology, Pittsburgh. I am grateful for stimulating discussions particularly with Patricia O'Brien, Charles Bishop,

Alan Marshall, Michael Shott, Susan Kent, Florence Shipek, Sheldon Smith, Peter Gardner, and Thomas Headland.

NOTES

1. I am NOT imputing fascist politics to any archaeologist. My point is that naïveté concerning the ideology behind programs to discover and apply "laws" governing human behavior, possibly to control people, has obfuscated political support that funds and publishes such projects.

2. These figures are from the early nineteenth century, when the Blackfoot population was recovering from the devastating 1780–1781 smallpox epidemic (Ewers 1958, 37), two generations after the horse had been introduced into Blackfoot life, a full century after first recorded contact with a European trader, and after half a century at least of pressure from eastern Indian groups moving westward in the face of European invasions. All these factors may have affected average community size and population distribution; on the other hand, insofar as the communities' subsistence continued to be based on corralling, they should reflect the adaptational range of size of such groups.

3. I am grateful to Sheldon Smith for suggesting the North studies to me.

4. Hence the extended concern with autonomy of members of "forager societies," discussed in Gardner (1991).

5. Stephen Loring correlates the depletion of South Atlantic sea mammals by early nineteenth century New England whalers (taking seals, also) with Ona impoverishment (pers. comm.).

REFERENCES

Allchin, Bridget. 1966. *The Stone-Tipped Arrow: Late Stone-Age Hunters of the Tropical Old World*. New York: Barnes and Noble.

Aristotle. 1946. *The Politics*. Translated by Ernest Barker. Reprint, London: Oxford University Press.

Barrett, Richard A. 1989. "The Paradoxical Anthropology of Leslie White." *American Anthropologist* 91:986–99.

Binford, Lewis A. 1980. "Willow Smoke and Dogs' Tails: Hunter-Gatherer Settlement Systems and Archaeological Site Formation." *American Antiquity* 45:4–20.

———. 1990. "Mobility, Housing, and Environment: A Comparative Study." *Journal of Anthropological Research* 46:119–52.

Blakeslee, Donald J. 1975. *The Plains Interband Trade System: An Ethnohistoric and Archaeological Investigation*. PhD dissertation, University of Wisconsin-Milwaukee.

Bowdler, Sandra. 1980. "Fish and Culture: A Tasmanian Polemic." *Mankind* 12:334–40.

Brink, Jack. n.d. "Bison Butchering and Food Processing at Head-Smashed-In Buffalo Jump, Alberta." Paper presented before the 48th Plains Anthropological Conference, Oklahoma City, 1990.

Dalton, George. 1965. "Primitive Money." *American Anthropologist* 67:44–65.

Davis, Leslie B. and Michael Wilson, eds. 1978. *Bison Procurement and Utilization: A Symposium*. Lincoln, NE: Plains Anthropologist Memoir 14.

Duke, Philip. 1991. *Points in Time*. Niwot, CO: University Press of Colorado.

Epp, Henry T. 1988. "Way of the Migrant Herds: Dual Dispersion Strategy Among Bison." *Plains Anthropologist* 33 (121): 309–20.

Ewers, John C. 1958. *The Blackfeet: Raiders of the Northern Plains*. Norman: University of Oklahoma Press.

Feit, Harvey A. 1990. "The Enduring Pursuit: Land, Social Relationships and Time in Anthropological Models of Hunter-Gatherers and Subarctic Hunters' Images." In *Sixth International Conference on Hunting and Gathering Societies: CHAGS 6*, 942–56. Fairbanks: University of Alaska, Department of Anthropology.

Ferguson, Arthur B. 1979. *Clio Unbound*. Durham, NC: Duke University Press.

Frank, Andre Gunder. 1991. "A Plea for World System History." *Journal of World History* 2:1–28.

Furet, François. 1984. *In the Workshop of History*. Translated by Jonathan Mandelbaum. Chicago: University of Chicago Press.

Gardner, Peter M. 1991. "Foragers' Pursuit of Individual Autonomy." *Current Anthropology* 32:543–72.

Gregg, Michael L., and Paul R. Picha. n.d. "Stones, Bones, Shells, and Other Objects of Value: Middle Woodland Resource Exchange as Viewed from the Northern Plains." Paper presented before the Midwest Archaeological Conference, La Crosse, WI, 1991.

Haraway, Donna. 1989. *Primate Visions*. New York: Routledge.

Henry, Donald O. 1989. *From Foraging to Agriculture: The Levant at the End of the Ice Age*. Philadelphia: University of Pennsylvania Press.

Higgs, Eric, and Michael R. Jarman. 1969. "The Origins of Agriculture: A Reconsideration." *Antiquity* 43 (172): 31–41.

Ingold, Tim. 1980. *Hunters, Pastoralists, and Ranchers*. Cambridge: Cambridge University Press.

Jones, Archer. 1987. *The Art of War in the Western World*. Urbana: University of Illinois Press.

Keene, Arthur S. 1991. "Archaeology and the Heritage of Man the Hunter." *Reviews in Anthropology* 16:133–47.

Kehoe, A. B. 1970. "The Function of Ceremonial Sexual Intercourse Among the Northern Plains Indians." *Plains Anthropologist* 15 (48): 99–103.

———. 1980. "The Giveaway Ceremony of Blackfoot and Plains Cree." *Plains Anthropologist* 25 (87): 17–26.

———. 1981. "Revisionist Anthropology: Aboriginal North America." *Current Anthropology* 22:503–17.

———. 1990. "Points and Lines." In *Powers of Observation: Alternate Views in Archaeology*, edited by Sarah M. Nelson and Alice B. Kehoe, 23–37. Washington, DC: Archeological Papers of the American Anthropological Association No. 2.

———. 1991a. "Contests of Power in Blackfoot Life and Mythology." In *Contests (Cosmos 6)*, edited by Andrew Duff-Cooper, 115–24. Edinburgh: University of Edinburgh Press.

———. 1991b. "The Invention of Prehistory." *Current Anthropology* 32:467–76.

———. 1995. "Blackfoot Persons." In *Women and Power in Native North America*, edited by Laura Klein and Lillian Ackerman, 113–25. Norman: University of Oklahoma Press.

———. n.d. "Processual and Postprocessual Archaeology: A Brief Critical Review." Paper presented before the Plains Conference, session "The PostProcessual Paradigm and Plains Archaeology," organized by Philip Duke and Michael Wilson, Sioux City, IA, 1989.

Kehoe, Thomas F. 1967. *The Boarding School Bison Drive Site*. Lincoln, NE: Plains Anthropologist Memoir 4.

———. 1973. *The Gull Lake Site: A Prehistoric Bison Drive Site in Southwestern Saskatchewan*. Milwaukee: Milwaukee Public Museum Publications in Anthropology and History, l.

Kennedy, Roger G. 1985. *Architecture, Men, Women, and Money in America 1600–1860*. New York: Random House.

Kent, Susan. 1992. "The Current Forager Controversy: Real Versus Ideal Views of Hunter-gatherers." *Man* 27:45–70.

Marshall, Alan G. n.d. "Wild Horticulture: The Nez Perce Subsistence Base." Paper presented before the American Anthropological Association, Chicago, IL, 1991.

Martin, John F. 1983. "Optimal Foraging Theory: A Review of Some Models and Their Applications." *American Anthropologist* 85:612–29.

McClintock, Walter. [1910] 1968. *The Old North Trail*. Lincoln: University of Nebraska Press.

McDonald, Jerry N. 1981. *North American Bison*. Berkeley: University of California Press.

McHugh, Tom. 1972. *The Time of the Buffalo*. Lincoln: University of Nebraska Press.

Meek, Ronald L. 1976. *Social Science and the Ignoble Savage*. Cambridge: Cambridge University Press.

Mercer, Lloyd J. 1982. "The Antebellum Interregional Trade Hypothesis: A reexamination of Theory and Evidence." In *Explorations in the New Economic History*, edited by Roger L. Ranson, Richard Sutch, and Gary M. Walton, 71–96. New York: Academic Press.

Moodie, D. W., and Arthur J. Ray. 1976. "Buffalo Migrations in the Canadian Plains." *Plains Anthropologist* 21 (71): 45–52.

Moodie, D. W. and Barry Kaye. 1977. "The Ac Ko Mok Ki Map." *The Beaver*, Outfit 307 (4): 5–15.

Moore, John H. 1989. "The Myth of the Lazy Indian: Native American Contributions to the U. S. Economy." *Nature, Society and Thought* 2 (2): 195–215.

O'Brien, Patricia J. n.d. a. "Exotic Resource Procurement in the Ramey State." Paper presented before the Central States Anthropological Society, St. Louis, MO, 1988.

———. n.d. b. "Routes and Trails of Cahokia's World-System." Paper presented before the Society for American Archaeology, Pittsburgh, PA, 1992.

Pinsky, Valerie. 1992. "Archaeology, Politics, and Boundary-Formation: The Boas Censure (1919) and the Development of American Archaeology during the Inter-war Years." In *Rediscovering Our Past: Essays on the History of American Archaeology*, edited by Jonathan E. Reyman, 161–89. Aldershot: Avebury.

Ruggles, Richard J. 1991. *A Country So Interesting*. Montreal: McGill-Queen's University Press.

Shott, Michael J. 1991. "Archaeological Implications of Revisionism in Ethnography." *Michigan Discussions in Anthropology* 10:1–10.

Smith, Eric Alden, and Bruce Winterhalder, eds. 1981. "New Perspectives on Hunter-Gatherer Socioecology." In *Hunter-Gatherer Foraging Strategies*. Chicago: University of Chicago Press.

Tanner, Helen Hornbeck. 1989. "The Land and Water Communication Systems of the Southeastern Indians." In *Powhatan's Mantle*, edited by Peter H. Wood, Gregory A. Waselkov, and M. Thomas Hatley, 6–20. Lincoln: University of Nebraska Press.

Taylor, Allan R. 1992. "Some New Old World Lists." *International Journal of American Linguistics* 58:312–16.

Uhlenbeck, C. C. 1912. *A New Series of Blackfoot Texts*. Amsterdam: Johannes Miller.

Verbickey-Todd, Eleanor. 1984. *Communal Buffalo Hunting Among the Plains Indians*. Edmonton: Archaeological Survey of Alberta, Occasional Paper No. 24.

Wimsatt, William C. 1982. "Reductionist Research Strategies and Their Biases in the Units of Selection Controversy." In *Conceptual Issues in Ecology*, edited by Esa Saarinen, 155–201. Dordrecht: D. Reidel.

Winterhalder, Bruce. 1981. "Optimal Foraging Strategies and Hunter-Gatherer Research in Anthropology: Theory and Models." In *Hunter-Gatherer Foraging Strategies*, edited by Eric Alden Smith and Bruce Winterhalder, 13–35. Chicago: University of Chicago Press.

.

Wissler, Clark. 1911. *The Social Life of the Blackfoot Indians*. New York: American Museum of Natural History, Anthropological Papers, vol. 7, Pt. I, 1–64.

Wissler, Clark, and D. C. Duvall. 1908. *Mythology of the Blackfoot Indians*. New York: American Museum of Natural History, Anthropological Papers, vol. 2, Pt. I: 5–163.

Wood, W. Raymond. 1980. "Plains Trade in Prehistoric and Protohistoric Intertribal Relations." In *Anthropology on the Great Plains*, edited by W. Raymond Wood and Margot Liberty, 98–109. Lincoln: University of Nebraska Press.

6. The Direct Ethnographic Approach to Archaeology on the Northern Plains

"The Direct Ethnographic Approach" developed from conversations and a 1977 conference session with Michael Stanislawski. As a proposed edited volume never materialized, we offered our paper to the *Plains Anthropologist*'s memoir series because we thought of our approach as paralleling the well-known Direct Historical Approach introduced into Plains archaeology by Duncan Strong (Strong 1940; see Lyman and O'Brien for a detailed history of that term). It seems worth reprinting here for our effort to promote working with local people, descendant or settler, to better understand cultural landscapes and weigh potentialities against observed data.

Tom Kehoe had been guided in this method by Claude Schaeffer, the director of the Museum of the Plains Indian, who hired Tom to carry out an archaeological survey of the Blackfeet Reservation where the museum stands. Schaeffer, in turn, had been a student of Frank Speck, who had been a student of Franz Boas. Speck, little noted now (but see Bruchac 2018, 140–75; Kehoe 2019, 249–71), recognized continuities between independent First Nations and their descendants, respectfully listening to them and observing persisting ways of life. To talk with Blackfoot in the 1950s about their grandparents' lives when bison herds were still corralled seems hardly a stretch today, yet at that time (and similarly now), ambitious archaeologists strove for Theory, dismissing the mundane as insignificant. Tom's master's thesis was on tipi rings, based on following Schaeffer's instructions to go to older people's homes and politely ask about nearby rings. Elders enjoyed speaking about and, on occasion, guiding the young man from the museum to see rings; one man showed him the tipi ring from the man's parents' tipi, preserved as a memorial near the son's home.

Straightforward as this seems, Plains archaeologist William Mulloy had insisted that such identifications are folklore, so to be scientific, we should term the multitude of tipi-diameter size rings on the Plains as "manifestations of unknown relationship" (Mulloy 1952, 137). Checking references in

Tom's thesis that was to be published (T. Kehoe 1958, 1960), we saw that Mulloy had overlooked small-print discussion following an early paper on the rings. Dr. Washington Matthews, the army surgeon who had lived for years in Sioux lands, politely told the speaker that during those years, Matthews had often seen tipis pulled up, leaving those rings of stones. Tom now had firsthand historical observation as "present process" to explain the archaeological data.

Living as we were with people whose grandparents were contemporary with Dr. Matthews, we pursued through ethnography the question of stone rings on the prairie. Capstone to the research was listening to the oldest person on the Siksika Reserve, Mrs. Duck Chief, who had lived in a bison hide tipi as a child. She explained that stones were used on hide tipis that stretched under the rocks, but could not be used when bison were gone, because stones rolled off taut canvas tents—those had to be pegged.

If it seems obvious that if direct descendants of the inhabitants of a site have continued to live in its territory. an archaeologist would talk with them, as Claude Schaeffer, Tom, and I did, Manifest Destiny colonialism had cut that string. American First Nations had been, according to Chief Justice John Marshall in 1823, "fierce savages, whose occupation was war, and whose subsistence was drawn chiefly from the forest. To leave them in possession of their country, was to leave the country a wilderness" (quoted in Williams 1990, 323n133). Boas and Speck were consciously revolutionaries against Anglo debasement of First Nations; that was taught as fact even in universities. I myself was told, quite frequently in the 1950s and '60s, that Indians of our time knew little of their forebears' cultures and wouldn't speak truthfully to whites; anthropologists' education had enabled Us to penetrate Their myths, and our trowels had revealed what no Indians could know. Indians were not seen in SAA meetings. The simple deduction that many thousands of tipi-size stone rings present on habitable campgrounds, indicating the stones were signs of tipis, was untenable in its very simplicity. Tom and I were fortunate to be mentored by a student of Frank Speck, the maverick who, as he phrased it, sat down in Indians' kitchens and drank coffee from their cups as they talked to him. It was the equivalent of Bronislaw Malinowski coming down from the veranda to mix with the people, practiced by Speck a decade before that Pole went to the Trobriands.

Moose Mountain "medicine wheel," the final example in the Direct Ethnography paper, received a lot of notice when we and our astronomer collaborator, Jack Eddy, reported it in 1977. Eddy (1977) wrote it for *National Geographic Magazine* as part of a National Geographic grant he obtained after realizing that the Big Horn medicine wheel in southern Montana has astronomical alignments. We get three paragraphs on the last page of the article. Eddy had submitted a paper on the Big Horn alignments to *Science* in 1974, Tom had reviewed it for the journal and recommended it, and seeing the similarities to the Moose Mountain site we had mapped in 1961, he contacted Eddy. During the next solstice, June 1975, we picked Jack up at the Regina airport and drove to the site, three hours away. Four days' observations confirmed the solstice alignments, plus five bright stars whose risings bracketed summer solstice *if the construction had been built around two thousand years ago*. Spectacular! The Big Horn construction is dated only three hundred years old.

Archaeoastronomy was the big new thing in the 1970s, sparked by the popular *Stonehenge Decoded* by Gerald Hawkins. Debate flared over whether so ancient a people as Neolithic Britons could have figured out the sun's cycle; Moose Mountain's antiquity was relevant to the debates but received very little notice. Overlooking endless wheat fields, the hill is far off any beaten tourist path and belongs to a First Nation that, to protect it, forbids visitors. Isolation is not the first reason for its obscurity: it's not mentioned in the authoritative archaeoastronomy texts by Anthony Aveni. When I asked Tony Aveni, in the book exhibits room at an SAA meeting, why not, he coolly replied, "Because it's not one of my sites." Gate-keeping.

The Direct Ethnographic Approach to Archaeology on the Northern Plains

In 1958, Thomas F. Kehoe published a report on investigations of tipi rings on the Northern Plains (Montana, North Dakota, Alberta, Saskatchewan.) Subtitling his work "The 'direct ethnological' approach applied to an archaeological problem," Kehoe explicated as a method of archaeological inquiry the principle of producing and testing hypotheses on archaeological data by discussing the data with persons active in the cultural tradition, ecological situation, or technological processes associated with the archaeological material. The method proved fruitful in each of our major projects of archaeological research. We shall discuss each after distinguishing our method, direct ethnographic inquiry, from other practices usually subsumed under the term ethno-archaeology.

Four Practices Involving Ethnology in Archaeological Interpretation

As we understand the labels, ethno-archaeology is the exploration of a present activity area by archaeological procedures: treating the material remains of contemporary behavior as if they constituted an archaeological site. The purposes of ethno-archaeology may be the testing of archaeological interpretations, as Robson Bonnichsen (1973) did at Millie's camp, or the discovery or corroboration of archaeological interpretations, as in our 1956 work at the Blackfeet North American Indian Days encampment (T. Kehoe 1958, 1960). Whatever the purposes or results, the essential criterion of ethnoarchaeology, *sensu strictu* is the availability of at least one person who actually participated in activity of the site to act as informant. True ethno-archaeology thereby has the virtue of infallibility.

Direct ethnographic inquiry is the method used when one does not expect to find persons who actually participated in the activities of the site investigated, but can find persons with firsthand familiarity with the cultural tradition, ecological adaptation, or artifact manufacturing techniques probably responsible for the archaeological data recovered. Direct ethnographic inquiry is a means of broadening the range of an archaeologist's interpretations by adding those of persons foreign to the archaeologist's own intellectual tradition. The informants' interpretations must be tested for goodness of fit to the data just as the archaeologist tests his own hypotheses. The method lacks the infallibility of true ethno-archaeology, but it does increase the probability that an archaeologist's conclusions are valid.

Both true ethno-archaeology and direct ethnographic inquiry must be distinguished from ethnohistory and ethnographic analogy. Ethnohistory uses documents and lacks the advantage of face-to-face interaction found in ethnographic inquiry: it is subject to the biases and lacunae of documents, and can generate new hypotheses only by inference, not by the stimulation of live discussion. Ethnographic analogy is farthest removed from the real activities of a particular archaeological site's formation. The archaeologist seeks parallels as suggested by the paradigms of his own tradition, without the fertilizing effect of contacts with outsiders. Ethnographic analogies have the highest probability of error of the four methods discussed here; even more than ethnohistory, they are confined within that portion of the received knowledge of the anthropological profession familiar to the particular fieldworker.

All four methods have been used by archaeologists working on the Plains. Ethnohistory has been most commonly employed, first during the 1930s to find contact-period sites from which the stylistic traditions of historic peoples could be determined, then after World War II to support Indian land claims. Within the massive documentations produced for these legal claims, there are occasional instances of direct ethnographic inquiry of Native persons to identify archaeologically manifested occupations, but the method of direct ethnographic inquiry is not highlighted. Ethnographic analogies have also been heavily used, generally drawn from accounts of Plains tribal life in the nineteenth century. These analogies are likely to be sound, given the ecological constraints of this marginal region and the descent of some tribes from the occupants of late sites, but not all Plains archaeologists have the thorough familiarity with the ethnographies and explorers' journals that must be the basis of valid analogies. Among those who have parleyed a good grounding in Plains ethnography and ethnohistory in the service of archaeological interpretations we may cite the late James H. Howard.

Direct Ethnographic Inquiry on Tipi Rings

T. F. Kehoe arrived on the Blackfeet Reservation in Montana in 1952 to become assistant curator of the Museum of the Plains Indian in the agency town, Browning. The director of the museum was the late Claude E. Schaeffer, an ethnologist who had trained with Frank Speck. Schaeffer expected Kehoe to add time depth to Schaeffer's own ethnohistorical and traditional ethnographic studies of Montana tribes by conducting archaeological surveys and tests on the reservation. The rings of stones popularly called tipi rings, abounding throughout the large reservation, seemed a suitable problem for initial investigation.

In 1952, the principal authority on Northern Plains prehistory, William Mulloy, had labeled the rings of stones "manifestations of unknown relationships" (Mulloy 1952, 137). Waldo Wedel, another eminent Plains archaeologist, remarked in reviewing Mulloy's paper, "I am inclined to agree with Mulloy that a good many of the tipi rings are probably of ceremonial, rather than practical, purpose" (Wedel 1953, 179). After surveying Alberta archaeology with Mulloy in 1955, Marie Wormington was quoted by Krieger (1956, 450) as concurring with Mulloy's opinion on tipi rings. This skepticism of the popular assumption that the rings were used to anchor tipi covers goes back to a paper published in 1889 by T. H. Lewis. Caution was commendable, but common sense argued that because there are many thousands of stone rings on the Northern Plains, a practical rather than esoteric function should be postulated.

T. F. Kehoe began his inquiry with a search of the historical literature. He found that Maximilian in 1833 noted that a circle of sods remained when the Blackfeet at Fort McKenzie took down their tents; that J. N. Nicollet made a similar observation in Minnesota in 1838; and that Henry Y. Hind stated in 1860, "The Plains Cree, in the day of their power and pride, had erected large skin tents, and strengthened them with rings of stones placed around the base" (Hind 1860, 1:338). At the close of the nineteenth century, Grinnell, McClintock, Schultz, Barrow, Denny, and McLean left observations of the Blackfeet custom of weighting tipi covers with stones. Early in this century, Wissler for the Blackfoot and Lewis for the Crow advanced this practical explanation for tipi rings. Even T. H. Lewis had retracted his opinion on the question of tipi rings only a year after his first paper, having been persuaded by Washington Matthews, who had been in the audience for the 1889 paper and had there declared that he "had seen boulders used for this purpose [weighting down lodge covers] in Dakota . . . while the Indians still followed the nomadic life" (Lewis 1889, 164–65). Mulloy and his followers apparently failed to read small print discussion of Lewis's paper in which Matthews's correction was advanced and accepted.

Such an array of documentation by the major explorers and ethnographers of the northern Plains was strong support for the popular ascription of a domestic function to the rings. Encouraged, Kehoe pursued two other lines of inquiry. One was archaeological, the extensive survey of undisturbed range land, mostly within the Blackfeet Reservation, to map and count tipi rings, relate their sitings to topographical features, and test some of them by excavation (which in this windy high country yielded a few flecks of charcoal and stone flakes within the rings). The other line of inquiry was direct ethnographic interviewing of Blackfoot on the Montana and Alberta reserves. This interviewing was what Kehoe termed the "direct ethnological approach" in his 1958 publication, modifying the concept of the direct historical approach used by William Duncan Strong in his classic work on Pawnee archaeology in Nebraska.

A few survivors from the pre-reservation nomadic period could still be found among the Blackfoot in the 1950s. They gave Kehoe information that corroborated the documentary data and added explanatory detail. Bull Head, a North Piegan band member, told that "These tipi rings were *iskiman* 'something to hold down the lodge' . . . The center rocks were called *appskitan,* 'confine the fire.'" Mrs. Duck Chief, then the oldest North Blackfoot, remembered, "Where old Indians pitched their tipis, they put the rocks around the tipi to keep it down. They don't do it nowadays; only old people with hide tipis used them, when the tipis were used often, for everyday. The hides stretched more than canvas, so the rocks didn't roll off as they would from tight canvas." (These sentences were translated from the Blackfoot by younger interpreters during the interviews.) Adam White Man, a South Piegan, took Kehoe to the White Man allotment on Badger Creek, on the Blackfeet Reservation, to show him a tipi ring that had been used by the first White Man, father of Adam, at the beginning of this century. The family had been protecting this ring as a memento. Mr. White Man identified the hearth within the ring, appearing as a slight discoloration in the soil, and the cooking hearth outside, 21 feet to the east, bounded by two rocks. He said that cooking had been done outside the tipi whenever weather permitted. Other Indians, such as Bull Head and George Bull Child—not to mention the government that made a monument of Chief Crowfoot's tipi ring at Blackfoot Crossing in Alberta—identified particular rings as having been used by known families to anchor tipis. Adam White Man pointed out the tipi rings clustered on Badger Creek north of Highway 89, which had been left from a Sun Dance held about 1891 when two bands camped together but each had a Sacred Woman using the traditional rocks to hold down her lodge cover.

A final phase of the tipi ring research was ethno-archaeological. We visited the 1956 North American Indian Days camp, at Browning, Montana, sponsored by the Blackfeet Tribe. There were thirty-nine tipis as well as numerous wall tents on the grounds. None of the tipis, which were all of canvas, used rocks to hold down the lodge cover, but several tipi owners weighted down the inner linings of their lodges with rocks. By measuring the tipis while erect and then their sites after they were taken down, we were able to demonstrate that removal of the fabric (in these cases, the inner linings) does regularly leave the anchoring rocks in a ring closely approximating the dimensions of the base of the structure. We also noted that the occupation area within the tipi retained taller grass than the heavily trodden ground outside it, with only a light path around the central hearth evidencing traffic within the lodge. The tipi floors had been protected by the bedding and robes laid over them, and additionally by the lack of other than sedentary activities within the lodges. Our final discovery was that very little imperishable material was abandoned in or near the tipis. This near absence of what could become archaeological data conformed to our experiences excavating tipi rings on the range.

Boulder Monuments

The success of the three-pronged research on tipi rings led us to use direct ethnographic inquiry as a normal phase of our subsequent work on the Northern Plains. Concurrently with the tipi ring study, T. F. Kehoe had been investigating the rock rings or cairns with radiating lines of rocks, popularly known as medicine wheels. Kehoe learned from Jim Weasel Tail, son of John C. Ewers's principal informant on Blood traditions, and from Adam White Man that the Blackfoot had constructed cairns with radiating rock lines as monuments to deceased chiefs (Kehoe 1954, 1972). Following Kehoe's lead, the Alberta historian Dempsey (1956) was able to record three "medicine wheel" monuments erected in 1900, 1932, and 1940 respectively to the late leaders Red Crow, Eagle Child, and Steel. Jim Weasel Tail recalled his father explaining to him that "The line of rocks show the different directions in which they go on the warpath—they were the dead chief's war deeds. If they kill someone, they pile rocks at the end of the rock line. If there is no rock pile present, then they just go to the enemy. Short lines are short trips. The whole thing is the monument, like George Washington's monument." Other Blackfoot informants said that the lines of rocks could represent the paths of people coming for help to the tipi of the wise and generous leader. Since many of the Northern Plains "wheel" monuments, including Steel's, consist only of a central rock cairn with four rock arms more or less in the form of a cross, it is likely that the elder Weasel Tail's particularistic explanation cannot fit all Plains "medicine wheels," many instead having the four opposing lines simply symbolizing the coming of people from all directions to their beloved leader.

A second class of boulder monuments on the Northern Plains are effigies. Those for which the origin is known memorialize historic events: a fight about 1872 between a North Blackfoot band called the Roasters and a Blood band called the Bear People; the murders of an adulterous Dakota couple and the avenging husband; the speech made by a Dakota chief after a great hunt; the killing of an Arikara by a Dakota; gang rapes of unfaithful Crow women by their husbands' comrades; and the failure of the brother of two Mandan heroes to kill even an antelope resting close to him (the heroes' battle was recorded by cutting sod and placing "small cobbles" in the excavated holes and on low mounds, to form "paths" and cairn-like monuments) (Kehoe and Kehoe 1959); the finding of a lost child (Forbis 1960, 122). Obviously, the exact function of such monuments can only be known by direct ethnographic inquiry, conducted in the present or recorded in the past. It is instructive that of these eight explained memorials of events, the two Mandan monuments consist only of mounds with paths; the Dakota speech is represented by a snake; the killing of the Arikara by a turtle with a path; and the remaining events by crude human effigies, cairns, and paths. Were the sample not so small, we might generalize that Northern Plains boulder effigies, human or animal, and cairns with rock "paths" where not astronomically aligned, were most likely built to commemorate noteworthy events. Given the inadequacy of the sample compared to the total number of boulder cairns, paths, and effigies on the Northern Plains, we can still argue that ethnographic inquiry has rendered it more probable that any boulder effigy or cairn-with-path in the region memorialized an event rather than served as totemic, myth, or religious symbol.

Bison Drives

T. F. Kehoe's principal research project has been bison drives (Kehoe 1967, 1973). Bison herds became extinct, for all practical purposes, in the early 1880s, and no one surviving into the second half of this century participated actively in bison drives, but this central concern of pre-reservation Plains

Indians was the subject of reminiscences for decades, and left a legacy of ritual. The monograph on Kehoe's first major bison pound excavation (Kehoe 1967) mined this rich source of interpretations for archaeological data, not only those obtained from Northern Plains drive sites, but by extension applicable to data from game pounds elsewhere.

The elder Weasel Tail slaughtered a bison in the last of the Blackfoot drives, about 1872, and gave Ewers much detail on drive procedures in an interview in 1943. During the excavation and analysis of the Boarding School Bison Drive site (24GL302), we obtained a great deal more detail by interviewing Jim Weasel Tail, Bull Head, and Chewing Black Bone, in the late 1950s the oldest South Piegan. Other Blackfoot contributed corroborative information, some of it elicited in direct examination of archaeological data. These interviews were deeply satisfying, the Blackfoot reveling in recalling what had been the focus of their people's life, we excited by the wealth of leads and enriching particulars pouring from their lips (see Kehoe 1967, 75–84).

Bison drive excavation data contrast with boulder effigies in that the latter can only be explained by ethnographic inquiry, while the former usually have clear functions—corral poles, arrowpoints, choppers, butchered bone, and so on. The value of ethnographic inquiry on bison drives was to literally flesh out the excavated materials, expanding upon construction of the pound and drive lane, the drive, impoundment, and slaughter of the herd, the butchering and distribution of the carcasses, the processing of the meat and bones, and the social structure and religious context of the drive. Coupled with data on bison and other bovine behavior and on ecological conditions, our rich understanding of Northern Plains bison drives yields principles useful in developing hypotheses to interpret herd kill sites of more ancient periods and on other continents.

Reciprocally the archaeological data, with its concrete exposition of technological trends, persistences, and innovations and its quantification of slaughter, provided the means to develop an interpretation of Northern Plains economy industrializing in response to markets on the Missouri and Saskatchewan (Kehoe 1973, 195–200, 1976). Here, the bias of Western tradition equating "nomadic" with "primitive" had obscured the technological and social-structural sophistication of the Northern Plains bison pound economy. Analysis of the archaeological data gave new shadings to the ethnographic information, resulting in a revisionist view of the Late Prehistoric and historic Northern Plains. The respect and empathy our informants engendered stimulated this rejection of traditional Western ethnocentrism.

A minor but interesting result of ethnographic inquiry on bison drives was Kehoe's (1965) addendum to Kenneth Oakley's paper (1965) on fossils in prehistoric occupations. Oakley had collated reports of fossils that suggest collection by Upper Paleolithic and later peoples and associated these with surviving folklore. Of particular note, to us, was Oakley's citation of fossil ammonites in Solutrean sites. Ammonites are the fetishes, called *iniskim*, kept by the Blackfoot in medicine bundles and formerly used to call bison to the pounds (now used to call prosperity in general). Calder found ammonites among the offerings in a cairn in Alberta, and did not hesitate to name them *iniskim* (Calder 1977, 164–65); Forbis had earlier (1960, 158) found ammonites inside Grassy Lake Cairn and the Ross occupation site in southern Alberta, and implied, but did not state, they are probably *iniskim*. Although according to Oakley's researches the ammonites are considered fossilized snakes in British folklore, we may suggest that to the Solutreans, as to the Blackfoot, they resembled curled-up sleeping bison, to be awakened when a drive was planned.

Solstice-Aligned Boulder Constructions

Another project was the investigation of solstice-aligned boulder constructions in Saskatchewan (Kehoe and Kehoe 1977, 1979). We began in collaboration with the astronomer John A. Eddy, who in 1974 published the astronomical alignments of the Big Horn Medicine Wheel in Wyoming. Asked to comment on Eddy's paper in *Science* (1974), T. F. Kehoe realized that the significant alignments in the Wyoming construction closely resembled the lines in a site we had mapped at Moose Mountain, Saskatchewan. Eddy joined us at this site, DkMq-2, for summer solstice, 1975, and confirmed the solstitial alignments with a transit and calculations as well as by direct observation. We then checked with a transit all the eleven known "medicine wheels" surviving in Saskatchewan, most of which we had mapped. Only one other "medicine wheel" and one boulder turtle effigy with cairns had rock lines that computed to fit astronomical alignments during solstice. The remainder of the summer of 1975 we spent traveling to various Indian reserves to inquire from former informants whether they recognized any of the rock constructions and whether their peoples had observed summer solstice. None of the Indians recognized any of the boulder constructions (unless one counts an Assiniboin lady who knew of Moose Mountain from reserve children taken to see an exhibit at the Saskatchewan Museum of Natural History). Jim Weasel Tail stated that the Saskatchewan constructions did not closely resemble the Blackfoot chiefs' monuments with which he was familiar, and he explicitly excluded the three solstice-aligned figures.

We did learn that the Plains Cree of the Battleford district recognize summer solstice with private prayer, and that until about 1929, there had been a "calendar man" on Poundmaker's Reserve who kept tally of the days of the year from June to June (Kehoe and Kehoe 1977, 91). This information cannot be directly applied to the Moose Mountain site, which we excavated in 1976 and have dated to 2650 radiocarbon years BP, nor to the undated but probably prehistoric Minton Turtle effigy, but it does suggest calendar keeping and solstice observances may have been common aboriginally. Neither is mentioned in Mandelbaum's standard ethnography of the Plains Cree (1940), although Mandelbaum worked primarily in the Battleford district, only a few years after the last "calendar man" died. As with bison drives, the combination of direct ethnographic inquiry and archaeological data has cast a new light on anthropological assumptions, in this case proving that calendar keeping tied to solstice observation was practiced by wholly nomadic, non-agricultural hunting peoples in the recent past and probably for at least two thousand years previously. This fact highlights the falsity of linking calendars and astronomy to complex sedentary societies, and emphasizes the importance of large social gatherings to nomads—for we postulate, on ethnographic analogy (Legesse 1973), that the purpose of solstice observance was to rectify calendar-keeping in order to bring together bands into an annual tribal rendezvous. Again, direct ethnographic inquiry on archaeological data has contributed to a revisionist view of the Northern Plains.

Conclusions

Our experience convinces us that wherever non-Western or conservative rural peoples remain in or near traditional territories, direct ethnographic inquiry is likely to be profitable to the archaeologist. It may explicitly elucidate archaeological data, as in our published reports, or it may be fruitful for broader theoretical issues, as Bonnichsen learned in Millie's camp. It may bring to the archaeologist's attention features or factors that he had not realized were significant. It will certainly enhance the interpreter's "feel" for the life fossilized in his data. And, at the very least, inquiry evidences a respect toward an excavator's neighbors and laborers that is usually then reciprocated.

We have been urged "the probable advantage of carrying on our archaeological investigations not only in a more systematic manner, but in one which rests firmly on an ethnological and ethnographical basis. The time is past when our major interest was in the specimen, the collection, the site as a thing in itself; our museums are no longer cabinets of curiosities. We are today concerned with the relations of things, with the whens and the whys and the hows; in finding the explanation of the arts and customs of historic times in the remnants which have been left us from the prehistoric; . . . in attempting to reconstruct the life of the past from its all too scanty remains. It is only through the known that we can comprehend the unknown, only from a study of the present that we can understand the past; and archaeological investigations therefore must be largely barren if pursued in isolation and independent of ethnology." So spoke the President of the American Anthropological Association in his formal address—December, 1913 (Dixon 1913, 565)!

NOTE

This article is reprinted from Volume 30, Reprints in Anthropology, J and L Reprint Company, 1985.

REFERENCES

Bonnichesen, Robson. 1973. "Millie's Camp: an experiment in archaeology." *World Archaeology* 4:277–91.

Calder, James M. 1977. "The Majorville Cairn and medicine wheel site, Alberta." National Museum of Canada, National Museum of Man *Mercury Series*, Archaeological Survey Paper No. 62.

Dempsey, Hugh A. 1956. "Stone 'medicine wheels'—memorials to Blackfoot war chiefs." *Journal of the Washington Academy of Sciences* 46 (6): 177–82.

Dixon, Roland B. 1913. "Some aspects of North American archaeology." *American Anthropologist* 15:549–66.

Eddy, John A. 1974. "Astronomical alignments of the Big Horn Medicine Wheel." *Science* 184:1035–43.

Forbis, Richard G. 1960. "Some Late sites in the Oldman River region, Alberta." *National Museum of Canada Bulletin* 162:119–64.

Hind, Henry Y. 1860. *Narrative of the Canadian Red River exploring expedition of 1857 and of the Assiniboine and Saskatchewan exploring expedition* of 1858. London.

Kehoe, Thomas F. 1954. "Stone 'medicine wheels' in southern Alberta and the adjacent portion of Montana: were they designed as grave markers?" *Journal of the Washington Academy of Sciences* 44:133–37.

———. 1958. "Tipi rings: the 'direct ethnological' approach applied to an archaeological problem." *American Anthropologist* 60:861–73.

———. 1960. "Stone tipi rings in north-central Montana and the adjacent portion of Alberta, Canada: their historical, ethnological and archeological aspects." *Bureau of American Ethnology Bulletin* 173:417–73.

———. 1965. "'Buffalo stones': An addendum to 'The folklore of fossils.'" *Antiquity* 39:212–13.

———. 1967. "The Boarding School Bison Drive site." *Plains Anthropologist Memoir* 4.

———. 1972. "Stone 'medicine wheel' monuments in the Northern Plains of North America." *Atti del xl Congresso Internazionale degli Americanisti* II:183–89.

———. 1973. "The Gull Lake site." *Milwaukee Public Museum Publications in Anthropology and History* 1.

———. 1976. "New interpretation of prehistoric Plains economy." Paper presented at the 75th annual meeting of the American Anthropological Association, Washington, DC.

Kehoe, Thomas F. and Alice B. 1959. "Boulder effigy monuments in the Northern Plains." *Journal of American Folklore* 72:115–27.

———. 1977. "Stones, solstices, and Sun Dance structures." *Plains Anthropologist* 22:85–95.

———. 1979. "Solstice-aligned boulder configurations in Saskatchewan." National Museums of Canada *Mercury Series*, Canadian Ethnology Service No. 48.

Krieger, Alex D. 1956. "Early man: Alberta." *American Antiquity* 21:450.

Legesse, Asmaron. 1973. *Gada*. New York: Free Press.

Lewis, T. H. 1889. "Stone monuments in southern Dakota." *American Anthropologist* 2:162–65.

———. 1890. "Stone monuments in northwestern Iowa and southwestern Minnesota." *American Anthropologist* 3:273–74.

Mandelbaum, David G. 1940. "The Plains Cree." *American Museum of Natural History Anthropological Papers* 37:155–316.

Mulloy, William T. 1952. "The northern Plains." In *Archeology of Eastern United States,* edited by J. B. Griffin, 124–38. Chicago: University of Chicago Press.

Oakley, Kenneth. 1965. "Folklore of Fossils." *Antiquity* 39:9–16.

Wedel, Waldo R. 1953. "[Review of] The Northern Plains [by] William Mulloy." American Antiquity 19:178–79.

PART 3. Archaeology Lives in Social Contexts

Archaeology is conducted as a science, yet it is a social phenomenon. Its principal data do not exist in nature.

Carl Sauer saw this clearly. Archaeologists' data are *artifacts*, Latin *arte factum*, made, implicitly, by people. An entire landscape can be an artifact. And it could not exist as it does, or did, except that communities of people agreed to engage in the activities that created the cultural landscape, just as small artifacts exist only through social conventions of manufacture and style. More: the practice of archaeology, how to recognize artifacts and cultural landscapes, are taught by people to other people; that is, by ostentation (Kehoe 1990a). Professors, especially the acknowledged influential ones, have been, until very recently, WASP men. Some assumed that Cahokia's great mounds were natural, fitting the colonialist claim that invading settlers were civilizing a land without artifacts (Kennedy 1994, 30).

In this chapter, I present my interpretation of Cahokia in a paper that was rejected without comment on its data or argument. Likewise, my research on the Kensington runestone (Kehoe 2005) was dismissed without argument on its data. Both artifacts should be immediately convincing to an unbiased eye: Cahokia because such geometric earth mounds cannot be natural in a floodplain, and the runestone because weathering is clearly visible along the text incisions in its very hard greywacke. Is it preposterous to claim that American scientists blatantly ignore potent data? Not anymore! Donald Trump revealed the extraordinary ability of the dominant class in the United States to obstruct factual knowledge. We saw its brutality on January 6, 2021.

It is crucial to understand that the United States, like other nation-states, created and maintains a structured ideology proclaiming its actuality as a people and the legitimacy of its occupation of territory. It is as Benedict Anderson put it in 1992: "In an anthropological spirit, then, I propose the following definition of the nation: it is an imagined political community—and imagined as both inherently limited and sovereign" (quoted in Eriksen 2016, 4). Anderson meant "imagined" as more a mental and linguistic construct than a physical area, therefore "limited and sovereign" would be *asserted* rather than empirically obvious. Immaterial in this sense of a pre-existing landscape with natural physical boundaries, the United States of America maintains its sovereignty over its claimed territory in part through its approved history. Those who earn their livelihood by writing histories of that territory jeopardize that income if their work fails to conform and confirm the imagined community. At the least, their work doesn't get published.

Whether Cahokia had a trade relationship with Cholula is not of immediate consequence to anyone. Rather, the issue is the tip of the Himalaya constructed of Manifest Destiny ideology, Anglo cultural dominance, white supremacy doctrines, xenophobia, racism with its persistent inequalities, and as the "Q-Anon Shaman" embodied on January 6, 2021, crude masculinity. Up until this millennium, most professional archaeologists grew up in middle-class or upper-class communities infused with the assumptions produced by these factors. They chose to be archaeologists, not historians, political scientists, nor philosophers. Few thought about Black lives, questioned military actions of the United States against First Nations, or considered there might be any reality other than Christian European beliefs.

European archaeologists had discovered earliest *Homo sapiens* lived in caves, making and using flaked stone tools—the Paleolithic era—then figured out how to make bows and arrows, art, shelters for living in the open, and eventually pottery and agriculture, "the Neolithic" (ground stone axes in addition to flaked stone). All these were found in America upon European invasion. What was not found in the Anglo domain were massive stone buildings, domesticated beasts (except dogs and turkeys), alphabetic writing, metallurgy, or a class system of laborers, literate investors and professionals, and rulers. From this evidence, Lewis Henry Morgan followed European convention to present a system, replete with the magical number three, of Savagery, Barbarism, and Civilization, only the two primitive stages developed in North America. Morgan's system impressed Major John Wesley Powell, Smithsonian scientist, who, along with many other Americans, accepted it as empirically supported.

Tautologically, American archaeologists found plenty of stone artifacts and potsherds, and as they read nineteenth-century travelers' journals and the salvage ethnographies following Grant's brutal imposition of peace by military force, archaeologists saw their data fit the Savage or Barbarian slots. Spanish sources described Civilizations in Latin America, with great stone buildings, cities, writing, and rulers, to which Morgan averred that the conquistadors had lied to impress their own king (Kehoe 1998, 174–75). Morgan gave archaeologists their schema, they found the evidence, therefore Morgan had correctly described North American First Nations.

The lineage from Morgan to mainstream American archaeology surprisingly curves to Friedrich Engels, to the University of Michigan professors Leslie White and Elman Service, and then around to Lewis Binford. White was an active member of the Socialist Labor Party, and Service was a member of the Communist Party and Young Communist League. Both believed in linear cultural evolution, and White became a fervent proponent for Morgan's work. White was a contentious man whose vigorous attacks and uncompromising self-assurance attracted students (Peace 2006) and even made him a pundit, selected to represent all the social sciences in NBC's 1947 radio series "The Scientists Speak." Service's teaching, although less grandiose, likewise enthralled students by these professors' staunch conviction that they knew the truth about human history. Neither man was a Marxist in the strict sense of Marx's own writings, since Marx focused on capitalist industrial society. Expected to be familiar with non-Western small societies, the two American anthropologists found Morgan's work more apropos. So did their students, equally schooled as children in American public schools' Manifest Destiny history (Kehoe 1990b).

Cultural Evolution's Entanglement with America

Anglo America conventionally is viewed as a Christian nation, founded in 1620 and 1630 by Protestants escaping religious battles in Europe. They and their descendants envisioned a Redeemer Nation, a City upon a Hill, as it has been asserted (Van Engen 2020). Perry Miller, a dominant historian of colonial America during the mid-twentieth century, titled his widely read 1956 book *Errand Into the Wilderness*, disregarding that Massachusetts Bay First Nations were raising corn, beans, and squashes in cleared fields and had fed the Puritans from these harvests. Miller's glorification of the English Puritans was published only three years before Leslie White's *The*

Evolution of Culture. In their disparate ways, they upheld the United States as great and good, as leader of the world.

Postwar America papered over the crisis of conscience spurred by its annihilation of Nagasaki and Hiroshima. World War II was a justified war against naked evil, as was America's Civil War. Nonetheless, veterans were haunted by their experiences of brutal slaughter. Henry Adams pondered upon the dissonance between that actuality and the ideals espoused by educated citizens, realizing that

> He was a Darwinist before the letter; a predestined follower of the tide. . . . The ideas were new and seemed to lead somewhere—to some great generalization. . . . He felt, like nine men in ten, an instinctive belief in Evolution. . . . Unbroken Evolution under uniform conditions pleased everyone—except curates and bishops. . . . Such a working system for the universe suited a young man who had just helped waste five or ten thousand million dollars and a million lives, more or less, to enforce unity and uniformity on people who objected to it; the idea was only too seductive in its perfection. (Adams [1907] 1918, 224–26)

For young Adams, it was Herbert Spencer's version of unbroken evolution that absolved him of guilt. For the vets enrolled in anthropology at the University of Michigan a century later, it was Leslie White's pseudo-scientific demonstration that an impersonal, empowering force drove humans. Harnessing energy was the key to evolution, particularly human cultural evolution. Mushroom clouds were signs in the heavens that America was the epitome of evolution.

So we see a zeitgeist: after a devastating war, perhaps even especially one with a just cause, survivors seize a doctrine exculpating them from blame. Caught up in the exciting revelation of inexorable progress, late-nineteenth-century and post-World War II educated people were comfortable with their status as leaders. The technologies they developed proved their mental abilities as shrewd men and built fortunes in industry. Science was king. Positivism was the label, sometimes attributed to Auguste Comte, who first popularized the word and proposed social engineering (Bourdeau 2023). The working definition of positivism was "propositions are meaningful if and only if they are about the relations of ideas or about matters that are subject to empirical verification or falsification" (Taliaferro 2023,

2.1). How could these educated leaders empirically verify Progress, the mystical Force that had produced their superior way of life?

Leslie White did it. His postwar book, *Evolution of Culture*, used equations: $C=ExT$ to express that Culture equals Energy (per capita per year) plus Technological efficiency, and $ExT \rightarrow P$, power; "a culture is high or low depending upon the amount of energy harnessed per capita per year" (White [1959] 2007, 42). Energy from fissioning atoms, using Technology, unquestionably led to America's Power. QED. Like Henry Adams, the vets in White's courses were seduced by the perfection of White's empirical demonstration of his true explanation for human history.

Did White's and Service's Marxism disturb their students? I talked with Roy Rappaport and Robert Carneiro, who told me they never noticed Marxism in White's lectures. Carneiro, in a series of letters exchanged in 2001, reflected upon the question, concluding that he was led to accept White's work as Truth because White spoke as a top authority in the hierarchy of American scholars. Hierarchy was inherent in the world Carneiro grew up in, he told me, an immigrant Catholic culture in New York. From his father up through priests, bishops, cardinals, to the Pope who spoke as God, Carneiro was raised to accept dicta from male authorities. White's own conviction that he had found Truth, propounded with vigor, fit the expectations of his Eisenhower-era students; science rationally argued was Truth.

More than White's and Service's Marxist connections was hidden from students. The United States was engaged in a Cold War against Russia, its mortal enemy. Physics and chemistry had won World War II. Therefore those disciplines deserved to be generously supported to continue their scientific progress toward munitions superiority in the new contest for global dominance. The National Science Foundation was created to not only support laboratory work but to channel science into a narrow "Positivist" model. NSF did not support social sciences, as a rule, unless projects were constructed within a Positivist model (Reisch 2005; Solovey 2012, 2013, 2020; Baker 2022). Note that this version of Positivism is not Comte's philosophy, which, to quite the contrary, intended to create a set of social sciences to ameliorate human lives in communities.

Behind the earmarking of money for the laboratory physical sciences was the CIA, abetted by the FBI (Price 2016). "Liberals" had been under surveillance and harassment, as part of the Cold War, since 1947 (Saunders 1999, 2); one was the Boasian anthropologist Gene (Regina) Weltfish, who was dismissed from her Columbia University faculty position when Senator Joseph McCarthy targeted her as a Communist (Price 2004, 110–35, 2022, 69–83). Her ordeal cautioned anthropologists, along with other citizens, to keep silent if they held socialist opinions. At least one archaeologist, Michael Coe, worked for the CIA, and his department head at Yale, George Peter Murdock, recruited students for the CIA (Price 2016, 160–62 on Coe, 248ff. on Murdock). These CIA operatives likewise kept silent on their clandestine work.

NSF has been the principal federal funding agency for archaeology, although NEH (National Endowment for the Humanities) also offers grants for archaeological field research. John Yellen became Director of NSF's Archaeology and Archaeometry Program in 1977, and of this writing, 2023, is still the director. SAA selected him for its Distinguished Service Award in 1992, claiming that "given his long tenure in this sensitive position, he has avoided politicizing the program, and has maintained a remarkably fair and unbiased perspective on the encouragement and funding of research" (SAA Bulletin 10(3):4). Yet even though he was shown by Joan Gero in 1982[1] that women received significantly fewer NSF grants for archaeology than men did, a 2017 report by an SAA task force on gender disparities recorded continuation of the same marked disparity between senior men and senior women in NSF grant awards (Goldstein et al., 2017). Why did nothing change at NSF?

NOTES

1. On Friday afternoon on April 16, 1982, session 31 of the SAA Annual Meeting was a symposium titled "The Socio-Politics of Archaeology," organized by Joan Gero and Michael Blakey, who were at the time graduate students in Anthropology at University of Massachusetts-Amherst. Participants were: Michael Blakey, Robert Paynter, D. M. Lacy, Robert Hasenstab, Olga Soffer, John Yellen, Joan Gero, Marsha Hanen, Jane Kelley, Martin Wobst, Arthur Keene, and Mark Leone as Discussant. (Program online at https://documents.saa.org/container/docs/default-source/doc-annualmeeting/abstract/1982.pdf?sfvrsn=b3916582_4, accessed 4/30/23). Papers from the session were published in Gero et al. 1983.

7. Chiefdoms

The clue to the persistence of the conservative colonialist mainstream in American archaeology may lie in the success of some applicants, primarily men, in consistently getting their projects funded by NSF. For example, take the recipient of SAA's 2023 Lifetime Achievement Award, Timothy Earle. His first NSF support was in 1967, an undergraduate participation field school stipend, through his last in 2010 as an NSF Foundation Grant, the year before he retired from his professorship at Northwestern University. His graduate studies at University of Michigan were supported by three years of NSF graduate fellowships, his fieldwork projects from 1982 through 2010, with a total of $554,000. Most of his writings argue for Service's scheme of cultural evolution, specifically for the "chiefdom" stage of clear hierarchy:

The Hierarchy
The tribe, which may encompass several camp-sized groups, is a hierarchy. Hierarchical organizations have a clearly defined leader, and often many strata of authority. They have clear lines of authority, and no inherent means to achieve consensus. They evolved as a means of providing a mechanism for relations with other tribes (including commerce and war), for conducting religious observances and to allow occupational specialization. But they had the fortuitous result of solving the problem of instability in large organizations. The tribal hierarchy made it possible for more than 50 people to live and work together, at the cost of personal and group autonomy. (Tuck and Earle 1996)

Let us now look at a senior woman archaeologist whose application for NSF fieldwork funding was rejected *eight* times. Carole Crumley's undergraduate work was at the University of Michigan in anthropology, graduating in 1966 at the top of her class in anthropology. She applied to do graduate work at University of Michigan but was not accepted; she then obtained an MA at the University of Calgary in 1967, supervised by Richard S. MacNeish. For doctoral work, she enrolled at the University of

Wisconsin (Madison), earning the degree in 1972 with a dissertation on "Celtic Social Structure," drawing upon literary sources to test inferences with archaeology. At Madison, she took courses in historical ecology with William Denevan, who trained with Carl Sauer's students. Crumley's fieldwork since beginning graduate study has been in Europe, focused since 1975 on the citadel site of Mont Dardon in southern Burgundy. With stratified occupations from the Neolithic through the Medieval period, the site supported a historical ecology approach; it is a landmark to the present communities around it, and Crumley linked with local and regional historical groups and local citizens. From 1977 on, she was a professor in anthropology at the University of North Carolina-Chapel Hill.

So far as professional qualifications go, Crumley appears as fully worthy of NSF archaeological fieldwork support as Earle. They are of the same generation. Both have been full professors at major research universities. Both had graduate and doctoral experience and continuing research at several sites abroad. Were Crumley's rejections due to her gender? Or was her work with documentary sources, her humanities orientation toward communities' values and sustainable subsistence practices, not "scientific" enough for NSF?

Or was it masculinity in our Indo-European culture? Kristian Kristiansen, the Danish archaeologist who, as it happens, collaborated with Timothy Earle in excavations of Bronze Age sites in Denmark, explained to a student why they focused on weapons:

> Kristian and I had an interesting conversation about the female costume in the Bronze Age. Kristian confided that he had once worked on the topic, but could not get it published, so he turned to swords instead and never looked back. He promised to send me a copy of his unpublished manuscript from 1975, which he claimed was his only unpublished manuscript. (Bergerbrant 2013, 755)

Earle co-published *The Evolution of Human Societies* in 1987 (a second edition was published in 2000); *Specialization, Exchange and Complex Societies* in 1987 (nine contributors including Earle as co-editor); *Chiefdoms: Power, Economy and Ideology* in 1991 (ten contributors including editor Earle); *How Chiefs Come to Power*[1] in 1997; and *A Primer on Chiefs and Chiefdoms*

(Principles of Archaeology) in 2021. These build on Elman Service's teaching at the University of Michigan, based on Lewis Henry Morgan's schema. Chiefs are men, patriarchies are unexamined premises in chiefdoms, and there is an evolutionary pathway to global dominance by the descendants of those Bronze Age warrior princes Earle and Kristiansen excavated.

Earle and Crumley have followed very different pathways in their researches. Earle's has been straight as he sought to establish a reality for Service's hypothesized evolutionary stages, excavating in Peru, Hawai'i, and Scandinavia. Crumley, too, has focused her research, but from a very different standpoint: historical ecology. In spite of undergraduate experience at the University of Michigan when White and Service were teaching, she was drawn to the Sauer perspective of cultural landscapes. Where Earle fit data into a format drawn from Morgan's nineteenth-century racist progression that denied the final culminating stage, the state, to colonized First Nations, Crumley framed her project within the archaeological sequence Neolithic-Bronze Age-Iron Age-Roman/Gaulish-"Dark Ages"-Medieval, which she found, through testing, are represented within Mont Dardon in France. For evidence of the last two thousand years, she and her associates had to work with documents and historians' analyses as well as the region's ecological and human alterations features.

These two careers in archaeology illustrate a fundamental difference between modes of practice. The physical sciences methodology dominated American archaeology from the 1960s until the retirements of its practitioners who had completed their doctorates in the last third of the twentieth century. During this half century, accepting it got one's bread buttered, while using Peirce's abductive process and analogies left its practitioners unfunded and uncited. Earle's focus on "chiefdoms" and chiefs is closer to the common idea of science as testing hypotheses, "hypothetico-deductive." Leslie White and Elman Service followed this practice, and Lewis Binford claimed it (Kehoe 1998, 133–41).

Crumley's Mont Dardon project is exemplary for method of the historical sciences. In the course of its analyses, she realized that the data corollary to the archaeology did not show any path to a hierarchy, any path to "complexity." What she and her colleague William Marquardt recognized were multiplicities, what Franz Boas had advocated as historical particularism. She introduced the word "heterarchy" to describe how communities recognized various forms of knowledge and expertise, on a variety of scales of range and frequencies of leadership (see especially Crumley and Marquardt 1987, 613–15; better known are her 1987 and 1995 papers). Earle read those two papers, citing them in his 1997 book (Earle 1997, 210), without apparently realizing that Crumley was challenging the core cultural-evolutionary paradigm.[2] He put "heterarchy" in the middle between egalitarianism and hierarchy, hewing to the white supremacy premise of Progress. It looks like putting down the woman, distorting her contribution, though he may simply not have grasped that the racist paradigm itself was actually unscientific.

What follows here is my paper that was rejected by both *American Anthropologist* and *Journal of Anthropological Research* in 2003.

Chiefdoms

An Artifact of Postmedieval European Preconceptions

The Chiefdom Model versus the Principle of Actualism

In a document promulgated, as it states,

> In Congress, July 4, 1776. The unanimous Declaration of the thirteen united States of America,
>
> When in the Course of human events, it becomes necessary for one people to dissolve the political bands which have connected them with another . . . a decent respect to the opinions of mankind requires that they should declare the causes which impel them to the separation. . . .
>
> The history of the present King of Great Britain is a history of repeated injuries and usurpations . . . . To prove this, let Facts be submitted to a candid world.

Jefferson then listed twenty-seven "Facts"; the last in the list claims,

> He [King of Great Britain] . . . has endeavoured to bring on the inhabitants of our frontiers, the merciless Indian Savages, whose known rule

of warfare, is an undistinguished destruction, of all ages, sexes and conditions.[3]

After this "Fact" in the Declaration of Independence, it's hardly surprising that Chief Justice John Marshall, in *Johnson v. McIntosh*, 1823, would state that

> the tribes of Indians inhabiting this country were fierce savages, whose occupation was war, and whose subsistence was drawn chiefly from the forest. To leave them in possession of their country, was to leave the country a wilderness; to govern them as a distinct people, was impossible. (quoted in Williams 1990, 323n133)

Marshall had as a second authority, Jedidiah Morse, whose standard geography text stated,

> When North-America was first visited by Europeans, it might be regarded, except Mexico, as one immense forest, inhabited by wild animals, and by a great number of savage tribes, who subsisted by hunting and fishing. (quoted in Short 1999, 31, from the 1819 Morse *Geography Made Easy*, 30th edition)

The authors of the Declaration of Independence, Jedidiah Morse, and Justice Marshall were speaking of the indigenous nations of the Southeast, those commonly known as the Five Civilized Tribes. These authorities' imperial propaganda underlies nineteenth-century ethnology (Wallace 1997, 28; 1999, 15, 327–29) and the flattened past, "a uniform nonpresent" (Kroeber 1952, 151) inhabited by savages.

A century later, marking in 1893 the quadricentennial of Columbus's American landing, Frederick Jackson Turner declared,

> [A]t the frontier, the environment is at first too strong for the man. He must accept the conditions which it furnishes or perish, and so he fits himself into the Indian clearings and follows the Indian trails. Little by little he transforms the wilderness. (quoted in Klein 1997, 79)

Working on his dissertation, in 1888, Turner had pictured American Indians emerging from the wilderness as untutored children to wonder at [the European's] goods and call him master—even as Caliban lay at the feet of Trinculo and the potent bottle on Prospero's enchanted island. (quoted in Klein 1997, 135)

Perhaps young Turner had read Daniel Wilson's 1873 *Caliban: The Missing Link*. Wilson, who introduced the word "prehistory" into English (in 1851) and outlined the basic method for American archaeology in his *Prehistoric Man* (1862, 1876), had concluded that the Caliban type was geologically ancient and extinct. Wilson, from a liberal Scottish reformist group, was a maverick. Recurrent late-nineteenth-century allusions to Shakespeare's bestial aborigine are a clue to Anglo-American images of their predecessors in this land and of their own self-image as the magus Prospero.

Where Daniel Wilson looked to geology for a model for a scientific archaeology, Turner used geology for explanation:

Indian villages . . . had been placed in positions suggested by nature. . . . Thus civilization in America has followed the arteries made by geology, pouring an ever richer tide through them, until at last the slender paths of aboriginal intercourse have been broadened and interwoven into the complex mazes of modern commercial lines; the wilderness has been interpenetrated by lines of civilization [leading to] economic and social consolidation. (quoted in Klein 1997, 141)

Turner's Quadricentennial keynote address, "The Significance of the Frontier," propounded enduring themes for the study of preconquest America: ecological determinism and Indians lacking the insignia of civilization. The Land of Prehistory beyond the frontier of Anglo-America had been modeled by Jefferson and Marshall well before Turner reiterated it.

Both dominant themes go back to the seventeenth century, particularly powerfully enunciated by John Locke (Williams 1990, 248). That Turner made his career by repeating them in 1893 tells us how highly charged ideologically they are, for Turner makes his statements *in spite of* twenty years of B.A.E. ethnographies, of Wilson's *Prehistoric Man*'s two thick volumes describing achievements of indigenous American civilizations, of Squier and Davis's *Ancient Monuments of the Mississippi Valley*. America continued to justify its conquests and dispossessions by projecting the Land of Prehistory as primeval wilderness where Merciless Savages hunted.

Canadian anthropologist Dara Culhane (1998, 180) comments that we assume, without question, that immigrants to the United States and Canada will learn these nations' language, will conform to their laws and customs, and expect to become citizens. Why then, she asks, was it not assumed in the seventeenth and eighteenth centuries, or indeed well into the nineteenth, that immigrants to North America would take residence in the existing indigenous nations, learn their languages, conform to their laws and customs, and become assimilated into their citizenry? Why are we not speaking Algonkian and paying taxes to one or another sachem?

American History

American history in a global perspective—latest fad in social science—begins well before 1492. Polynesians surely discovered America, unfortunately for them already inhabited (Green 1998, 109). Seagoing fishermen were in the North Atlantic in the first millennium AD, and probably earlier (Kehoe 1971). Phoenicians or North Africans may have ventured across the mid-Atlantic, their voyages lost to history when Rome declared, "Carthago deleta est." Even Alfred Kidder admitted that it "is illogical" to deny contacts between the so-called Old and New Worlds (Kidder 1936, 151). Anglo denial of First Nations' history extends to disregard the extent of sixteenth century Spanish, French, and privateers' activities along the Atlantic region of the Southeast (Lewis and Loomie 1953).

America cut off from the world until 1492 is essential for the chartering myth of wilderness. Like other animals in the wilderness, Indian savages have no history other than paleontological. It was Herder, in the 1780s, who formulated the contrast between historic nations and the *Volk* living outside time as literate Europeans know it (Adams 1998, 279), a dichotomy traced by Arthur Lovejoy and George Boas (1935) back to our earliest surviving sources in eighth century BCE Greece. The seventeenth-century Enlightenment postulated universal principles but made alphabetic literacy the touchstone for historical consciousness; communities that did not preserve their histories in written texts were classed as people without history, and by extension of the importance of texts, without law, religion, or political structure. The logic of the dichotomy extends, it seems, to archaeologists working with the relics of people without history, asking them to use terms different from those customary for historically constructed nations. In England, for example, when we get to the prehistoric century before the Roman invasions, the kingdom of Wessex becomes a chiefdom.[4] Conversely, now that we can read their texts, the Maya have "kingdoms," replacing Eric Thompson's "autonomous city states" ruled by pairs of "chiefs" (Thompson 1954, 81).

Here is the nub of the problem. Are we justified in employing one set of terms for the literate nations for whom we have written documents, and another set of terms for nations without these fossilized historical data?[5] In Talal Asad's landmark *Anthropology and the Colonial Encounter*, Stephan Feuchtwang acidly pointed out that "Literacy . . . besides defining [anthropology's] subject-matter . . . preliterate peoples . . . [ensures] the lack of challenge by its subjects, unable to read the finished work" (Feuchtwang 1973, 79). Now that our subjects can and do read anthropology, the postcolonial situation is forcing us to critical discussion (Wylie 1995, 268) of anthropology's usage of the term "chief" (e.g., Carucci 1986; White and Lindstrom 1997; van Rouveroy, van Nieuwaal, and Dijk 1999). The boundary of prehistory lies on a slippery slope.

The Chiefdom Model

Struggling for footing on that slope, Americanist archaeologists for the past forty years have used the categories in Elman Service's small and well-written textbook, *Primitive Social Organization* (1962) ("Political Anthropology for Dummies", I'd say). Joan Vincent remarked of the Service and Sahlins "popular and simple taxonomy" (1990, 312) that, "as so often happened when historical processes proved hard to grasp, the quick fix was provided by evolutionism" (Vincent 1990, 330). That evolutionism was diffused primarily from the University of Michigan after World War II, by students inspired by Leslie White (Carneiro 1981, 224). The era being the beginning of the Cold War and of McCarthy's witch-hunts, it is not surprising that Leslie White concealed the fact that he was a card-carrying member of the Socialist Labor party and an active contributor, under a pseudonym, to its newsletter (Peace 1993). He did not conceal where his sympathies lay in 1960:

Although the United States was born in armed revolt . . . , in mid-twentieth century it is determined that no other country shall do likewise, and the communist revolution which is spreading throughout much of the world is always called "aggression," and is opposed. (White 1960, vi)

This is in his Foreword to Sahlins's and Service's *Evolution and Culture*. Whether Timothy Earle is cognizant of it I do not know, but William Peace's research into Leslie White's career leaves no doubt that White was fervently teaching the inevitability of, in Service's words, an "ideally conceived, more democratic socialism" purged only of Stalinist terrorism (Service 1960, 119). Not really Marxist, for he was oblivious to class conflicts, White revitalized nineteenth-century evolutionism. Though fundamentally imperialist and racist, not to mention out-of-sync with tenets of evolutionary biology, it has been innocently absorbed by mainstream American archaeologists.

Naming four stages of political evolution, soon collapsed into three (Service 1971), Service stimulated archaeologists to worry the implicit question of how people had got from one stage to the next.[6] Sahlins's more expansive exposition of "chiefdoms" claims them to be "a classic kind of evolutionary progress" (Sahlins 1968, 26) "occupy[ing] a position in cultural evolution" (Sahlins 1968, 4). Our Founding Fathers' "Fact" that only Merciless Savages inhabited the Land of Prehistory beyond our frontiers established the conditioning premise that states would never be found there. Archaeologists looked for bands and chiefdoms[7] in North America, leaving the question of how states evolved to researchers working in Latin America and Eurasia.

Timothy Earle is presently chief of the archaeologists pursuing the study of social evolution by focusing on what they label "chiefdoms." Earle states, "A general theory of social evolution can begin with the study of what factors determine the success (or failure) of leaders attempting to centralize and thus control social systems" (Earle 1997, 208; see also Carneiro 1998, 20). He cites Ehrenreich, Crumley, and Levy (1995) when remarking, "Complex societies are not so much hierarchical as they are 'heterarchical,'" then explains, "meaning simply that segments have separate internal hierarchies that deflect overall social centrality" (Earle 1997, 1). Yet in the cited publication, Crumley differed significantly: "Heterarchy may be defined as the relation of elements to one another when they are unranked or when they possess the potential for being ranked in a number of different ways" (Crumley 1995, 3, also 1987, 163, where she emphasizes a "*dialectical relation* between ranked and counterpoised power"). She explicitly discusses her "dissatisfaction" with Service's cultural evolutionary model and speaks of the "social formation of larger polities" rather than of "chiefdoms and states" (Crumley 1995, 4). Earle appropriated Crumley's word without accepting her defined meaning.

Carole Crumley zeroed in on the crux of the "problem" of chiefdoms when she reviewed several archaeological theorists whom she saw

> attempt[ing] to "break out" complexity from notions of progress deeply embedded in cultural evolutionism. . . . These authors would seem to concur that all societies are (at least periodically) complex. (Crumley 1987, 163)

This was exactly my argument in a 1981 *Current Anthropology* article, "Revisionist Anthropology: Aboriginal North America" (Kehoe 1981, 505) and in my 1993 paper on hunter-gatherers in *Research in Economic Anthropology* (Kehoe 1993, 93–94, both reprinted in this book). In these papers, I cite Aristotle's discussion of the *polis* for its outline of the functions carried out through governance:

1. it has recognized rights to territory from which subsistence may be drawn,
2. its members engage in food production (not necessarily agriculture),
3. its members engage in arts and crafts production,
4. it uses arms, to maintain internal order and to protect against foreign aggression,
5. it sponsors public worship, and
6. "most vitally necessary, is a method of deciding what is demanded by the public interest and what is just in men's private dealings" (Aristotle 1946, 299).

The *polis* can entertain foreign visitors, traders and workers, so long as their numbers do not overwhelm the citizens (Aristotle 1946. 292).

Using Aristotle's outline, I found that Plains Indian nations such as the Blackfoot maintained polities through an annual summer rendezvous where several thousand people would gather for trade, recreation, rituals, adjudication of disputes, and negotiation of alliances. These rendez-vous camps manifested a polity otherwise latent while the people lived in task-group hunting bands; it was through rendezvous that previously agricultural nations such as the Cheyenne retained national structure after removal to the shortgrass Plains (Moore 1996, 163). Archaeological traces of the rendezvous camps consist of sites with hundreds of tipi rings (e.g., T. Kehoe 1960, 449). Scheduling trekking to the annual camp may be the reason for the astronomical observatories popularly called medicine wheels, such as Moose Mountain (Kehoe and Kehoe 1979).

Service's 1962 textbook definition of chiefdoms is that they "are *redistributional societies* with a permanent central agency of coordination . . . [which can] act to foster and preserve the integration of the society for the sake of integration alone" (Service 1962, 144, his italics). His key term, redistribution, is taken from Karl Polanyi's contrast between reciprocal and redistributive economic structures, but as Joan Vincent noted, Service ignored the two other structures Polanyi included, markets and house-holding (Vincent 1990, 330). Service did then discuss "regional exchange" encouraging higher productivity,

> which in turn stimulates the tendency toward redistribution from a central authority. . . . The above emphasis on regional exchange is again a way of stressing the significance of the superorganic aspect of the environment as part of the total adaptive situation. (Service 1961, 147)

By omitting markets, Service perpetuated the dichotomy between impe-rial nations ("systems of predatory expansion" in the words of Leacock and Lee [1982, 6]) and those they overwhelmed—his bands, tribes, and chiefdoms—forever beyond the frontier in the Land of Prehistory.

The Late Prehistoric and Protohistoric Southeast

Contemporary archaeologists working in the Southeast have inherited these two extraordinary propositions, that the Five Civilized Tribes and all their predecessors and neighbor nations were Merciless Savages in a wilderness, and that there is a "superorganic aspect of the environment" fostering "leaders attempting to centralize and thus control social systems." Service's mentor, Leslie White, visited Stalin's Russia in 1929 and put it succinctly to his Socialist Labor Party comrades reading *New Masses* (1931):

"cultural processes grind steadily on . . . [to] the next stage of political evolution" (quoted in Peace 1993, 129).

The concept of stages of cultural evolution is, and has always been, ideologically loaded, whether among the classical Greeks with their Golden, Silver, Bronze, and Iron Ages (Lovejoy and Boas 1935, 24–30), Enlightenment philosophes (Meek 1976), Lewis Henry Morgan (Kehoe 1998, 176), or Leslie White. William Adams's analysis of the history of anthropology emphasizes,

> Early anthropologists not only added greatly to the store of ethnographic and archaeological evidence, they also arranged that evidence in orderly progressions to provide seemingly irrefutable confirmation for what had long been only a philosophical doctrine. (Adams 1998, 72)

Adams adds, that by mid-twentieth century, most anthropologists had become disillusioned with evolutionary stage theory, although "archaeologists remained firmly wedded" (Adams 1998, 64).

Smithsonian ethnologist William Sturtevant recently stated, "There is evidently no case of a chiefdom directly observed by a modern ethnographer. . . . American chiefdoms are an artifact of postmedieval European preconceptions" (Sturtevant 1998, 138, 140). Such plain words should be enough: the concept of "chiefdoms" is without empirical substantiation. Disregarding his warning, archaeologists have been deductively slotting data into a "chiefdom stage" and then proffering the data to allegedly validate it (e.g., Earle 1997, 17–66): a tautology. Worse, in the past decade some Southeastern ethnohistorians (e.g., Hudson 1997; La Vere 1998) have pushed their data into this hypothetical construct, naively assuming that what looks like fifty million archaeologists can't be wrong.

The foundation of the historical sciences is the principle of actualism. In a magisterial essay on actualism, Simpson declared that "hypotheticodeductive explanation" is "quite inacceptable in the practice of historical science" (Simpson 1970, 86). For the study of American prehistory, hypotheses uncritically formulated within the Anglo political convention fabricated by John Locke, carried on by Jefferson and Marshall, are going to be "thinking within the box." Lakoff and Johnson remark (1999, 88) that "if [researchers] are not aware of how a priori philosophy shapes their scientific worldviews, they will simply not notice its effects." Imputing reality to logical models such as "chiefdom stage" can be (consciously or unwittingly) a hegemonic strategy. Models are heuristic, simplified analogies; "to understand modelling . . . in science it is necessary to consider the practical purposes of the users" (Barnes, Bloor, and Henry 1996, 109). Richard Fardon reminds us that "Anthropology necessarily reproduced versions of assumptions deeply embedded in a predatory European culture" (Fardon 1990, 6). Our historical circumstances render work with American data to be fraught with assumptions from our chartering myth. To be scientific, interpretation of archaeological data should depend, first and foremost, upon fit to actual ethnographic analogies (Moore 1994, 129–31).

One step toward actualism is to take seriously the usages of our sixteenth and seventeenth century sources. Centralized, absolutist monarchies did not develop in Europe until late in the seventeenth century (Friedrichs 2000, 66–67). Captain John Smith, of Jamestown, and Hernando de Soto knew that their nations had, only a few centuries earlier, consisted of several quite independent kingdoms, seven in first-millennium England and more in medieval Spain. Smith, in Virginia, called Wahunsonacock, the Powhatan, a king (Barker 1992, 68), and carried out an exchange of kingly robes between him and England's king, James the Sixth and First (as they call him in Scotland). Smith was highly conscious of rank and status, protesting that he was well aware a commoner like himself should not presume to seek marriage with a king's daughter such as Pocahontas (Lemay 1991, 126).

Opechancanough, who succeeded Wahunsonacock's immediate heir, Itopatin, was said by Virginia Colony historian Robert Beverley to have been "a Prince of a Foreign Nation, and came to [Chesapeake Bay] a great Way from the South-West. And by these Accounts, we suppose him to have come from the *Spanish Indians,* some-where near *Mexico*" (quoted in Lewis and Loomie 1953, 59). An earlier Virginia chronicler, Raphe Hamor, stated in 1615 that "*the Spaniards* . . . name is odious among [the Chickahominy of Chesapeake Bay], for Powhatan's father was driven by them from the *west-Indies* into these parts [Chesapeake]" (quoted in Lewis and Loomie 1953, 58; "west-Indies" at that time signified Spanish-held Mesoamerica as well as the Caribbean). Spanish chroniclers used the Arawak term cacique, implying obvious similarities between Caribbean notables and those met in the Southeast.[8] This title they gave to the Chesapeake noble, Paquinquineo (Hoffman 2002, 42) they picked up in 1560, baptized

"Don Luis," and returned to his homeland in 1570, after he had passed the decade in "various islands" of the Caribbean, including Havana, and in Spain. Whether Opechancanough was "Don Luis," or even related to him (Lewis and Loomie 1953, 60), it is a historical fact that throughout the sixteenth century, i.e., before Jamestown's 1607 settlement, Atlantic-seaboard Algonkians saw hundreds of Europeans and their ships—Spanish explorers and galleons, privateers and buccaneers—and very possibly Mesoamerican kings fled from Spanish conquests, if Hamor and Beverley are correct. The cosmopolitan "Don Luis," once introduced into the Spanish royal court, returned to live with his people a generation before Jamestown. Theirs was a position in the sixteenth-century world-system rather than "a position in cultural evolution."

The principle of actualism comes most strongly into play when archaeological data are triangulated between sophisticated and well-supported studies of highly documented historical eras, e.g., Susan Reynolds's work on medieval political concepts (1994, 1997), and politically sensitive ethnographies of First Nations, such as the work of John H. Moore. (It really helps to have some fairly extended ethnographic experience oneself, to have hung out with Indian people.) Actualistic research brings in a range of sobering analogies, from Thorstein Veblen's point that the upper upper class distinguishes itself from nouveau riche by "resort to subtler contrivances," as he put it (Kehoe 1999), to examples of peripatetic capitals (Kehoe 2002)—a range of cases calling for alternative working hypotheses toward inference to the best explanation (Kelley and Hanen 1988, 276–77). Specifically relating to Mississippian polities, we may consider John Moore's description of the Cheyenne Council of Forty-Four, the nation's august governing body. Men recruited to this society "are supposed to be humble, modest, and constantly in service to the people . . . generous to the point of giving away all their possessions" (Moore 1996a, 162). Archaeologists will be happy to know that when John Black Owl, the embodiment of chiefly behavior during Moore's fieldwork, died, his funeral was the largest Moore had seen, and although his home had been small and poor, the pile of blankets and shawls mourners deposited beside the casket was so high it looked like a Northwest Coast potlatch (Moore 1996a, 162–63). Exactly how the Council of Forty-Four was constituted is a matter of some controversy, in part because of political upheavals during two centuries of United States colonization pressures, but basically it seems to be the congress of representatives from the named bands of the Cheyenne nation. The Cheyenne Council seems to resemble the Five Nations Iroquois Council, and perhaps that analogy can be extended at least to the villages and groups of villages peripheral to the Mississippian kingdoms (e.g., Blitz 1993, on central Tombigbee sites).

The Osage seem to have had a supreme council similar to that of the Cheyenne. Their No$^{n'}$-ho^n-zhi^n-ga representing the twenty-four clans of the Osage nation constituted their House of Mystery. Like the Cheyenne chiefs, the No$^{n'}$-ho^n-zhi^n-ga comported themselves modestly and could appear materially impoverished. When La Flesche was working with them, the Osage had just revolutionized their culture (Callahan 1990) to accommodate defeat in war, contrasting with the necessarily overweening dominance of warfare during the previous two or more centuries. There are powerful echoes of Cahokia in La Flesche's texts.[9] The arguments of Patricia O'Brien and Guy Gibbon, and Robert Hall although he hesitates on the word, and my own observations, persuade me that Cahokia was a state, perhaps the only polity in Anglo America fully deserving that appellation (Kehoe 1998, 163). It collapsed after a couple of centuries, from which ensued the balkanization met in the Southeast by sixteenth-century Europeans. The question is, given the power of Osage texts to illuminate Cahokia, could Cahokia have been governed through a House of Mystery constituted by the congress of representatives of its clans? The United States is governed by a Congress of representatives, with a titular head living in a Great House walled off from commoners, and a Great Plaza stretching from that Great House to the House of Congress.

There is one important difference between the icons of governing power in Washington DC and Cahokia: the United States revolutionized the charter of power by secularizing it. Benjamin Franklin expunged the word "sacred" from the Declaration of Independence. Monarchs, anointed with holy oil, ruled by divine mandate; comparably, the Seven Chiefs of the Omaha Nation governed by supernaturally granted authority, embodied in their Venerable Man pole (Fletcher and La Flesche 1911, 243). Gordon

Childe distinguished between "chief" and "king" in that chiefs, "though invested with authority," would be "expected to share with his fellows in most of the fatigues and dangers of economic life and war," whereas "A king on the contrary should . . . be raised above society, exempt from all manual tasks, and entitled to command. . . . royal burials should be marked by singular rites and exceptional constructions" (Childe 1958, 13). Coosa and Cofitachequi, and those other tribute-demanding centers whose rulers were carried on litters, by these criteria merit the designation "kingdom." Mound 72 at Cahokia, and the Great Mortuary at Spiro, contain litters. This one artifact, historically documented and associated with only a few burials, "singular rites and exceptional construction," may be postulated as a key to recognizing kingdoms in the Southeast: polities headed by an office imbued with charisma.

Looking across the spectrum with the many regional sets of sites lacking evidence of litters or singular tombs, an ethnohistoric perspective notes the persistence of the Woodland dispersed farmstead/hamlet settlement pattern (Herring 1990) and the prevalence of alliances. To take one instance, John Moore's analysis of Mvskoke through ethnohistoric and ethnographic data distinguishes *etvlwa* "town" marked by ceremonial ground and sacred fire, and *talofa*, "village" or settlement unmarked by ground, fire, or the political and ritual status communicated by these icons (Moore 1996b, 4–5). A *talofa* normally recognizes an *etvlwa* mother ground for ritual activities and political action. Shifts in trading advantage and resource profitability, similar to what happens to county seats when the interstate bypasses them and then Walmart invades, as well as conquests and defeats in war, would have affected the standing of towns and settlements (Moore 1996b, 7). Rather than grand theory,[10] the oscillating fortunes of Southeastern kingdoms, mother towns, and alliances deserve actualistic interpretation.

Indian people in the Southeast, like many contemporaries in the world (Leach 1954, Turner 1969), seem to have cherished a republican ethos struggling with the notion of divinely empowered sovereigns. Kings rule in consultation with ministers and council; in Philip and Alexander's Macedonia,

> although as chief priest, chief judge, commander in chief, and political leader, the king embodied the state, he was constrained in practice to

function in consultation with his *hetairoi* . . . [in] *synedrion* or council. . . . it was the privilege and duty of the nobles to attend the king as his *hetairoi* (companions) both in war and peace, as cavalry fighters and officers, or as councillors and boon companions. (Billows 1990, 19)

Susan Reynolds (1997, 254, 262), like Gordon Childe before her, emphasizes the king incarnating the regnal community (the "king's two bodies," corpus mysticum [Kantorowicz 1957]), drawing its subjects' allegiance in spite of considerable political power in the hands of landed nobles, free towns, and even peasant communes. Thus there is no simple dichotomy between kingdoms and republics. Shakespeare's historical dramas vividly portray how murderously contested the divine mandate can be. Whether in the Southeast we are looking at the residue of Wars of the Roses between contending noble houses (Lévi-Strauss 1982), or wars between kingdoms, or between alliances of sovereign districts, as scientists we should not slap upon those polities a term that is, as Sturtevant pronounced, an "artifact of postmedieval European preconceptions."

Delgamuukw

To close, I want to say—no, shout! "This really matters!" The bald propaganda of our Founding Fathers and Chief Justice Marshall's remarkably inventive legalisms got reinforced by the doctrine of Manifest Destiny (Kehoe 1998, 65) and the construction of anthropology as the discipline legitimating the White Man's Burden (Kehoe 1998, 90, quoting Major Powell[11]). The general public and even the learned professions still do not realize how Eurocentric American society has been and remains, how much was at stake when spinmeister John Locke's treatises overrode the international principle of first discovery that should give title to First Nations. The wake-up call clanged in British Columbia in 1991 when Chief Justice Allan McEachern of the British Columbia Supreme Court ruled, in *Delgamuukw v. Regina*,

It is common, when one thinks of Indian land claims, to think of Indians living off the land in pristine wilderness. . . . Similarly, it would not be accurate to assume that even pre-contact existence in the territory was in the least bit idyllic . . . there is no doubt, to quote Hobbs [*sic*], that aboriginal life in the territory was, at best, "nasty, brutish and short". . . .

It is asked whether a nation may lawfully take possession of some part of a vast country in which there are none but erratic nations, whose scanty population is incapable of occupying the whole? . . . Their unsettled habitation . . . cannot be accounted a true and legal possession, and the people of Europe . . . finding land of which the Savage stood in no particular need, and of which they made no actual and constant use, were lawfully entitled to take possession. . . . Some tribes are so low in the scale of social organization that their usages and conceptions of rights and duties are not to be reconciled with the institutions or the legal ideas of civilized society. . . . I do not accept the ancestors "on the ground" behaved as they did because of "institutions." Rather I find they more likely acted as they did because of survival instincts. . . . the Indians of the territory were, by historical standards, a primitive people without any form of writing, horses, or wheeled wagons. . . . Aboriginal life, in my view, was far from stable. . . . It is my conclusion that Gitksan and Wet'suwet'en laws and customs are not sufficiently certain to permit a finding they or their ancestors governed the territory. (quoted in Culhane 1998, 236, 239, 246–49)

The plaintiffs appealed McEachern's decision to the British Columbia Court of Appeal, which in 1993 ruled that McEachern had erred in finding extinguishment of aboriginal title. Then in December, 1997, the Supreme Court of Canada ruled that McEachern erred in refusing to give weight to the plaintiffs' formal oral histories, Gitksan *adaawk* and Wet'suwet'en sung *kungax*, and ordered a new trial.

Chief Justice McEachern, in his *Reasons for Judgment* in Delgamuukw, did not, so far as I know, cite Johnson and Earle's chapter on Northwest Coast in their 1987 *Evolution of Human Societies*, pigeonholing Northwest Coast societies as "Big Man Collectivities" (Kehoe 1998, 185–87). Their text, ignoring a generation of ethnohistorical research and still uncorrected in the recent second edition, purveys the same nineteenth-century imperialist unilinear evolutionism familiar to McEachern. Real people, thousands of Tsimshian and Wet'suwet'en, were really injured by McEachern ruling they are people without history. Sturtevant had spoken out back in 1979 on our responsibility in First Nations' claims at law (Sturtevant

1983). Strong-arming data into a priori logic, oblivious of the real-world import of supposedly scientific interpretations, can be morally negligent.

But this is an academic journal. Let us push aside dispossessed Gitksan and Wet'suwet'en wailing. Our debate concerns the legitimacy of modeling Southeastern archaeological data upon an "artifact of postmedieval European preconceptions." Archaeology should be a historical science, and if it is to be scientific, it must align data along the principle of actualism. Simpson explained,

> We ... observe present configurations and from them infer configurations that preceded them. . . . In the total study of . . . any history, there are three phases:
>
> (1) obtaining and studying the historical data, . . .
> (2) determination of present processes, . . . and
> (3) confrontation of (1) and (2) with a view to ordering, filling in, and explaining the history. (Simpson 1970, 81, 84–85)

We have historical data from sixteenth, seventeenth, and eighteenth century observers. We can observe present processes, contemporary and as recorded in ethnographies, in surviving Indian nations, transported though many of them have been. Subordinating these actual data to a European doctrine is not scientific. And it can be pernicious.

Acknowledgments

I thank Lynne Sullivan, program chair for the 2001 Southeastern Archaeological Conference, for inviting me to make "chiefdoms" the subject of the conference's evening lecture, November 16, 2001; this paper is a revision of that lecture. David Anderson, Bettina Arnold, Alex Barker, Robert Carneiro, Carole Crumley, Warren DeBoer, Guy Gibbon, Robert Jeske, Patricia O'Brien, Tim Pauketat, Kent Reilly, and Andrea Stone have been especially collegial in discussing the topic. My correspondence with Bob Carneiro, begun in the summer of 2001 as I worked on the lecture, delved deep into our formative influences, spurred by the mortal impact of the Two Towers collapse, 9/11/01, not far from Bob's apartment; suffice it here to say that Bob recalled being unconcerned, when a student, about Leslie White's politics, supposedly of no import to his scientific theory.

1. In this book, Earle describes how men came to power: "He steals away from the dinner table, rudely shuts out the family, and thinks about style when others need love" (Earle 1997, viii). This was indeed the pattern in the twentieth century for archaeologists. Those of us who were mothers, cooks, washer-uppers . . . "homemakers" were presumed to not be archaeologists.

2. "The concept of heterarchy (Crumley 1987; Ehrenreich, Crumley, and Levy 1995) that for many intermediate-level societies, power is diffuse, not because leaders do not try to centralize the political institutions, but because the different sources of power are difficult to monopolize and bring together" (Earle 1997, 210). Crumley is quite clear that heterarchy is a normal and common principle of *distributed power* (Crumley 1987, 156–57), structurally and conceptually dialectically opposed to hierarchy. See also Marquardt 2019.

3. Jefferson is described by historian Peter S. Onuf (1997, 141) as "uncompromising, self-righteous, and dangerously doctrinaire."

4. German archaeologists, in contrast, assumed their Iron Age had a feudal structure they projected from the medieval period. Copying Schliemann, his Princes' Graves in Mycenae, they labeled Iron Age "Princes" in "Furstengraben" and "Furstensitzen" (Bettina Arnold, personal communication 7/11/01).

5. Does writing revolutionize a society? Neither Gordon Childe (1950) nor Alfred Kroeber (1962, 58) privileged writing above other criteria of the urban revolution. Tawantinsuyo, the state ruled by the Inca, is said to have a history at least from 1438 (Bruhns 1994, 331) although apparently it had no writing.

6. Leslie White's (1959, 40) simple universal prime mover, harnessing energy, would seem to be a factor accessible to archaeological measurement. One would suppose White's disciples would have worked to operationalize the principle, use it to categorize archaeological cultures, and develop quantified transition points. Why did White not demand or inspire this from his students? Sahlins and Service (1960, 21) said, "We . . . do not know how to specify the operations required to ascertain this measure."

7. The genealogy of the term "chiefdom" is thoroughly covered for American usage in, e.g., Alex Barker's dissertation (Barker 1999), in Chapter 10 of my *Critical History* (Kehoe 1998, 172–87), and more broadly by Joan Vincent (1990, 325–35).

8. By the nineteenth century, Spaniards were using the term ironically for local political bosses in Spain (Page 1991, 63–64).

9. See the strong congruence between his section on "The Weaver" in the Shrine of the Waxo'be (La Flesche 1930, 682–99), and the Keller figurine from the BBB Motor site. I discuss the congruences at length in Kehoe 2007.

10. Long before David Anderson (Anderson 1994, 9), Kroeber (1939, 225) was fascinated by the question of cycling, crediting Flinders Petrie, in a 1911 publication

called *The Revolutions of Civilizations,* with an early detailed effort to "derive . . . a recurrent pattern" from examining "a number of civilizations." Continuing the quest, Kroeber hoped

> If it ever proves possible to find some objective measure of culture intensity . . . the relative strength of the two factors of cultural evolution and devolution would be computable, and the history of nonhistoric peoples and cultures could be better projected than now. (Kroeber 1939, 225)

Kroeber came to realize, in *Configurations of Culture Growth,* that historical factors dominated the cases he examined.

11. "When civilized man first came to America the continent was partially occupied by savage tribes, who obtained subsistence by hunting, by fishing, by gathering vegetal products, and by rude garden culture in cultivating small patches of ground. Semi-nomadic occupancy for such purposes was their tenure to the soil.

"On the organization of the present government [United States] such theories of natural law were entertained that even this imperfect occupancy was held to be sufficient title. . . . The attempts to educate the Indians and teach them the ways of civilization have . . . disappointed their enthusiastic promoters. . . . The great boon to the savage tribes . . . has been the presence of civilization, which, under the laws of acculturation, has irresistibly improved their culture by substituting new and civilized for old and savage. . . . The industries and social institutions of the pristine Indians have largely been destroyed, and they are groping their way to civilized life." (Powell 1881, xxvii, xxviii, xxx)

REFERENCES

Adams, William Y. 1998. *The Philosophical Roots of Anthropology.* Stanford: Stanford University Center for the Study of Language and Information.

Anderson, David G. 1994. *The Savannah River Chiefdoms: Political Change in the Late Prehistoric Southeast.* Tuscaloosa: University of Alabama Press.

Aristotle. 1946. *The Politics.* Translated by Ernest Baker. London: Oxford University Press.

Arnold, Bettina, and D. Blair Gibson. 1995. "Introduction: Beyond the Mists: Forging an Ethnological Approach to Celtic Studies." In *Celtic Chiefdom, Celtic State,* edited by Bettina Arnold and D. Blair Gibson, 1–10. Cambridge: Cambridge University Press.

Barker, Alexander Wade. 1992. "Powhatan's Pursestrings: On the Meaning of Surplus in a Seventeenth Century Algonkian Chiefdom." *In Lords of the Southeast: Social Inequality and the Native Elites of Southeastern North America,* edited by Alex W. Barker and Timothy R. Pauketat, 61–80. Washington DC: Archeological Papers of the American Anthropological Association Number 3.

———. 1999. *Chiefdoms and the Economics of Perversity*. PhD dissertation, University of Michigan.

Barker, Alex W., and Timothy R. Pauketat, eds. 1992. *Lords of the Southeast: Social Inequality and the Native Elites of Southeastern North America*. Washington DC: Archeological Papers of the American Anthropological Association Number 3.

Barnes, Barry, David Bloor, and John Henry. 1996. *Scientific Knowledge*. Chicago: University of Chicago Press.

Billows, Richard A. 1990. *Antigonos the One-Eyed and the Creation of the Hellenistic State*. Berkeley: University of California Press.

Blitz, John H. 1993. *Ancient Chiefdoms of the Tombigbee*. Tuscaloosa: University of Alabama Press.

Bruhns, Karen Olsen. 1994. *Ancient South America*. Cambridge: Cambridge University Press.

Callahan, Alice Anne. 1990. *The Osage Ceremonial Dance I'n-Lon-Schka*. Norman: University of Oklahoma Press.

Carneiro, Robert L. 1998. "What Happened at the Flashpoint?" In *Chiefdoms and Chieftaincy in the Americas*, edited by Elsa M. Redmond, 18–42. Gainesville: University Press of Florida.

Carucci, James. 1986. "Prehistoric Complex Societies in Micronesia: Where Have All the Chiefdoms Gone?" Paper presented to 51st annual meeting of the Society for American Archaeology, New Orleans, April 24, 1986.

Childe, V. Gordon. 1950. "The Urban Revolution." *Town Planning Review* 21(1): 3–17.

———. 1958. *The Prehistory of European Society*. Harmondsworth: Penguin.

Crumley, Carole L. 1987. "A Dialectical Critique of Hierarchy." In *Power Relations and State Formation*, edited by Thomas C. Patterson and Christine W. Gailey, 155–69. Washington DC: Archeology Section/American Anthropological Association.

———. 1995. "Heterarchy and the Analysis of Complex Societies." In *Heterarchy and the Analysis of Complex Societies*, edited by Robert M. Ehrenreich, Carole L. Crumley, and Janet E. Levy, 1–5. Washington DC: Archeological Papers of the American Anthropological Association Number 6.

Culhane, Dara. 1998. *The Pleasure of the Crown: Anthropology, Law, and First Nations*. Burnaby BC: Talonbooks.

Daly, Douglas C., and John D. Mitchell. 2000. "Lowland Vegetation of Tropical South America." In *Imperfect Balance*, edited by David L. Lentz, 391–453. New York: Columbia University Press.

Earle, Timothy. 1991. "The Evolution of Chiefdoms." In *Chiefdoms: Power, Economy, and Ideology*, edited by Timothy Earle, 1–15. Cambridge: Cambridge University Press.

———. 1997. *How Chiefs Come to Power: The Political Economy in Prehistory*. Stanford: Stanford University Press.

Fardon, Richard. 1990. "General Introduction." In *Localizing Strategies: Regional Traditions of Ethnographic Writing*, edited by Richard Fardon, 1–35. Washington DC: Smithsonian Institution Press.

Feldman, Lawrence H. 2000. *Lost Shores, Forgotten Peoples: Spanish Explorations of the South East Maya Lowlands*. Durham NC: Duke University Press.

Feuchtwang, Stephan. 1973. "The Colonial Formation of British Social Anthropology." In *Anthropology and the Colonial Encounter*, edited by Talal Asad, 71–100. London: Ithaca.

Fletcher, Alice C., and Francis La Flesche. 1911. "The Omaha Tribe." In *27th Annual Report, Bureau of American Ethnology, Smithsonian Institution*, 17–660. Washington DC: Government Printing Office. Lincoln: University of Nebraska Press facsimile edition, 1972.

Friedrichs, Christopher R. 2000. *Urban Politics in Early Modern Europe*. London: Routledge.

Green, Roger C. 1998. "Rapahui Origins Prior to European Contact: The View from Eastern Polynesia." In *Easter Island and East Polynesian Prehistory*, edited by Patricia Vargas Casanova, 87–110. Santiago: Universidad de Chile, Instituto de Estudios Isla de Pascua.

Herring, Joseph B. 1990. *The Enduring Indians of Kansas*. Lawrence: University Press of Kansas.

Hoffman, Paul E. 2002. *Florida's Frontiers*. Bloomington: Indiana University Press.

Hudson, Charles M., Jr. 1997. *Knights of Spain, Warriors of the Sun*. Athens: University of Georgia Press.

Johnson, Allen W., and Timothy Earle. [1987] 2000. *The Evolution of Human Society: From Foraging Group to Agrarian State*. Stanford: Stanford University Press.

Kantorowicz, Ernst H. 1957. *The King's Two Bodies*. Princeton: Princeton University Press.

Kehoe, Alice Beck. 1971. "Small Boats Upon the North Atlantic." In *Man Across the Sea*, edited by Carroll L. Riley, J. Charles Kelley, Campbell W. Pennington, and Robert L. Rands, 275–92. Austin: University of Texas Press.

———. 1981. "Revisionist Anthropology: Aboriginal North America." *Current Anthropology* 22 (5): 503–17.

———. 1993. "How the Ancient Peigans Lived." In *Research in Economic Anthropology* 14, edited by Barry Isaac, 87–105. Greenwich CT: JAI Press.

———. 1998. *The Land of Prehistory: A Critical History of American Archaeology*. New York: Routledge.

———. 1999. "A Resort to Subtler Contrivances." In *Manifesting Power*, edited by Tracy Sweely, 17–29. London: Routledge.

———. 2002. "Theaters of Power." In *The Dynamics of Power*, edited by Maria O'Donovan, 259–72. Carbondale: Southern Illinois University Press.

————. 2007. "Osage Texts and Cahokia Data." In *Ancient Objects and Sacred Realms*, edited by F. Kent Reilly III and James Garber, 246–61. Austin: University of Texas Press.

Kehoe, Alice Beck and Mary Beth Emmerichs, eds. 1999. *Assembling the Past*. Albuquerque: University of New Mexico Press.

Kehoe, Alice B., and Thomas F. Kehoe. 1979. "Solstice-Aligned Boulder Configurations in Saskatchewan." Ottawa: Canadian Ethnology Service Paper No. 48, Mercury Series, National Museum of Man.

Kehoe, Thomas F. 1960. *Stone Tipi Rings in North-Central Montana and the Adjacent Portion of Alberta, Canada: Their Historical, Ethnological, and Archeological Aspects*. Washington DC: Smithsonian Institution Bureau of American Ethnology, Anthropological Paper No. 62, Bulletin 173, 417–74.

Kelley, Jane H. and Marsha P. Hanen. 1988. *Archaeology and the Methodology of Science*. Albuquerque: University of New Mexico Press.

Kennedy, Roger G. 1994. *Hidden Cities*. New York: Free Press and Penguin.

Kidder, Alfred V. 1936. "Speculations on New World Prehistory." In *Essays in Anthropology Presented to A. L. Kroeber*, edited by Robert H. Lowie, 143–51. Berkeley: University of California Press.

Klein, Kerwin Lee. 1997. *Frontiers of Historical Imagination: Narrating the European Conquest of Native America, 1890–1990*. Berkeley: University of California Press.

Kroeber, Alfred L. 1939. *Cultural and Natural Areas of Native North America*. Berkeley: University of California Press.

————. 1944. *Configurations of Culture Growth*. Berkeley: University of California Press.

————. 1952. *The Nature of Culture*. Chicago: University of Chicago Press.

Lakoff, George, and Mark Johnson. 1999. *Philosophy in the Flesh*. New York: Basic Books.

La Flesche, Francis. 1930. "The Osage Tribe: Rite of the Wa-Xo'-Be." In *Smithsonian Institution, 45th Annual Report, Bureau of American Ethnology*, 528–833. Washington DC: Government Printing Office.

La Vere, David. 1998. *The Caddo Chiefdoms: Caddo Economics and Politics, 700–1835*. Lincoln: University of Nebraska Press.

Leach, Edmund R. 1954. *Political Systems of Highland Burma: A Study of Kachin Social Structure*. London: Bell and Sons.

Leacock, Eleanor, and Richard Lee. 1982. "Introduction." In *Politics and History in Band Societies*, edited by Eleanor Leacock and Richard Lee, 1–20. Cambridge: Cambridge University Press.

Lemay, J. A. Leo. 1991. *The "American Dream" of Captain John Smith*. Charlottesville: University Press of Virginia.

Lévi-Strauss, Claude. 1982. *The Way of the Masks*. Translated by Sylvia Modelski. Seattle: University of Washington Press.

Lewis, Clifford M., S.J., and Albert J. Loomie, S.J. 1953. *The Spanish Jesuit Mission in Virginia, 1570–1572*. Chapel Hill: University of North Carolina Press.

Lovejoy, Arthur O., and George Boas. 1935. *Primitivism and Related Ideas in Antiquity*. Baltimore: Johns Hopkins University Press.

Meek, Ronald L. 1976. *Social Science and the Ignoble Savage*. Cambridge: Cambridge University Press.

Moore, John H. 1994. "Ethnoarchaeology of the Lamar Peoples." In *Perspectives on the Southeast*, edited by Patricia B. Kwachka, 126–41. Athens: University of Georgia Press.

———. 1996a. *The Cheyenne*. Oxford: Blackwell.

———. 1996b. "The Mvskoke Ethnogenetic Engine." Paper presented at annual meeting, American Anthropological Association, Chicago.

Onuf, Peter S. 1997. "Thomas Jefferson, Missouri, and the 'Empire for Liberty.'" In *Thomas Jefferson and the Changing West: From Conquest to Conservation*, edited by James P. Ronda, 111–53. St. Louis: Missouri Historical Society Press.

O'Shea, John M., and Alex W. Barker. 1996. "Measuring Social Complexity and Variation: A Categorical Imperative?" In *Emergent Complexity: The Evolution of Intermediate Societies*, edited by Jeanne Arnold, 13–24. Ann Arbor: International Monographs in Prehistory, Archaeological Series No. 9.

Page, Edward C. 1991. *Localism and Centralism in Europe*. Oxford: Oxford University Press.

Peace, William J. 1993. "Leslie White and Evolutionary Theory." *Dialectical Anthropology* 18:123–51.

Powell, J. W. 1881. "Report of the Director." In *First Annual Report, Bureau of Ethnology, 1879–80*, xi–xxxiii. Washington DC: Government Printing Office.

Redmond, Elsa M., ed. 1998. *Chiefdoms and Chieftaincy in the Americas*. Gainesville: University of Florida Press.

Renfrew, Colin. 1986. "Introduction: Peer Polity Interaction and Socio-political Change." In *Peer Polity Interaction and Socio-political Change*, edited by Colin Renfrew and John F. Cherry, 1–18. Cambridge: Cambridge University Press.

Reynolds, Susan. 1994. *Fiefs and Vassals: The Medieval Evidence Reinterpreted*. New York: Oxford University Press.

———. 1997. *Kingdoms and Communities in Western Europe, 900–1300*. Second edition. Oxford: Oxford University Press.

Sahlins, Marshall D. 1968. *Tribesmen*. Englewood Cliffs NJ: Prentice-Hall.

Service, Elman R. 1960. "The Law of Evolutionary Potential." In *Evolution and Culture*, edited by Marshall Sahlins and Elman R. Service, 93–122. Ann Arbor: University of Michigan Press.

———. 1962. *Primitive Social Organization: An Evolutionary Perspective*. New York: Random House.

———. 1971. "Our Contemporary Ancestors: Extant Stages and Extinct Ages." Reprinted in *Elman R. Service, Cultural Evolutionism*, 151–57. New York: Holt, Rinehart and Winston. First published 1967 in *War: The Anthropology of Armed Conflict and Aggression*, edited by Morton Fried, Marvin Harris, and Robert Murphy, 160–167. Doubleday, New York.

Short, John Rennie. 1999. "A New Mode of Thinking: Creating a National Geography in the Early Republic." In *Surveying the Record: North American Scientific Exploration to 1930*, edited by Edward C. Carter II, 19–50. Philadelphia: Memoirs of the American Philosophical Society, volume 231.

Simpson, George Gaylord. 1970. "Uniformitarianism. An Inquiry into Principle, Theory, and Method in Geohistory and Biohistory." In *Essays in Evolution and Genetics in Honor of Theodosius Dobzhansky*, edited by Max K. Hecht and William C. Steere, 43–96. New York: Appleton-Century-Crofts.

Smith, Marvin T. 2000. *Coosa*. Gainesville: University Press of Florida.

Sturtevant, William C. 1983. "Tribe and State in the Sixteenth and Twentieth Centuries." In *The Development of Political Organization in Native North America*, edited by Elisabeth Tooker, 3–16. Washington DC: American Ethnological Society.

———. 1998. "Tupinambá Chiefdoms?" In *Chiefdoms and Chieftaincy in the Americas*, edited by Elsa M. Redmond, 138–149. Gainesville: University Press of Florida.

Thompson, J. Eric S. 1954. *The Rise and Fall of Maya Civilization*. Norman: University of Oklahoma Press.

Turner, Victor W. 1969. *The Ritual Process: Structure and Anti-Structure*. London: Routledge and Kegan Paul.

van Rouveroy van Nieuwaal, E. Adriaan B., and Rijk van Dijk, eds. 1999. *African Chieftaincy in a New Socio-Political Landscape*. African Studies Centre Leiden. Hamburg: Lit.

Veblen, Thorstein. [1899] 1931. *The Theory of the Leisure Class*. New York: Modern Library.

Vincent, Joan. 1990. *Anthropology and Politics*. Tucson: University of Arizona Press.

Wallace, Anthony F. C. 1997. "'The Obtaining Lands': Thomas Jefferson and the Native Americans." In *Thomas Jefferson and the Changing West: From Conquest to Conservation*, edited by James P. Ronda, 25–41. St. Louis: Missouri Historical Society Press.

———. 1999. *Jefferson and the Indians*. Cambridge: Belknap.

Ware, John A., and Eric Blinman. 2000. "Cultural Collapse and Reorganization: The Origin and Spread of Pueblo Ritual Sodalities." In *The Archaeology of Regional Interaction: Religion, Warfare, and Exchange Across the American Southwest and Beyond*, edited by Michelle Hegmon, 381–409. Niwot: University Press of Colorado.

White, Geoffrey M., and Lamont Lindstrom, eds. 1997. *Chiefs Today: Traditional Pacific Leadership and the Postcolonial State*. Stanford: Stanford University Press.

White, Leslie A. 1959. *The Evolution of Culture*. New York: McGraw-Hill.

———. 1960. "Foreword." In *Evolution and Culture*, edited by Marshall Sahlins and Elman R. Service, v-xii. Ann Arbor: University of Michigan Press.

Williams, Robert A., Jr. 1990. *The American Indian in Western Legal Thought*. New York: Oxford University Press.

Wilson, Daniel. 1873. *Caliban: The Missing Link*. London: Macmillan.

———. [1862] 1876. *Prehistoric Man*. London: Macmillan.

Wylie, Alison. 1995. "Alternative Histories: Epistemic Disunity and Political Integrity." In *Making Alternative Histories: The Practice of Archaeology and History in Non-Western Settings*, edited by Peter R. Schmidt and Thomas C. Patterson, 255–72. Santa Fe: School of American Research Press.

8. Cahokia from a Postcolonial Standpoint

Let us turn now to one of my most rejected and ignored research interpretations: that Cahokia was a state trading with Cholula in Mexico. In developing this statement, I follow the method of historical sciences. In opposing my interpretation, nearly all North American archaeologists naively accept Manifest Destiny ideology that no North American First Nations—or in Morgan's case, *no* American natives—progressed to the culminating stage of evolution, the state of Civilization. A second factor is the "border wall" between Anglos and Latins, the invisible college of English-language scholars who do not fraternize with those south of the Rio Grande.

Cahokia in Illinois and its age-mate Chaco in New Mexico, both c. 1040–1200 CE, are anomalies. Peirce's method of abduction begins with surprising facts, that is, anomalies. First anomaly: both sites are extraordinarily large and have the most impressive architecture in Anglo America. Second anomaly: their beginnings and their terminations coincide closely. *What else in America stands out in this time period?* South of temperate America, according to the history recorded from the Aztecs by Spanish friars, in this time period a Toltec empire flourished. Aztec historians said the Toltec empire's capital was Tula in Hidalgo. In Mexico in this period, the largest city is Cholula in Puebla, not Tula. Why did the Aztecs not talk about Cholula? What do we know about Cholula? We know that Cortés was urged by his Tlaxcalan allies to use his soldiers and allies to massacre Cholulans, which he did, slaughtering over a thousand, men, women, children, gathered—they thought—to meet and hear his plans. Thus the largest competitor to the Mexica (Aztecs) and their allies was cut down and cut out of the as-told-to-Spaniards history of Mexico.

Now we can build a working hypothesis derived from empirical data. What was Cholula like in the Early Postclassic, c. 950–1200? There are two lienzos (annotated cloth maps prepared for land claims by native nobility under Spanish rule) titled *Historias de los Toltecas-Chichimecas*. They describe a foreign empire, the Olmeca-Xicallancas,[1] ruling in Cholula during the dates in question. This nation had invaded from the east; its homeland was in present Veracruz along the Gulf of Mexico. During its rule, it made Cholula even more magnificent than it had been, its conical pyramid the largest pyramid in the entire world, its markets the greatest in Mesoamerica. Its brilliant featherwork—garments, headdresses, banners—were the finest in the world, and abundant in the market. The *Historias* picture two Tolteca priests who had been allowed to continue serving under the conquerors, deciding to travel to the holy Seven Caves in the far northwest to beg for allies in a reconquest of Cholula. At the Seven Caves, the hovering goddess pities them and tells the Chichimec warriors, with their formidable longbows, to go with the priests. Finally arriving back in Cholula, the Toltecs attack the city, their bowmen's arrows killing the city's defenders before they can engage with their atlatl darts and hand-held swords. The Olmeca-Xicallancas were deposed, and a period of political unrest ensued, until finally the Mexica established Tenochtitlan and fought to dominate Mexico.

At this point, our hypothesis is that the Olmeca-Xicallanca, as part of their strategy to dominate Mesoamerica, encouraged or maybe sponsored merchants to explore far beyond the usual neighboring countries. This postulate draws upon the historic Mexica economy where the state-honored *pochteca*, merchants who carried knowledge of economies and politics as well as goods. We can reasonably postulate that merchants linked Cholula on Mexico's Central Plateau with the Gulf Coast, homeland of Cholula's ruling invaders. From its ports, they could travel to Mobile Bay (Alabama) or up the Mississippi delta. Totonac words for "town, plaza" and "maize" in Lower Mississippi languages demonstrate contact with Mexican Gulf Coast traders (Kaufman 2019, 35, 152–53, 168, 203; Kaufman 2023); Totonac is one of the languages of Mexico's coastal Northeast, though we don't know whether it was the language of the Olmeca-Xicallanca.

River-based transportation routes had been established in temperate North America at least by the era of Poverty Point (on a bayou in northern Louisiana) in the second millennium BCE. We deduce this by the number and variety of artifacts in Poverty Point made in materials from distant sources best traveled by boat. Clarence Webb (1968) and James A. Ford, the primary excavators of Poverty Point, interpreted the impressive site as Mesoamerican relationships enriching a well-established "late Archaic" polity (Webb 1968, 318). More recent archaeologists working at the site no longer recognized possibly significant Mesoamerican contacts; this may reflect the premise of autochthonous development that has dominated Anglo American archaeology since the 1970s.

Fundamentally, it is crucial to realize that the political boundary between the United States and Mexico wasn't established until 1848. Southeastern United States forms the north shores of the Gulf of Mexico, and well-known land routes tied eastern Texas to northwest Mexico (Kelley 1955; Barr 2011; Barr 2017; Carpenter 2020). It is likewise crucial to realize that Eurasia as a single land mass developed its societies within its own ecumene, while temperate North America's histories developed with few contacts to Eurasia. Models of states derived from Eurasian histories should not be assumed to fit North American societies. Juliana Barr's meticulous research, cited above, makes this clear. My 2021 paper on Cahokia was rejected by both *American Antiquity* and *American Anthropologist* editors without sending me any peer reviews.[2] Absent any engagement with my data and argument, I can only surmise that these rejections were prompted by the paper's opposition to Anglo America's dominant paradigm derived from Morgan's racist categorization.

A year after these rejections, Timothy Pauketat sent me the PDF of his latest book, then titled "The Maya and the Mississippi: On the Road to Medieval America" and formatted as if already published. His acknowledgments tell how his research was generously funded, and thanks the many universities around the world whose staffs hosted him and the Santa Fe Institute that supported seminars he led. "With the support of SFI Founder and Nobel laureate Murray Gell-Mann, George [Gumerman] made these discussions happen, with the generous underwriting of the SFI and Jerry Murdock. The insightful indigenous archaeologist and gentleman Robert L. Hall was at a couple of these meetings, and his studies are often referenced in this book. The resulting big historical narrative that I espouse was also preceded and inspired by work of anthropologist Alice Kehoe, who has long directed me to look deeper into the pan-American past" (Pauketat n.d., 11–12). The published book, by Oxford University Press in 2023, is titled *Gods of Thunder*. On page xii is this same paragraph, but the final sentence, acknowledging me, is not there: I was excised.

Gods of Thunder is, as advertised, bold. It does indeed challenge mainstream American archaeology's denial, since the 1970s, of Mesoamerican contacts with eastern North America. It does cite my argument for Ramey knives being Mexican sacrificial knives (Pauketat calls them "daggers"), and an endnote suggests contrasting my view with a paper by James A. Brown. What Pauketat does not acknowledge is our common humanity with American First Nations. As in his more recent published papers (cited in my paper in this chapter, "Postcolonial Cahokia"), he espouses the romantic idea that spirituality dominated, and dominates, "indigenous Americans"; trade was secondary. Seizing the cusp of the moment, *Gods of Thunder* proposes that climate change (the Medieval Warm Period) devastated Mayan lands, stimulating a revivalist movement carrying bundled objects of power far into all the less-affected lands to the north. In the book's epigraph, Pauketat quotes *Black Elk Speaks*, the 1932 as-told-to book by John Neihardt, that "everything an Indian does is in a circle" (Pauketat 2023); circles are the leitmotif of the supposed religious movement and everything circular proves his thesis.[3] Not even an endnote cites DeMallie's 1985 critical study of Neihardt's romanticized version of Nick Black Elk's talks with the popular "poet laureate of Nebraska."

Timothy Pauketat is mired in the marshy wetlands he sees as prime movers of human histories. Perhaps it is better than staying within the fortress of Manifest Destiny, seeing "chiefdoms." Whichever, I cannot accept *Gods of Thunder* as a likely exposition of what happened in medieval Nuclear America (see my paper here for that term). My dissertation was on the Ghost Dance religious movement led by the Paiute prophet Wovoka from 1889 until his death in 1932. Its published version was *The Ghost Dance: Ethnohistory and Revitalization* (Kehoe 1989). I also, much later, researched Christianity (Kehoe 2012); its original spread was mostly matters of wars and politics. Wovoka's movement was a struggle for resilience, more than revitalization. Neither Wovoka's movement nor the spread of Christianity seem particularly apropos for the multiplicities of adaptions to medieval climate change. Fundamentally, that enabled maize to be grown on an agricultural scale in the temperate zone, supporting larger populations and concomitantly, more trade. The surprising fact of a Tollan in the middle of temperate America cannot be attributed to the romantic notion that American Indians do everything in circles. The fact is, Central Cahokia, the Tollan, is a set of rectangular grids.

Cahokia from a Postcolonial Standpoint

Land Acknowledgement: I write this as a resident at the traditional trading port of Milwaukee, held by Menominee and welcoming Potawatomi, Anishinaabeg, Dakota, and foreigners.

In 1095, at Clermont in France, Pope Urban II called Christian knights and soldiers to crusade against Muslim armies threatening Constantinople. The Cross—that instrument of torture Rome used to publicly assert its domination—was Urban's symbol, worn as badge by every man recruited to the Roman Church's army. Nearly four centuries later, when Columbus reported unrecognized lands populated by non-Christians, Pope Alexander VI had an established policy: heathens should be subordinated to Christian monarchs. On May 4, 1493, he issued *Inter Caetera*, authorizing Christian kings to Christianize the peoples of the lands reported by Columbus "wherein dwell very many peoples living in peace, and, as reported, going unclothed, and not eating flesh." This was the Doctrine of Discovery, discussed and debated thereafter as Europeans constructed their purported international laws and continued "just wars" to take over "tribes," as had Rome's earlier emperors.

"Going unclothed" was already a stigma signaling an Edenic paradise lost to Christians by its inhabitants' sin. It became a trope for America's First Nations, *sauvages* roaming a wilderness in defiance of God's imposition of labor upon humankind. John Locke, spinmeister to the Earl of Shaftesbury and his colonizing ventures, pronounced written title to land necessary for legitimate occupations (Locke [1689] 2003; Kehoe 2010). Eighteenth-century philosophes accepted the medieval Great Chain of Being linking, in order, monkeys, apes, primitive humans, and culminating in civilized literate European men (Lovejoy 1936). Accepting also the concept of relict primitive peoples, possibly nobly pure but more likely dull-witted or even depraved, conjectural histories of humankind were published by several Scots natural philosophers in the late eighteenth century, and in the later nineteenth century by English anthropologists. The Scots lived in centers of Industrial Revolution radical social change, the English at the peak of British imperial expansion (Flandreau 2016).

In America, industrialization and colonial expansion moved in tandem, linked by railroads—"the railway train in motion, which may be called the triumph of civilization," wrote Lewis Henry Morgan (1877, 553).

Morgan, John Lubbock, and Edward Tylor—the first two active capitalist investors, the third supported by a family-owned factory—accepted the Darwinian premise that humans, like other organisms, had evolved. Educated white men, the apex of the Great Chain of Being, now were explained by an evolution that left behind, yet still living, more primitive races, as ferns, fishes, and reptiles remain viable although evolved millions of years before mammals. As fishes cannot walk upon land, primitive human races lack capacity for more recently evolved thinking and actions. Apex men's high status is reflected in their layers of garments. Unclothed bodies were primitive, partially clothed barbaric, and a fully covered body a sign of a maximally evolved mind.

Progress from primitive simple organisms through stages to more complex creatures, implicitly the Great Chain of Being, was a given for most nineteenth-century European and Euro-American thinkers. Herbert Spencer, the most popular evolutionist, presumed a Vital Force driving this Progress that especially flourished in the northern hemisphere's temperate zones. What had been "natural philosophy" became "science" without dropping the presuppositions imprinted in Christian ideologies (Jin 2016). Colonization in the service of empires was the natural order.

Morgan's work served two purposes for Americans. He firmly asserted that no American First Nation ever achieved anything more impressive than the conquered Iroquoian villages he knew; "the Spanish writers . . . fabricate[d] the Aztec monarchy" (Morgan 1877, 213). All Native America lay within the inferior statuses of Savage and Barbarian. Morgan's second service to his America was to propound the critical value of private property, sine qua non of civilization, although "a mere property career is not the final destiny of mankind" (1877, 551–52). Archaeologists working in the Americas should not expect to see any evidence for political and economic structures comparable to Europe's nation-states (Lekson 2018, 3–10).

Classification was a mania for Enlightenment scientist; the terra nullius that officially was America required them. Kroeber sent out his University of California graduate students with a long list of classes of data to collect facts and artifacts. One was Julian Steward, who aimed to use his data from

Shoshone and Gosiute in the Great Basin to exemplify the lowest stage of human society, the patriarchal band. His field experience revealed an even more primitive political economy, the family group (Steward 1938, 230). John Wesley Powell and a co-worker had published extensive field observations of the same region nearly a century before, only a few years after Mormon settlement had appropriated the Numas' fertile valleys. "Formerly, they were organized into nations, or confederacies, under the influence of great chiefs," Powell had stated. Steward rejected that (1938, 252), theory erasing corollaries of field data (Kehoe 1999; see also Kerns 2003).

The tenet that the world can be explained through a singular disciplinary approach, "science," persisted in the West. It underlay the U.S. National Science Foundation, "a vigorous defender of the unity-of-science position and an outspoken advocate of value neutrality as the only legitimate investigative stance in scientific inquiry," while privately its first director, "[Harry] Alpert worried out loud that this stance tended to give scholarship a conservative direction" (Solovey 2020, 73). Although unity-of-science has been rejected specifically for archaeology by Alison Wylie (2002), for its untenable philosophical position and for disjunction with actual archaeological practices, NSF funding kept this fundamentally colonialist construct strong in American archaeology.

Elman Service, described as "the most influential cultural evolutionist of the past half-century [1950–1999]" (Harding 1999, 163), perpetuated nineteenth-century racist evolutionism.

[Service's] chiefdom concept, in particular, proved very fertile in the hands of archaeologists. Service's model, focusing on the integration of multiple local groups, hereditary leadership, social hierarchy, cycles of expansion and decline, sumptuary rules, and redistributive economy, suggested an extensive research agenda. (Harding 1999, 162)

That model is band-tribe-chiefdom-[state]. North American First Nations' diversity stretched the two categories of savagery and barbarism, so Service extended Morgan's scheme's "barbarism." Adding "chiefdom" accommodated early contact descriptions of kingdoms while maintaining the dictum that no North American nations progressed farther than barbarism.

Words matter. Jamestown colonizers knew the words "king" and "chief." From an England still remembering its division into seven kingdoms, they saw the Powhatan to be a king. Gordon Childe distinguished chiefs from kings (Childe 1958, 13), and sixteenth-century entradas into the Southeast clearly describe kings and queens, by Childe's criteria (e.g., Power 2004, 114–16). "Tribe," however, suits the Doctrine of Discovery paradigm, for as Morton Fried noted, the word has "pejorative shading" indicating "primitive or barbaric people" (Fried 1975, 7). For this reason, Canada officially designates its encapsulated pre-conquest nations "First Nations." The United States federal government has not yet (2021) "woke" to its abusive terminology, although increasingly, its "Indian tribes" are themselves adopting the term "nation."

Spurred by the assertion of tribal sovereignties in the 1975 Indian Self-Determination and Education Assistance Act, First Nations people demanded repatriation of their forebears' remains, grave goods. and holy objects. The Society for American Archaeology organized sessions at its 1980s annual meetings to discuss the ethics, legal issues, and likely effects of repatriation. Panel members included self-appointed spokesman Vine Deloria, Jr., protestors such as Maria Pearson from Iowa speaking from personal grief at trashed burials, and representatives from American Indian organizations. Session rooms were packed, debates continued in the corridors and back home in archaeologists' home states. Finally, in 1990, NAGPRA, the Native American Graves Protection and Repatriation Act, was passed by the United States Congress. Archaeologists have been forced by law to engage with injustices born of the Doctrine of Discovery.

Cahokia

Until as late as 1921, some geologists gave as their professional opinion that the mounds on the Cahokia floodplain were natural drift accumulations, not constructed (Hall 1991, 4). What are now horrifying destructions of mounds, using horse-drawn drags, by Warren Moorehead in the 1920s revealed the mounds were built and contained human skeletons and artifacts (Moorehead 2000). Then little was done for decades. Interstate highway development impacted Cahokia as a bypass highway around St. Louis, I-270, was projected across the American Bottom. Federal Aid

Interstate, FAI-270, beginning 1975, was one of the largest cultural resource mitigation projects in North America, later to be linked with extensive mitigation excavation where a new bridge over the Mississippi was to be built (Emerson et al. 2018). Avocationals in the St. Louis region, supported by professionals, achieved United Nations recognition in 1982 of Cahokia as a World Heritage Site, enhancing state protection. Withall, the question of sampling remains: FAI-270 and ISAS-IDOT work was limited to the zones endangered by the highway projects; a great deal of Cahokia, even within the state park, has been destroyed; the boundaries of the city not only have not been identified, we don't know how Cahokians conceptualized them (O'Brien 1994).

Leading interpreters on Cahokia as I write, in 2021, are Thomas Emerson, for many years head of the Illinois State Archaeological Survey; Timothy Pauketat, professor of anthropology, University of Illinois-Champaign/Urbana and now Emerson's successor at Illinois Archaeological Survey; and James Brown, professor of anthropology emeritus, Northwestern University, working with John Kelly of Washington University. Emerson superintended the research of a large staff as Illinois State Archaeologist; Pauketat directed a number of doctoral students conducting research in and near Cahokia; Brown is an authority on the Spiro site, on the Arkansas River in Oklahoma, and has written extensively on Mississippian and Hopewell in the Midwest; Kelly, living in ancient Cahokia's west side, has conducted excavations at Cahokia Mounds for many years. Earlier, Patricia O'Brien, whose dissertation was based on Cahokia ceramics, argued against the standard label "complex chiefdom," propounding that Cahokia was the capital of a territorial state (O'Brien 1991, 1992, 1993, 1994).

Missing from this coterie of archaeologists is a First Nations person. In a parallel universe of discourse, the Osage Nation lays claim to Cahokia, according to its own historians and its THPO, Dr. Andrea Hunter, PhD, RPA.[4] The Osage are one of five nations whose languages make up Dhegihan Siouan, the others being Omaha, Ponca, Kansa (Kaw), and Quapaw. Presumably at the time of Cahokia, these had not separated into the post-contact groups.

Ponca historian Louis Headman recorded the origins history of the Dhegihans from Kenneth Headman (1891–1984), an elder considered authoritative on their history:

They [Dhegihans] kept coming west [from the Ohio Valley] and come to a big river—Nisude t'age [the Mississippi River]. . . . They came to a place what is now called Missouri. That's where the Missouri River flows into the Mississippi. There is a big hill there, and they know about it already. It is called P'ahe zide [red hill]. As long as we have heard about it, it has always been called that. It is at St. Louis, Missouri. That is why they call St. Louis P'ahe zide now. (Headman 2020, 3)

Dr. Hunter, in the Osage Nation Historic Preservation Office's 2013 claim under NAGPRA to human remains from Pike County, Missouri (north of St. Louis), summarized their history:

During the Late Woodland period, A.D. 400 to A.D. 500, the Dhegiha tribes (minus the Quapaw) migrated up the central Mississippi River valley settling in the St. Louis area as well as traveling outward from the valley following the various river drainages into the interior of what are now Missouri and Illinois. During the latter part of the Late Woodland (A.D. 900) and Emergent Mississippian, (A.D. 1000) periods, larger groups of the Dhegiha Siouan tribes focused their settlement strategy in the Cahokia/St. Louis area. At the onset of the Mississippian period, A.D. 1000, those who would later become the Omaha and Ponca tribes separated from the other two remaining Dhegiha Siouan tribes. At some point after the Omaha and Ponca departure, the Kaw separated and traveled up the Missouri River during the Middle Mississippian period, A.D. 1200-A.D. 1250. Those who would later become the Osage were the last remaining Dhegiha Siouan tribe in the Cahokia/St. Louis area. At the end of the Mississippian period, A.D. 1300, the Osage shifted their settlement pattern and moved westward to focus primarily within the central and western portions of the state of Missouri. At the onset of the historic period large groups of the Osage were located along the Missouri and Osage rivers. (Osage Nation 2013)

These accounts are consistent with linguists' analyses of Siouan language history (Kaufman 2019, 39–43).

Current interpretations of Cahokia can be placed on a continuum:

- Osage Nation: Cahokia may perhaps be best called a realm, that is, a large territory held by a polity. It would have been governed, in

Dhegihan tradition, by a council of representatives from the constituent clans, chaired by a member from the clan designated to provide the officer. He and the council would have appointed executive officers to carry out council directives. Priests from the clans carried out its ritual calendar and other duties maintaining sustaining relationships with other beings and forces; women filled some priestly roles (Kehoe 2007). Maize agriculture added to Eastern Agricultural Complex cultigens provided subsistence (Fritz 2019). Widespread trade was vital to its economy. Men of the nation formed its army, defending its trade as well as its borders.

- Thomas Emerson: With the 2018 publication of the massive final report on the East St. Louis excavations, *Revealing Greater Cahokia*, Emerson retired from forty-five years of Illinois archaeology. His work at Cahokia began in 1978 as a site director on the FAI-270 project, and his dissertation was published in 1997 as *Cahokia and the Archaeology of Power*. Timely publishing has been a priority with Emerson during his administration of Illinois archaeology. In his summary chapter in the 2018 volume, he reviews his changing interpretations of Cahokia, rejecting "chiefdom" but also rejecting "state" in favor of declaring Cahokia should be termed a "city" (Emerson 2018, 523–25). In 2023, he published a refined interpretation of the alleged relationship between Cahokia and Spiro, rejecting the Phillips and Brown schema (Emerson 2023, see next paragraph).

- James Brown with John Kelly: Brown was a student of Lewis Binford at the University of Chicago. As senior American archaeologist at Northwestern University, he has followed trends and ideas discussed among his peers working at major Midwest and Southeast sites. His principal contributions to archaeological data have been his documentation of the excavations at the Spiro Mounds on the Arkansas River in easternmost Oklahoma (Brown 1996; Phillips and Brown 1978). Spiro is considered the westernmost great Mississippian site, its spectacular artifacts in its Craig Mound constituting a strong component of what is termed Mississippian, so James Brown became recognized as an authority on Mississippian art (e.g., Brown 2007). Teaming with John Kelly who has long-term continuing excavations in central Cahokia, Brown applies his interpretations developed in collaboration with Phillips on Spiro data, to current discussions of Cahokia.

- Timothy Pauketat has been intrigued by Cahokia since boyhood. In spite of obtaining his PhD from the University of Michigan where Elman Service taught, Pauketat was uncomfortable with Service's simplistic Morgan-derived schema. Beginning with *An Archaeology of the Cosmos: Rethinking Agency and Religion in Ancient America* (2012), he adopted a standpoint premising religious beliefs to be central to American First Nations. Increasingly engaged with Deleuze and other European philosophers, Pauketat asserts that "Cahokia at its urban climax was a vibrant assemblage of human and other-than-human causal powers" (Pauketat 2018, 481).

Taking the American Bottom large floodplain, where the Missouri disgorges into the Mississippi, as the environs of Cahokia (Emerson in Emerson et al. 2018, 36), it is clear that all the archaeology conducted there is only a sample of its human history. Little is known of its western portion, blanketed by the city of St. Louis. Even the central Great Plaza and its mounds suffered substantial reductions through most of the twentieth century. Our data are highly constrained by exigencies of funding: in no way can the actual projects be considered an adequate scientific sampling. For this reason, we as archaeologists should question the derivation of interpretations and their strength in regard to actual hard data. Nor can Osage Nation's history be dismissed; its people and other Siouans have known Cahokia for centuries.

Cahokia From a Postcolonial Standpoint

A postcolonial interpretation of archaeological data from the American Bottom and surrounding lands disengages the European academic premise of an evolutionary progress of life forms from simple to complex. Organic evolution produces extraordinary diversity from effects of apparently random mutations (Kemp 2015). For human societies, historical particularism recognizes similar effects from individuals' novel behaviors and interactions with other people. As Wilson and Sullivan put it, the trend has been to *historicize* the archaeological record, looking not to unilinear cultural evolutionism nor to ecological determinism but to myriads of personal encounters in the past (Wilson and Sullivan 2017, 8–9).

Cahokia is not an anomaly. It is a real, abandoned city. Its center of great rectangular plazas surrounded by mounds is unique in temperate-zone North America, but a standard urban plan in Mexico. It did not "emerge" like a hatching bird, and its rapid growth in the mid-eleventh century was a historical event comparable to the similarly rapid growth of St. Louis in the mid-nineteenth. It is parsimonious to begin with the powerful fact that both cities are located at the central hub of transportation routes across North America. The Ohio rises in the Appalachians, where the Siouans say they originated, traveling down the O'hai, as they call that river. The Missouri links the midcontinent to the Rockies and transmontane trade routes. The Mississippi rises in the north and flows into the Gulf of Mexico. Cahokia is ideally situated to command trade from all sectors of the continent and from Mesoamerica. The remarkable coincidence of its dates for its Mesoamerican-plan monumental center, with the dates for Olmeca-Xicallanca control of Cholula, point to an active connection. St. Louis and Mexico are today connected through trade and labor movements. On the principles of historical sciences,[5] these observations may explain the connections a thousand years ago.

Taking Historical Examples Seriously

The Fall of Rome was followed by the Dark Ages of many small kingdoms and the spread of Christianity through Europe. It's a not-unreasonable parallel to Cahokia, its collapse, the balkanization of the former major polity's territory into small kingdoms, and the spread of the Mississippian Ideological Interaction Sphere (formerly known as SECC, South East Ceremonial Complex). If we take this parallel deeper, we encounter multiplicities of local histories on Rome's borderlands and vast trade reaches, and Islam's rise to the east and south—histories that from a postcolonial standpoint might sharpen our view of Cahokia. It's time to cut the apron strings to Anglo Christianity, ditch John Locke, rip up the Great Chain of Being, toss out Morgan.

To understand Cahokia and Mississippian, the first step is to accept that Cahokia was not "emergent" Mississippian. It was Late Woodland with an intrusive Mexican Tollan (see below). Not "Terminal Late Woodland" because Late Woodland, its "primary forest efficiency" (Caldwell 1958; Dye and Watson 2010), continued in much of eastern America. Specifically, that characterized Toltec Mounds Plum Bayou (Alspauch 2014), often mentioned as a possible source of some of Cahokia's population; incidentally, Toltec Mounds is on the lower Arkansas River, later a route for Mexican green obsidian and, further upriver, Spiro and Etzanoa, historically in Caddoan lands.

Cahokia as a City

Cahokia's central zone in its eastern portion is unique north of Mesoamerica in its grid plan of rectangular plazas ringed by mounds: this zone looks like a Mesoamerican Tollan. "Tollan" is the term for the Mexican ideal city, in "a place of reeds and rushes" with abundant resources of water and land. Lake and river systems facilitate trade (López Austin and López Luján 2000). Both Teotihuacan and Tenochtitlan were Tollans in the Basin of Mexico's marshy lake system; a Mesoamerican traveler would have seen the marshes of the American Bottom to be a beautiful "place of reeds and rushes," ideal for maize agriculture using the common system of ridges and ditches, ideal for hosting traders using the continent's principal waterways. Cahokia's Tollan center dates to the era of Olmeca-Xicallanca rulership at Cholula, the Early Postclassic, when this originally eastern Mexican nation aggressively built the trading empire the Aztecs labeled "Toltec" (McCafferty 2000, 2007, 2017; McCafferty and Chiykowski 2008; Mountjoy 1987; Testard 2017; Turner 2016).

There are also, in the eastern American Bottom, small sites called Terminal Late Woodland "nodal sites" or "villages" by Emerson (2018, 53). His base map, his Figure 14.2, shows these sites clustering along the eastern edge of the floodplain. They resemble a major trading town of the type identified by Blakeslee as Etzanoa (2018), somewhat earlier by Odell (2002), and by Barr (2017). Both the towns and Barr's subjects are in Caddoan territory, but this type of town that consists of households along a river terrace for several kilometers, without a single large plaza or marketplace, may have been common among mid-continent North American First Nations.

Around 1700, the sites at Blood Run on the Big Sioux River between South Dakota and Iowa were recognized, although debated, as constituting a Big Town (Henning and Schnepf 2014). David Overstreet suggests, in conversations, that such a Big Town may have been constituted in the Late Precontact period along the Suamico River just above its outlet into Green Bay, Wisconsin (Overstreet and Henning, personal communication, 2020–2021). The conundrum of Hopewell apparently lacking towns may be answered by seeing the series of farmsteads along the rivers in southern Ohio as such extended towns. Barr (2017) explains how Caddoans protected their towns by posting soldiers along trade routes, a stratagem that fits O'Brien's (1994) identification of possible Cahokian polity symbols, thunderbird and cross-in-circle territorial marker, at points where approaches to the American Bottom could be manned with soldiers.

If, as seems reasonable, around 1000 CE a major trading town occupied the eastern side of the American Bottom below the confluence of the Missouri and Mississippi, how may we account for the Tollan in its midst? Did Cholulan traders exploring sources and markets on waterways debouching in the Gulf of Mexico, stop at the trading town along the eastern edge of the ideal location and propose an alliance? Or did Dhegihans ambitious to build economic domination travel down the Mississippi, across the northern Gulf to the Olmeca-Xicallanca original homeland in the Huasteca and along the principal route inland to Cholula? Whoever initiated the trading relationship, Cahokians could ship slaves and deerhides (Kehoe 2013; Lapham 2005) downriver to sell in Mexican markets—the slaves paddling and portering—and return home with some of Cholula's famous featherwork and textiles. A few had their incisors filed in the Mexican fashion of the time (Hedman et al. 2011). Alas for archaeologists, in each direction the valuables were highly perishable.

Cahokia as an agricultural polity farming maize

Alfred Kroeber and his Berkeley colleague Carl Sauer recognized a huge area of the Americas as Nuclear America (Kroeber 1939, 221, noting Sauer's 1936 similar idea), sharing the cultivation of *Zea mays*. An extraordinary characteristic of cultivated maize is that the plant cannot propagate itself; its seed kernels must be planted sufficiently apart to allow seedlings to grow. Within this immense zone there had been innumerable human-to-human instruction events passing on not only maize seeds but also knowledge of their cultivation (Brown 2006). Maize cultivation was not "emergent," it was a historical practice shared within communities of practice spanning the greater part of two continents. Cahokians continued to farm, along with maize, the Eastern Agricultural Complex in a polyculture practice traditional in the Eastern Woodlands (Mueller et al. 2019).

Cahokia as a Trading Center

Philip Curtin, in his *Cross-cultural Trade in World History*, found that "the most common institutional form after the coming of city life was the trade settlement" (Curtin 1984, 2). Spanish invaders recorded a variety of trade personnel and the high status accorded *pochteca*, merchant businessmen (Hassig 1985, 117; Hirth and Pillsbury 2013). Already in Teotihuacán, many persons and goods came from the Gulf, a major producer of cotton and cotton garments prized by the elite, along with "the profusion and diversity of marine shells" and "marine fish" (Manzanilla 2015, 9211, 9213). Gulf lowlands are home to tropical birds with brilliant feathers, including quetzals and macaws, supplying the gloriously colorful headdresses and body ornaments that have persisted into today's powwow regalia.

Cahokia's center is planned on an orthogonal rectangular grid, with the principal plazas rectangular and their largest mounds arraigned along the rectangle sides, unique among built environments of First Nations north of Mexico. Given that earth architecture on a monumental scale was already nearly three millennia old (Poverty Point) by 1000 CE, and Cahokia's engineering and veneers are in that tradition rather than Mexican (Kehoe and Bruhns 2002), the building of Central Cahokia likely was by indigenous methods, although on the Mexican Tollan design. Its great mounds of layered colored earths may have personified, not the mountains surrounding Mexican cities but the massive thunderclouds moving in from the meeting of the rivers, so memorable to anyone caught in a storm there, as Osage priests memorialized them (Kehoe 2007).

Osage dominated historic Midwest trade (Rollings 1992, 282–83); Cahokia likely did similarly, plus overseeing Cholula Olmeca-Xicallanca trade into the Mississippi Valley. Ironically, that leg of Cahokia's state economy precipitated its downfall at the end of the twelfth century: Cholula fell to reconquest by the Tolteca with Chichimec allies, and its Early Postclassic Gulf Coast-linked trading empire collapsed. Cahokia's floodplain was highly vulnerable to attack. Whether retaliating against slave raids

(Kehoe 2013), or simply aggrandizing, nations at Cahokia's state borders would be tempted by its farmlands and its unparalleled transportation nexus. So far as available evidence goes, Cahokia's Dhegihans moved en masse up the Missouri to the nearest defensible and desirable territory, likely part of Cahokia's polity, the Osage Plains and Ozark Plateau. No major power attempted to control the river nexus until the United States purchased it as Louisiana Territory in 1804.

Surely the termination of so large and dominating a city as Cahokia was as dramatic as its sudden genesis two centuries before. What happened has been muffled by the persisting premise that North American First Nations evolved organically through Morgan's stages, making Cahokia a way station to the "tribes" met by Anglo colonists. Emerson's and Pauketat's and Alt's (2020) Durkheimian tenet that common religious focus created Cahokia, led to Emerson's astounding interpretation,

> Strong fortifications and burned villages were outward signs of increasing factionalism. Ultimately, it was the breaking of the social bonds uniting these diverse people . . . . Given the lack of a smoking gun implicating environmental-derived factors, we posit that *internal* divisions among social, political, ethnic, and religious factions provide a more reasonable description of events that led to Cahokia's dissolution. (Emerson and Hedman 2016, 147, 166, emphasis added)

Usually, "strong fortifications and burned villages" are interpreted as evidence of attacks by enemies *outside* the polity (cf. vivid and well-documented discussion by Duncan and Reilly 2020). Denying any Mexican connection and also the aggressions fomented by state-supported trade disconnects Cahokia from the powerful Osage of the seventeenth century; it drops Cahokia out of history.

"Mississippian"

Thirteenth-century eastern North America saw changes toward the cultural and political features observed by Spanish explorers in the sixteenth century. In the Mississippian era, 1200–1700 (Brain n.d.), maize agriculture was common, small kingdoms the political form, trade strongly established along both riverine and overland routes and facilitated by Mobilian Trade Language, a Muskogean-based lingua franca. Prominently shared iconography, the South East Ceremonial Complex (SECC) (Power 2004; King et al. 2007; but see Brain 2008), more recently termed Mississippian Ideological Interaction Sphere (Duncan 2020, 196), could have been diffused through Mobilian (Drechsel 1997). Significantly, the Mississippian era did not have any city comparable to Cahokia; Ocmulgee in Georgia, too, was abandoned.

A slow shift in interpreting Late Precontact Eastern and Midwestern sites is marked by a pair of edited volumes, *Mississippian Emergence* (Smith 1990) and *Mississippian Beginnings* (Wilson 2017). The recent volume states that "'Mississippian' did not 'emerge' from a Woodland base. . . . Mississippianization consisted of new traditions and cosmologies" spread by people moving and meeting (Wilson and Sullivan 2017, 2). Morgan's model of inherent evolution through stages is incompatible with the abundance of recent data from large-scale excavations such as FAI-270, many smaller excavations conducted by contract archaeologists, newer techniques such as flotation, and increasingly numerous and refined dating technologies. These fail to show any sweeping introduction of cult, style, or maize-based subsistence agriculture, either during Cahokia's two centuries or after its collapse. Instead, the data show multiplicities of local histories tied by trade (demonstrated archaeologically) and sharing of rituals and belief systems (inferred from iconographic artifacts and recorded traditions). Neither unilinear cultural evolutionism nor ecological determinism but myriads of personal encounters in the past account for the nations met by European invaders (Wilson and Sullivan 2017, 8–9).

The concept of "communities of practice" explains many data that vex Midwestern archaeologists. The term originated with anthropologists Jean Lave and Etienne Wenger analyzing apprenticeship as a mode of learning (Wenger 2011). Oceanic archaeologists seized the term to explain what had been called Lapita culture, recognizing that the widely diffused sherds are more parsimoniously understood to represent the spread of a technology, not an ethnic group (Specht et al. 2014):

> couched in terms of "geographical mobility" . . . in which there is constant movement of people and goods between communities for a range of purposes and of varying duration and distance without necessarily involving permanent residential relocations. . . . These networks are

conduits for transfers of goods and raw materials, beliefs and rituals, songs and dances, languages, people, and genes. (Specht et al., 92)

Globular shell-tempered cooking pots are best interpreted as technology associated with maize agriculture. Such pots are better for boiling hominy than the Woodland grit-tempered conical pots *that persist alongside* the globular shell-tempered pots, but not to the degree that cooking maize *demands* shell temper and globular pots (e.g., Schirmer 2016; Feathers 2006; Michelaki 2007). Shell-tempered pottery's high variability in mid-continent North America, both in timing of appearance and in whether a dominant practice, suggests its makers were communities of practice whose potters needed to consider also, political associations and realities through which they understood their clays, methods, products, and social place.

Mesoamerican Postclassic concepts and images circulated among First Nations north of both the Rio Grande and the Gulf of Mexico (Hall 1997, especially 84–85). Feathered Serpents as Underwater Power, portrayed also as giant felines with serpent tails, are ubiquitous within the mid-continent watersheds and eastward. Quetzalcoatl, identified by his necklace of big beads and conch columella pendant, a prominent deity in Postclassic Mesoamerica, frequently appears in publications on Mississippian shell engravings, but he is actually not common in Mississippian art, and possibly all these engravings were done by a single artist at Spiro and distributed through its trade (Kehoe 2018). Spiro's location on the Arkansas River gave it a direct route to Mexico and also to Pecos and other Pueblos via the Santa Fe Trail. Cahokia had reverted to marshy fields during Spiro's florescence.

Conclusion: Interpreting Cahokia

Before radiocarbon dating, archaeologists' primary goal was ordering sites through time and spatial clusters. With these tasks facilitated by laboratories and computer programs, academic archaeologists became free to turn to Théorie, to borrow Lekson's shorthand for French philosophes' abstruse metaphysics (Lekson 2018, 169–71). I concur with Artur Ribeiro that "metaphysical speculation and the discussion of ontology holds little value for archaeology" (Ribeiro 2019, 25). Not only are they far from empirical, they obstruct postcolonial historicity. Emphasizing religion rather than economics and its political supports, today's principal interpreters of Cahokia "Other" the Cahokians from Us.

Cahokia is awesome. It is a UNESCO World Heritage site. Yet it is not a U.S. National Monument, only a Historic Landmark. Few Americans have heard of it. The Doctrine of Discovery licensed subjugation of America's First Nations (Jeffers 2013). John Locke's 1689 treatise defended his patron's seizures of the lands of both English villagers and American nations, becoming the founding document for Anglo conquests and Jefferson's policy of removals (Kehoe 2010; Williams 1990; Wallace 1999). That vision of the United States stretching from sea to sea became Manifest Destiny with the Mexican War. Anglo supremacy's leit-motif erased Cahokia from American history (Kennedy 1994). Only when federal antiquities laws forced a belt highway to avoid demolishing the great mounds and funded a major archaeological salvage project, was Cahokia seen.

The Border Wall built in 1846 by Anglo aggression against Mexico squashed historical ties between Anglo North America and Latin America (e.g., Heaney 2016). We now have indubitable evidence of macaws from southeastern Mexico in Chaco in northern New Mexico, New Mexican turquoise in central Mexico, and Pachuca green obsidian in Spiro (Barker et al. 2002). Nonetheless, the filed teeth from the Cahokia area are not accepted as strong evidence of Mexican relations, although James B. Griffin had so considered them (Griffin 1966).

It's time to repudiate the 1493 Doctrine of Discovery. Time to disown Anglo Manifest Destiny, time to dismiss imperialist unilinear cultural evolutionism. On-the-ground evidence for a likely Late Woodland Big Town with an outpost Mexican Tollan on the American Bottom, suggest the capital of a Dhegihan state ancestral to the Osage and affiliated First Nations. More than a century ago, Boas insisted on historical particularism, a postcolonial standpoint *avant la lettre*. It fits a historical science. It's time to be woke.

NOTES

1. No one knows what this East Coast nation called itself. Mesoamerican scholars like to put "Olmeca-Xicallanca" in scare quotes. See Chadwick 2013 for discussion.

2. The *American Anthropologist* editor, Elizabeth Chin, said that this paper needed an explanation of what "postcolonialism" is. One would suppose that readers of that journal would be familiar with the term, or if not, would Google it. Having cut the paper down to AA's limit of eight thousand words *including* bibliography, I felt I could not cut out more to put in an explanation of "postcolonialism."

3. Pauketat's excavation at what he calls Emerald Acropolis, a ridge site a day's walk from Cahokia, revealed small circular constructions adjacent to houses. He insists they were sweatbaths. His slides shown at the 2022 Society for American Archaeology showed the floors are clean, no pit nor evidence of heat, nor are there hearths outside the circle where rocks could be heated. To me, the circular structures adjacent to houses would be most parsimoniously interpreted to be granaries. Pauketat did not identify any granaries in his interpretation. In his book, he does not cite or discuss the classic study of the sweatbath by Ivan Lopatin (1960), which concludes that the American First Nations sweatbath is closely similar to that of northwestern Europe, especially Finland (but not Saami). Given the wide extent of this particular custom in the Americas, its limited extent in Europe and absence elsewhere before Russian expansion, the sweat bath may have been taken to northwest Europe from America by Norse traders and hunters during their settlements in Greenland, 985-c. 1450. Sweatbaths among American First Nations are a means of cleansing, especially before rituals. Ordinarily, people bathed in rivers and streams, often daily.

4. RPA is the Register of Professional Archaeologists. It registers professionally trained and recognized archaeologists, and is used by contract archaeology (CRM) businesses to vet applicants for positions in their companies. Dr. Hunter is thus established as academically and professionally credentialed.

5. The methods of historical sciences (Simpson 1970; D. Turner 2007; Currie 2018; and the work of Alison Wylie, 2002 and including her co-edited books with Chapman, 2014 and especially 2016) are necessary to make the strongest, parsimonious interpretations archaeological data will allow. Ethnographic and historic analogies provide archaeologists with full sets of relevant observations, as living organisms do for paleontologists. These issues were discussed in Kehoe 1998.

REFERENCES

Alspaugh, Kara Rister. 2014. *The Terminal Woodland: Examining Late Occupation on Mound D at Toltec Mounds (3LN42), Central Arkansas.* Master's thesis, University of Alabama, Tuscaloosa.

Barker, Alex W., Craig E. Skinner, M. Steven Shackley, Michael D. Glascock, J. Daniel Rogers. 2002. "Mesoamerican Origin for an Obsidian Scraper from the Precolumbian Southeastern United States." *American Antiquity* 67 (1): 103–8.

Barr, Juliana. 2017. "There's No Such Thing as 'Prehistory': What the Longue Durée of Caddo and Pueblo History Tells Us about Colonial America." *William and Mary Quarterly* 74 (2): 203–40.

Blakeslee, Donald J. 2018. "The Miguel Map Revisited." *Plains Anthropologist* 63 (243): 67–84.

Brain, Jeffrey P. 2008. Review of *Southeastern Ceremonial Complex: Chronology, Content, Context* by Adam King. *Southeastern Archaeology* 27 (1): 158–61.

———. n.d. "Tunica Origins." Unpublished paper, sent to author, January 2018.

Brown, Cecil H. 2006. "Glottochronology and the Chronology of Maize in the Americas." In *Histories of Maize*, edited by J. E. Staller, R. H. Tykot, and B. F. Benz, 647–63. Amsterdam: Elsevier/Academic Press.

Caldwell, Joseph R. 1958. *Trend and Tradition in the Prehistory of the Eastern United States*. Menasha Wisconsin: American Anthropological Association, Memoir No. 88.

Chapman, Robert, and Alison Wylie, eds. 2014. *Material Evidence: Learning from Archaeological Practice*. London: Routledge.

———. 2016. *Evidential Reasoning in Archaeology*. New York: Bloomsbury Academic.

Currie, Adrian. 2018. *Rock, Bone, Ruin*. Cambridge MA: MIT Press.

Curtin, Philip D. 1984. *Cross-Cultural Trade in World History*. Cambridge: Cambridge University Press.

Drechsel, Emanuel J. 1997. *Mobilian Jargon: Linguistic and Sociohistorical Aspects of a Native American Pidgin*. New York: Oxford University Press.

Duncan, James R. 2020. "The Long-Nosed Ear Ornaments: Their Depth of Meaning." In *Recovering Ancient Spiro*, edited by Eric D. Singleton and F. Kent Reilly III, 194–203. Oklahoma City: National Cowboy and Western Heritage Museum.

Duncan, James R., and F. Kent Reilly III. 2020. "The Turtle, a Clever Warrior (Who Can Overcome Strong Fortifications)." In *Recovering Ancient Spiro*, edited by Eric D. Singleton and F. Kent Reilly III, 116–33. Oklahoma City: National Cowboy and Western Heritage Museum.

Emerson, Thomas E. 1997. *Cahokia and the Archaeology of Power*. Tuscaloosa: University of Alabama Press.

———. 2023. "The Origins of Engraved Marine Shell Cups, Copper Repoussé Plates, and Ritual Centers: Disentangling Early Cahokia Symbolism from Post-AD 1200 SECC Iconography." *Southeastern Archaeology* 42 (2): 83–104.

Emerson, Thomas E., and Kristin M. Hedman. 2016. "The Dangers of Diversity: The Consolidation and Dissolution of Cahokia, Native North America's First Urban Polity." In *Beyond Collapse: Archaeological Perspectives on Resilience, Revitalization, and Transformation in Complex Societies*, edited by Ronald K. Faulseit, 147–74. Center for Archaeological Investigations, Occasional Paper No. 42. Carbondale: Southern Illinois University.

Emerson, Thomas E., Brad H. Koldehoff, and Tamira K. Brennan, eds. 2018. *Revealing Greater Cahokia, North America's First Native City: Rediscovery and Large-Scale Excavations of the East St. Louis Precinct* (ISAS-IDOT). Urbana: Illinois State Archaeological Survey.

Feathers, James K. 2006. "Explaining Shell-Tempered Pottery in Prehistoric Eastern North America." *Journal of Archaeological Method and Theory* 3 (2): 89–133.

Flandreau, Marc. 2016. *Anthropologists in the Stock Exchange: A Financial History of Victorian Science.* Chicago: University Press of Chicago.

Fried, Morton H. 1975. *The Notion of Tribe.* Menlo Park, CA: Cummings.

Fritz, Gayle J. 2019. *Feeding Cahokia: Early Agriculture in the North American Heartland.* Tuscaloosa: University of Alabama Press.

Griffin, James B. 1966. "Mesoamerica and the Eastern United States in Prehistoric Times." In *Handbook of Middle American Indians*, vol. 4, edited by Gordon F. Ekholm and Gordon R. Willey, 111–31. Austin: University of Texas Press.

Hall, Robert L. 1991. "Cahokia Identity and Interaction Models of Cahokia Mississippian." In *Cahokia and the Hinterlands: Middle Mississippian Cultures of the Midwest*, edited by Thomas E. Emerson and R. Barry Lewis, 1–34. Urbana: University of Illinois Press.

———. 1997. *An Archaeology of the Soul.* Urbana: University of Illinois Press.

Hassig, Ross. 1985. *Trade, Tribute, and Transportation.* Norman: University of Oklahoma Press.

Headman, Louis V. 2020. *Walks on the Ground: A Tribal History of the Ponca Nation.* Lincoln: University of Nebraska Press.

Heaney, Christopher. 2016. "A Peru of Their Own: English Grave-Opening and Indian Sovereignty in Early America." *William and Mary Quarterly*, third series, 73 (4): 609–46.

Hedman, Kristin M., Julie A. Bukowski, and Dawn E. Cobb. 2011. "A Study of Modified Teeth from Archaeological Sites in Illinois: Recent and Archival Examples." Poster presented at 80th meeting of American Association of Physical Anthropologists, Minneapolis MN, April 2011.

Heyden, Doris. 1983. "Reeds and Rushes." In *Flora and Fauna Imagery in Precolumbian Cultures: Iconography and Function.* Oxford: B. A. R. Proceedings, International Series 171.

Hirth, Kenneth G., and Joanne Pillsbury, eds. 2013. *Merchants, Markets, and Exchange in the Pre-Columbian World.* Washington DC: Dumbarton Oaks.

Jeffers, Joshua J. 2013. "Of Laws and Land: The Doctrine of Discovery in History and Historiography." *Maryland Historical Magazine: The Journal of the Maryland Historical Society*, 108 (1): 91–115.

Jin, Dengjian. 2016. *The Great Knowledge Transcendence.* New York: Palgrave/Macmillan.

Kaufman, David V. 2019. *Clues to Lower Mississippi Valley Histories: Language, Archaeology, and Ethnography*. Lincoln: University of Nebraska Press.

Kehoe, Alice B. 1998. *The Land of Prehistory: A Critical History of American Archaeology*. New York: Routledge.

———. 2003. "An Artifact of Postmedieval European Preconceptions: The Chiefdom Model versus the Principle of Actualism." Available on Academia.

———. 2007. "Osage Texts and Cahokia Data." In *Ancient Objects and Sacred Realms*, edited by F. Kent Reilly III and James Garber, 246–61. Austin: University of Texas Press.

———. 2010. "Deconstructing John Locke." In *Postcolonial Perspectives in Archaeology*, edited by Peter Bikouis, Dominic Lacroix, and Meaghan M. Peuramaki-Brown, 125–32. Calgary: University of Calgary Archaeological Association.

———. 2013. "'Slaves' and Slave-raiding on the Northern Plains and Rupert's Land." In *Human Expeditions: Inspired by Bruce Trigger*, edited by Stephen Chrisomalis and André Costopoulos, 31–40. Toronto: University of Toronto Press.

———. 2018. "The Ehecailacocozcatl Wind Jewel—Quetzalcoatl in Mississippian America?" Paper presented at Midwest Mesoamerican meeting, Chicago, March 17, 2018.

Kehoe, Alice B., and Karen Olsen Bruhns. 2002. "Cahokia: A Mesoamerican City?" In *The Archaeology of Contact: Processes and Consequences*, edited by Kurtis Lesick, Barbara Kulle, Christine Cluney, and Meaghan Peuramaki-Brown, 287–92. Calgary: Archaeological Association of the University of Calgary.

Kemp, Tom S. 2015. *The Origin of Higher Taxa: Palaeobiological, Developmental, and Ecological Perspectives*. Chicago: University of Chicago Press.

Kennedy, Roger G. 1994. *Hidden Cities: The Discovery and Loss of Ancient North American Cities*. New York: Free Press.

King, Adam, ed. 2007. *Southeastern Ceremonial Complex: Chronology, Content, Context*. Tuscaloosa: University of Alabama Press.

Kroeber, Alfred L. 1939. *Cultural and Natural Areas of North America*. Berkeley: University of California Press.

Lapham, Heather A. 2005. *Hunting for Hides*. Tuscaloosa: University of Alabama Press.

Lekson, Stephen H. 2018. *A Study of Southwestern Archaeology*. Salt Lake City: University of Utah Press.

López Austin, Alfredo, and Leonard López Luján. 2000. "The Myth and Reality of Zuyuá: The Feathered Serpent and Mesoamerican Transformations from the Classic to the Postclassic." In *Mesoamerica's Classic Heritage: From Teotihuacan to the Aztecs*, edited by David Carrasco, Lindsay Jones, and Scott Sessions, 21–84. Boulder: University Press of Colorado.

Lovejoy, Arthur O. 1936. *The Great Chain of Being*. Cambridge MA: Harvard University Press.

Manzanilla, Linda R. 2015. "Cooperation and tensions in multiethnic corporate societies using Teotihuacan, Central Mexico, as a case study." *PNAS* 112 (30): 9210–15.

McCafferty, Geoffrey G. 2000. "Tollan Cholollan and the Legacy of Legitimacy during the Classic-Postclassic Transition." In *Mesoamerica's Classic Heritage: From Teotihuacan to the Aztecs*, edited by David Carrasco, Lindsay Jones, and Scott Sessions, 341–67. Boulder: University Press of Colorado.

———. 2007. "So What Else is New? A Cholula-centric Perspective on Lowland/Highland Interaction during the Classic/Postclassic Transition." In *Twin Tollans: Chichén Itzá, Tula, and the Epiclassic to Early Postclassic Mesoamerican World*, edited by Cynthia Kristan-Graham and Jeff Kowalski, 429–59. Cambridge MA: Harvard University Press.

———. 2017. "The Early Postclassic of Cholula: Results from the UA-1 Household Compounds." Society for American Archaeology 86th annual meeting, April, online.

McCafferty, Geoffrey, and Tanya Chiykowski. 2008. "Mayan Migrants to Tollan Cholollan." Paper presented at the 2008 Canadian Archaeological Association Peterborough, ON.

Michelaki, Kostalena. 2007. "More than Meets the Eye: Reconsidering Variability in Iroquoian Ceramics." *Canadian Journal of Archaeology / Journal Canadien d'Archéologie* 31 (2): 143–70.

Moorehead, Warren King. 2000. *The Cahokia Mounds*. Tuscaloosa: University of Alabama Press.

Morgan, Lewis Henry. [1877] 1985. *Ancient Society*. Classics of Anthropology facsimile edition. Tucson: University of Arizona Press.

Mountjoy, Joseph. 1987. "The Collapse of the Classic at Cholula as seen from Cerro Zapotecas." *Notas Mesoamericanas* 10:119–51.

Mueller, Natalie G., Andrea White, and Peter Szilagy. 2019. "Experimental Cultivation of Eastern North America's Lost Crops: Insights into Agricultural Practice and Yield Potential." *Journal of Ethnobiology* 39 (4): 549–66.

O'Brien, Patricia J. 1991. "Early State Economics: Cahokia, Capital of the Ramey State." In *Early State Economics*, Political and Legal Anthropology Series, Vol. 8, edited by Henri J.M. Claessen and Pieter van de Velde, 143–76. New Brunswick, NJ: Transaction Publishers.

———. 1992. "The World-System of Cahokia Within the Middle Mississippian Tradition." In *Precapitalist World Systems*, edited by Christopher Chase-Dunn. Special issue of *Review* (3): 389–417.

———. 1993. "Cultural Taxonomy, Cross-Cultural Types, and Cahokia." In *Highways to the Past: Essays on Illinois Archaeology in Honor of Charles J. Bareis*, edited by Thomas E. Emerson, Andrew C. Fortier and Dale L. McElrath. *Illinois Archaeology* 5 (1–2): 481–97.

———. 1994. "Prehistoric Politics: Petroglyphs and the Political Boundaries of Cahokia." *Gateway Heritage* 15 (1): 30–47.

Odell, George H. 2002. *La Harpe's Post: A Tale of French-Wichita Contact on the Eastern Plains.* Tuscaloosa: University of Alabama Press.

Osage Nation. 2013. Excerpt from: *Osage Nation NAGPRA Claim for Human Remains Removed from the Clarksville Mound Group (23P16), Pike County, Missouri* by Andrea A. Hunter, James Munkres, and Barker Fariss, 1–60. Pawhuska, OK: Osage Nation Historic Preservation Office. https://www.osagenation-nsn.gov /who-we-are/historic-preservation/osage-cultural-history.

Pauketat, Timothy R. 2003. "Resettled Farmers and the Making of a Mississippian Polity." *American Antiquity* 68:39–66.

———. 2012. *An Archaeology of the Cosmos: Rethinking Agency and Religion in Ancient America.* London: Routledge.

———. 2018. "Thinking Through the Ashes, Architecture, and Artifacts of Ancient East St. Louis." In *Revealing Greater Cahokia, North America's First Native City: Rediscovery and Large-Scale Excavations of the East St. Louis Precinct (ISAS-IDOT)*, edited by Thomas E. Emerson, Brad H. Koldehoff, and Tamira K. Brennan, 463–86. Urbana: Illinois State Archaeological Survey.

Pauketat, Timothy R., and Susan M. Alt, eds. 2020. *New Materialisms, Ancient Urbanisms.* New York: Routledge.

Phillips, Philip, and James A. Brown. 1978. *Pre-Columbian Shell Engravings From the Craig Mound at Spiro, Oklahoma.* Cambridge MA: Peabody Museum of Archaeology and Ethnology, Harvard University.

Power, Susan C. 2004. *Early Art of the Southeastern Indians: Feathered Serpents and Winged Beings.* Athens: University of Georgia Press.

Reisch, George A. 2005. *How the Cold War Transformed Philosophy of Science.* New York: Cambridge University Press.

Reisch, George A. 2019. *The Politics of Paradigms: Thomas S. Kuhn, James B. Conant, and the Cold War "Struggle for Men's Minds".* Albany: SUNY Press.

Ribeiro, Artur. 2019. "Archaeology and the new Metaphysical Dogmas: Comments on Ontologies and Reality." *Forum Kritische Archäologie* 8:25–38.

Rollings, Willard H. 1992. *The Osage: An Ethnohistorical Study of Hegemony on the Prairie-Plains.* Columbia: University of Missouri Press.

Ross, Dorothy. 1991. *The Origins of American Social Science.* Cambridge: Cambridge University Press.

Schirmer, Ronald C. 2016. "Radiocarbon Dating Early Oneota Sites in Southern Minnesota." Report for Grant #1501–05965 of the Clean Water, Land, and Legacy Amendment.

Service, Elman R. 1962. *Primitive Social Organization, An Evolutionary Perspective.* New York: Random House.

Simpson, George Gaylord. 1970. "Uniformitarianism. An Inquiry into Principle, Theory, and Method in Geohistory and Biohistory." In *Essays in Evolution and Genetics in Honor of Theodosius Dobzhansky*, edited by Max K. Hecht and William C. Steere, 43–96. New York: Appleton-Century-Crofts.

Smith, Bruce D., ed. 1990. *The Mississippian Emergence*. Washington DC: Smithsonian Institution Press.

Solovey, Mark. 2013. *Shaky Foundations: the Politics-Patronage-Social Science Nexus in Cold War America*. New Brunswick NJ: Rutgers University Press.

———. 2020. *Social Science for What?: Battles over Public Funding for the "Other Sciences" at the National Science Foundation*. Cambridge: MIT Press.

Specht, Jim, Tim Denham, James Goff, and John Edward Terrell. 2014. "Deconstructing the Lapita Cultural Complex in the Bismarck Archipelago." *Journal of Archaeological Research* 22:89–140.

Testard, Juliette. 2017. "Arqueología, fuentes etnohistóricas y retóricas de legitimización: un ensayo reflexivo sobre los olmecas xicalancas." *Anales de Antropología* 51:142–53.

Turner, Andrew. 2016. *Cultures at the Crossroads: Art, Religion, and Interregional Interaction in Central Mexico, AD 600–900*. Unpublished Ph.D. dissertation, University of California-Riverside.

Turner, Derek. 2007. *Making Prehistory: Historical Science and the Scientific Realism Debate*. New York: Cambridge University Press.

Wallace, Anthony F. C. 1999. *Jefferson and the Indians*. Cambridge: Belknap Press.

Wenger, Etienne. 2011. *Communities of Practice: A Brief Introduction*. Online: https://scholarsbank.uoregon.edu/xmlui/bitstream/handle/1794/11736/A%20brief%20introduction%20to%20coP.pdf?sequence=1&isAllowed=y.

Williams, Robert A., Jr. 1990. *The American Indian in Western Legal Thought: The Discourses of Conquest*. New Haven: Yale University Press.

Wilson, Gregory E., ed. 2017. *Mississippian Beginnings*. Gainesville: University of Florida Press.

Wilson, Gregory E., and Lynne P. Sullivan. 2017. "Mississippian Origins." In *Mississippian Beginnings*, edited by Gregory E. Wilson, 1–28. Gainesville: University of Florida Press.

Wylie, Alison. 2002. *Thinking From Things: Essays in the Philosophy of Archaeology*. Berkeley: University of California Press.

PART 4. Postcolonial

Scientific Standpoint and Moral Imperative

9. Delgamuukw

Delgamuukw is a name that should cause every North American archaeologist to cringe in horror. In 1991, the Chief Justice of British Columbia
ruled that the Delgam Uukw and his Gitksan nation had no claim to the
timber surrounding their reserve village because their forebears were so
primitive that they had no territory. In 1991, not 1891! The nation and their
neighbors the Wet'suwet'en appealed the ruling, and in 1997 the Supreme
Court of Canada held in their favor on grounds of procedural errors in
the trial.[1] Justice McEachern's flagrant racism was not directly addressed.

Worse, in Vancouver McEachern was hailed as a great jurist and
appointed Chancellor of the University of British Columbia. Disregarding
strong protests from faculty and students, McEachern was *reappointed* to
a second term as chancellor; he died in office in 2008. The WASP Anglo
power elite in British Columbia made it blatantly clear that they would
not yield their conquests. Canada as a nation has pursued Truth and
Reconciliation with its First Nations farther than has the United States,
yet in federally constituted nations oppositional politicians can override
national policies.

Like my colleagues in Canada who shared with me, their shock and
anger, I was deeply disturbed by the gross ignorance entombed in McEachern's final ruling. See it in this excerpt from a presentation I made to the
Society for Historical Archaeology in 2010:

> Chief Justice Allan McEachern of the British Columbia Supreme Court
> stated, in *Delgamuukw v. Regina,*
>
>> It is common, when one thinks of Indian land claims, to think of
>> Indians living off the land in pristine wilderness. . . . Similarly, it
>> would not be accurate to assume that even pre-contact existence in
>> the territory was in the least bit idyllic . . . there is no doubt, to quote
>> Hobbs [sic], that aboriginal life in the territory was, at best, "nasty,
>> brutish and short". . . . It is asked whether a nation may lawfully take
>> possession of some part of a vast country in which there are none but

erratic nations, whose scanty population is incapable of occupying the whole? . . . Their unsettled habitation . . . cannot be accounted a true and legal possession, and the people of Europe . . . finding land of which the Savage stood in no particular need, and of which they made no actual and constant use, were lawfully entitled to take possession. . . . Some tribes are so low in the scale of social organization that their usages and conceptions of rights and duties are not to be reconciled with the institutions or the legal ideas of civilized society. . . . I do not accept the ancestors "on the ground" behaved as they did because of "institutions." Rather I find they more likely acted as they did because of survival instincts. . . . the Indians of the territory were, by historical standards, a primitive people without any form of writing, horses, or wheeled wagons. . . . Aboriginal life, in my view, was far from stable. . . . It is my conclusion that Gitksan and Wet'suwet'en laws and customs are not sufficiently certain to permit a finding they or their ancestors governed the territory. (quoted in Culhane 1998, 236, 239, 246–49)

The case had been brought by two British Columbia First Nations, Gitxsan and Wet'suwet'en, seeking rights, including timber, to the territory surrounding their villages. McEachern ruled against their claims on the grounds he declared. When did he speak thus? *1991*!

Earl Muldoe, the Delgam Uukw House hereditary Chief, and the heads of fifty other Houses within the two nations on the upper Skeena River in interior British Columbia, filed their case in 1984. Receiving the adverse judgement in 1991, they appealed to the provincial Court of Appeals and to Canada's Supreme Court, the latter ordering, in 1997, a new trial on procedural error, McEachern's refusal to entertain oral histories from the nations' appointed traditional historians. McEachern disdaining Gitxsan *adaawk* and Wet'suwet'en sung *kungax* follows from his astonishing reliance on nineteenth-century cant of conquest. John Lubbock might have written the brief.

Even more appalling than McEachern's judgment is that he *was honored* following the Appeals Court's and Canadian Supreme Court's reversals of his ruling! After the Supreme Court ruled against his judgement, Allan McEachern (1926–2008) was twice elected Chancellor of the University of British Columbia, serving in that office from 2002 until his death in 2008. Students and faculty protested, to no avail. It had been part of UBC's graduation ceremony for students to walk across the stage and kneel in front of the chancellor, who would tap each on the shoulder with his hat. Native students refused to kneel to him. The university then dropped that part of the ritual (personal communication, Arthur J. Ray, February 12, 2010).

One of University of British Columbia's historians, Arthur J. Ray, was called to testify in *Delgamuukw*. The trial shocked him into researching court cases on Indian title. He states,

> how Aboriginal history should be periodized . . . is a crucial question because chronologies are based on key Western notions about Aboriginal history. For many years it was common practice for scholars to divide their chronologies into three basic units: the Prehistoric, the Protohistoric, and the Historic periods. This scheme, derived from archeology, was intended to reflect two primary considerations: first, the intensity of Native—European contact and the disruptions that resulted from it; second, the absence or presence of documentary sources to facilitate the study of those processes. . . . For two main reasons, Native people have long objected to this framework. First, it suggests that they were without history and that their cultures were static before Europeans arrived. Second, it is a Eurocentric perception of their history that does not take into account varied Aboriginal historical traditions. As a partial concession to their objections, it has become a common practice to use the terms Pre-Contact, Proto-Contact, and Contact, but this modification does not address Aboriginal concerns in a fundamental way. (Arthur J. Ray, personal communication, 2008)

The clash between First Nations' actual histories and our legacy from Western imperialism recurs again and again in the courts. It is not a question of the accuracy of *adaawk* and *kungax* compared to, for example, the accuracy of Gibbon's *The History of the Decline and Fall of the Roman Empire*, it is a matter of recognizing a priori that every nation, large or small, literate or not, has histories—and not a single text graven on stone, but multiple histories.

McEachern's words were widely quoted in Canada and taken as true by even educated people. In 2003, I met with a prominent lawyer in Regina, Saskatchewan, Tony Merchant, whose Merchant Law Firm was preparing a class-action suit against the government of Canada on behalf of First Nations people who had allegedly suffered psychological abuse in the government's residential schools for Indian children. A lawyer in his firm, named Patrick Alberts, and an intern joined their employer to discuss my serving as expert witness in the case.[2] Mr. Merchant explained to his employees that Indians are primitive, that their languages are unable to communicate all that ours can, that they have no religion, nor understand territorial possession. I carefully and respectfully countered these statements, aghast that he would undertake the lawsuit when he knew so little. He did listen with some surprise to my corrections and indicated his employees should accept them.

Something about Merchant's litany of primitive characteristics sounded familiar. Yes, they echoed McEachern's Reasons for Judgment. A lawyer himself, Tony Merchant would have consulted the British Columbia Chief Justice's recent final opinion while preparing the class-action suit. The Supreme Court's dismissal of the judgment, on procedural grounds, did not address its gross inaccuracies. British Columbia elite's high praise for their colleague would indicate to a provincial lawyer that the statements in the Judgment were sound. *Delgamuukw v. Regina* (the Queen) not only denied the Gitksan and Wet'suwet'en people their rights, it supported utterly demeaning colonialist propaganda that they had been brute savages.

Canada's prime minister Justin Trudeau, serving since 2015, is son to Pierre Trudeau, who as prime minister in 1969 announced in a White Paper that he would assimilate the country's Indians into full participation in the dominant, Anglo/French culture. Outcries against the abrogation of treaties and denial of personal freedom erupted across Canada. Pierre Trudeau withdrew the policy and made amends by liberally sending money to First Nations organizations, greatly strengthening their political weight. Justin Trudeau takes care to show his support for the country's First Nations, who now have the Chief of the Assembly of First Nations sitting with the premiers of the provinces in First Ministers Conferences with him.

Pierre Trudeau's fiasco was a seismic shift in Canada's policies with, and about, its First Nations, yet *Delgamuukw* highlighted the bedrock racism of European-colonized nation-states. The remarkable transcript of the trial, published by Don Monet and Skanu'uk (Ardythe Wilson 1992), wrenches gut and heart as we read the *adaawk* histories of the petitioning Houses, recited by their Chiefs. These are particular histories, not stages in an evolution toward Us. All American First Nations—like every other human community—have deeptime histories that for many, can only be revealed through archaeology pursued as historical science with fullest use of ethnographies and descendant knowledge.

NOTES

1. A bold study of sovereignties, by Wood and Rossiter (2022) raises the fundamental question of whether the Crown actually has, legally, *any* sovereignty over most of Canada. Britain invaded the territories of hundreds of nations, encouraged settlement by European migrants, forced the smaller nations to sign treaties acknowledging Crown power, all resting upon the 1493 papal bull asserting Christian domination. Such a statement by a Pope would have no legal standing in international courts not only today, but even in the eighteenth century during colonial wars.

2. Merchant Law Firm was one of the largest in Canada, with offices in many cities. The Canadian government's 1996 Royal Commission on Aboriginal Peoples report and the 1998 consequent Aboriginal Action Plan with a Statement of Reconciliation, opened many avenues for lawyers to assist First Nations. The Action Plan targeted Indian residential schools as particularly damaging to the thousands of children forced to attend. Merchant saw substantial legal fees might accrue to successful suits by former students. He invested heavily in exploring and planning such a suit, only to have it moot when the government announced it would recompense former students for their suffering. My fee for researching and writing an expert witness paper on the residential schools, particularly in Saskatchewan, was paid in three installments, as the nearly bankrupt firm struggled to survive.

   This was the only time I was asked to be expert witness in a lawsuit. Merchant had asked a professor in First Nations University in Regina, but he had demurred because the lead plaintiff in the suit had been one of his students. The professor, long my colleague, suggested me, since my dissertation research had involved both ethnographic and archival work on several reserves including the plaintiff's own, Standing Buffalo.

REFERENCES

Culhane, Dara. 1998. *The Pleasure of the Crown: Anthropology, Law, and First Nations.* Burnaby BC: Talonbooks.

Monet, Don, and Skanu'u (Ardythe Wilson). 1992. *Colonialism on Trial: Indigenous Land Rights and the Gitksan and Wet'suwet'en Sovereignty Case.* Philadelphia: New Society Publishers.

10. The Muted Class
Unshackling Tradition

At this point, I turn to another paper, "The Muted Class: Unshackling Tradition." The Delgam Uukw and the several dozen other House Chiefs testifying in *Delgamuukw v. Regina* were muted by McEachern's ruling that their words "are not to be reconciled with . . . civil society."

My paper here was written for a conference of women in archaeology, with the papers published in 1992 in *Exploring Gender Through Archaeology*, edited by Cheryl Claassen. Prehistory Press in Madison, Wisconsin, is the publisher; it's still listed in the Madison Chamber of Commerce website although its own website gives only a phone number and street address, nothing on the page opens with a click on Reviews. Such obscurity merited inclusion in this book.

My title echoes my earlier paper, 1983, "The Shackles of Tradition" (Kehoe 1983a), in *The Hidden Half*, edited by Patricia Albers and Beatrice Medicine. That book came out of a landmark session in the 1977 Plains Anthropological Association annual meeting. We few women working professionally in Plains archaeology and ethnography decided to band together, show our strength; the session was reasonably well attended (that is, around twenty people) although not talked about by the men. Albers, a senior academic at University of Minnesota, shopped the manuscript of our papers around until finally the independent University Press of America agreed to publish it *if* guaranteed selling at least five hundred copies. Could we all assign it to our classes? Would that amount to selling five hundred copies? No. Albers at last told the Press she would personally buy whatever copies would be needed to make up the total (about two hundred, it appeared). When the book at last came out, it sold so well that a second printing was produced! Indeed, a turning point had been reached—or should I say a wall breached?

Claassen organized an open conference for women doing archaeology, in 1991, 1993, and 1995 at her school, Appalachian State University in Boone,

North Carolina. Picturesque in the southern Appalachians, Boone was of course not easy to travel to, nor likely to be a good place to advertise oneself seeking academic positions. In spite of these discouragements, there was a good turnout of women happy to be with their own kind and eager to progress the issues both of women's employment and of interpreting archaeological data. There were also two men attendees, Kenneth Sassaman and Brian Hayden. After the three conferences in Boone, one was held in Las Vegas and the last in Sonoma, California in 2002. By that time, feminist archaeology was solidly ensconced to the degree that, on the one hand, a group of California hippie-garbed feminists attacked scholar Cynthia Eller for her research demonstrating that a supposed original, prehistoric matriarchy is a myth (Eller 2001),[1] and on another angle, the three "feminist" archaeologists at University of California-Berkeley, Meg Conkey, Rosemary Joyce, and Ruth Tringham, drove to Sonoma together, marched in, gave their papers in sequence and then marched out to drive back to Berkeley. Such elitism was as outside feminism as we lived it, as was the attack on a serious and collegial woman scholar.

"Gender" archaeology had exploded in 1989 at the University of Calgary's annual Chacmool Archaeology conference. Organized by Calgary's graduate students as part of their training, the theme of "gender" was daring; the students were gently warned that few might come. Instead, about three hundred participated, the air fizzing with dramatic proof that "gender" was a hot topic, women mattered! My own paper, included in the published volume (that needed to be reprinted for continuing demand), was on recognizing fabrics in archaeological data, such as fabric-impressed Woodland sherds, a gendered topic because archaeologists assumed that in North America women made pottery. Upshot of the Calgary conference was that women had voices, women could publish! Euphoria is exhilarating . . . but, would women be *heard*?

"The Muted Class" was, and remains, a sobering distinction between speaking and being heard. Edwin Ardener, its published author, was a distinguished British anthropologist who, as was common during the colonial period, did fieldwork in his empire's overseas colonies, Cameroon in the Ardeners' case. Shirley Ardener, his wife, accompanied him, sometimes being acknowledged as collaborator. She edited the 1975 volume in which her husband's contribution on muting appeared, and addressed muting in

her next edited feminist volume, 1978.[2] I met the couple at a 1980 graduate student conference in Cambridge, to which Edwin was invited as key
speaker, primarily (I think) on the basis of his Malinowski Lecture published in 1971, "The New Anthropology and Its Critics." A memorable conference, it was organized by Ian Hodder's first bevy of students, including
Mike Parker-Pearson, Danny Miller, Henrietta Moore, and Chris Tilley.[3]
To my surprise, Edwin Ardener spoke in a lounge, seated informally before
the students, with Shirley beside him, seated lower. Professor Ardener's
voice was low; everyone had to strain to hear him. Later, my close colleague
Dena Dincauze, who had spent a year as a Fulbright scholar in Cambridge,
clued me in: Oxford dons spoke low, so that the room would quiet and
everyone would have to focus on them just to hear them. Dincauze herself
used this tactic to force people—men—to listen to her, and it worked. As
Edwin thus spoke, a couple times Shirley tried to interpolate a comment,
only to have him stop speaking, turn to look down at her with a withering
look, then resume what he had been saying. He muted her.

Having read Shirley's edited books, I asked her whether we could meet
and talk. Certainly, she said with a smile, let's lunch at such-and-such restau-
rant on the High Street. It was filled with women, housewives they seemed,
who had been shopping. Shirley's dress and coat fit in. After all, she is listed
in the online list of Wellcome Medals, of the Anthropological Institute of
Great Britain and Ireland, in this way: "1962 Ardener, Mrs S.G. 'The comparative study of rotating credit associations.' JRAI 1964. 94, pp. 201–29."[4] No
other medalist has a prefix to their initials, not even other women winners.
Our lunch conversation was a clear, focused description of Shirley's work to
establish women in anthropological discourse, from the Institute of Social
Anthropology begun in 1972, officially by Edwin as an Oxford professor, and
a seminar on the social anthropology of women meeting at Oxford's Queen
Elizabeth House, then in 1983 The Centre for Cross-Cultural Research on
Women, finally in 2000 becoming the International Gender Studies Centre.
Her career was honored in 1991 with the Order of the British Empire.

Shirley emphasized to me that conferences on women should have two
rooms, a formal lecture room and an adjacent informal room for tea breaks
and conversations. That the conferences should be jointly organized by a
senior, experienced woman and a junior scholar, the junior woman to be
co-editor of publications of conference papers, and advancement of junior

women scholars a purpose of the conferences. She told me that the tea breaks in relaxed surroundings were as important as the formal presentations to build collegial relationships. In other words, Shirley Ardener used her extraordinary mind and sensibilities for decades to unmute women, even in the high realm of Oxford University—in collusion with Edwin. Though Appalachian State University was far from Oxford in every way, I did my best to work with Cheryl Claassen in the mission we shared with Shirley Ardener.

The Muted Class
Unshackling Tradition

Dominant groups dominate discourse. Subordinated groups whose discourse differs from the dominant mode may not be heard; Edwin Ardener (1975) termed them "muted groups." Shirley Ardener explained, in her introduction to *Defining Females* (1978), that muted groups are not deficient in their capacity for language, nor are they necessarily more quiet than the dominant group. "The 'mutedness' of one group may be regarded as the inverse of the 'deafness' of the dominant group, as the 'invisibility' of the former's achievements is an expression of the 'blindness' of the latter. Words which continually fall upon deaf ears may, of course, in the end become unspoken, or even unthought" (S. Ardener 1978, 20). I want to suggest here that the concept of mutedness is a powerful entrée into the field of scholarship focusing on women, whether we are discussing women as subjects of research or women as scholars.

Dominant Discourse Muting Gender, Race, and Class

Let us first note that in 1989, the Modern Language Association published a handbook on *Language, Gender, and Professional Writing* (Frank and Treichler 1989) that gave its imprimatur to the standard of non-sexist writing. The handbook illustrated the absurdity of traditional formal practice with excerpts such as this:

> The central issue in man's evolution was bipedalism. When man thrust himself erect, he truly became *Homo erectus*: for he discovered front-

to-front copulation. And woman in her turn was rewarded by orgasm, unknown to all other species. (Frank and Treichler 1989, 189)

Not to mention, "Man, being a mammal, breast-feeds his young" (Frank and Treichler 1989, 4). These examples do more than flag foolishness; from the Ardeners' perspective, they show how thoroughly the dominant class has expropriated the accomplishments of the subordinated class, in this case, of women.

We who are women are members of a class for whom formal higher education was until this century generally proscribed. What was on top of our heads—our long and tediously arranged hair—was our crowning glory; what was inside our heads was muted. Take this 1921 note from a male professor at Smith College:

> Mme. Curie is to be here tomorrow.... The average student, however, *I imagine* to be much more interested in the Prom.... These students seem much less interested in the pursuit of learning than in avoiding as far as possible its pursuit of them (quoted in Rossiter 1982, 357n59, my italics).

The philosopher Marjorie Glicksman Grene recounts a story typical of women who persisted in scholarly interests rather than Proms:

> Alasdair MacIntyre ... was lecturer in philosophy ... when ... I myself fell luckily into a temporary lectureship.... I was teaching Descartes to Kant ... and MacIntyre had drummed into the students the thesis "There is no philosophy from St. Thomas to Hegel." Every time I came close to convincing the class that something in *my* period was worth attending to, I could just see their dear little minds ticking over: "But MacIntyre says there *is* no philosophy from St. Thomas to Hegel." (Grene 1986, 356)

Parenthetically, we can point out that Grene's notion of luck seems rather perverse. She studied at Harvard, at Freiburg with Heidegger and at Heidelberg with Jaspers, and upon completing her doctorate (in 1935), wrote to 129 schools seeking a position. "[N]obody gives jobs to women in philosophy," she was told, but a small junior college did take her, and then the University of Chicago as an instructor during World War II, until the boys came back and she was, as she says, "forcibly retired." For fifteen years, she was "exiled from her profession," struggling on a "shabby, back-breaking, debt-ridden farm" until Michael Polanyi hired her as his research assistant in Manchester (Grene 1986, 355–56).

The standard histories of archaeology seem to avoid as far as possible the pursuit of identifying women's contributions to the discipline. Willey and Sabloff's sole reference, in their *History of American Archaeology*, to Memoir No. 1 of the Society for American Archaeology, the work of a woman, is via somebody else's citation:

> It was John W. Bennett who realized the functionalist implications of Martin's and Rouse's writings. In 1943, he published an article . . . in which . . . he referred to archaeological uses of the concept of *accultur-ation*, by T. M. N. Lewis and Madeline Kneberg in Tennessee (1941) and by D. L. Keur (1941) in the southwestern United States. (Willey and Sabloff 1980, 135, their italics)

What happened to Dorothy Keur? She gave up attempting to work in archaeology and used her husband's connections to carry out ethnographic study—pioneering study, as had been her Big Bead Mesa work—in Holland and the Caribbean. And Madeline Kneberg? She and Lewis rate a second reference (Willey and Sabloff 1980, 138) via Walter Taylor's praise of them.

At the 1987 Carbondale conference "Writing the History of Archaeology," I brought up Willey and Sabloff's muting of women's contributions. In the published version of the conference, editor Andrew Christenson (1989, 76) states, "of 562 individuals whose gender I could determine in the index of Willey and Sabloff (1980), 31 (6%) were female and of 405 individuals in Daniel's (1981) index, only 12 (3%) were female." Christenson continues (1989, 76–77), "These data do not necessarily indicate any gender bias in these volumes because we do not know the actual gender ratio of archaeologists for the times and locations covered." Ratios seem hardly relevant beside the historical fact that Keur's monograph inaugurated the memoir series of the preeminent organization of American archaeologists.

When I began planning a women's studies course in my university, it seemed to me that the course could best be considered revisionist history. I wanted to share with the students information on interesting people who had raised radical questions. This to me was another way of teaching anthropology, the discipline that raises profoundly radical questions about human nature and societies. My students had read about Tom Paine; I wanted them to know the ideas and the tragic life of his fellow writer for the *Analytical Review*, Mary Wollstonecraft (whose *Vindication of the Rights of Women* appeared in 1790, a year before Paine's *Rights of Man*). They had heard of Susan B. Anthony and perhaps Elizabeth Cady Stanton, two respectable middle-class ladies, and I wanted them to hear about Victoria Claflin Woodhull, not respectable in the eyes of the dominant class but the first woman to run for president of the United States (with ex-slave Frederick Douglass as her running mate), first woman stockbroker on Wall Street, first to publish in America an English translation of Marx and Engels's *Communist Manifesto*. Revisionist history is the history of muted groups.

What about the anthropology component of my course? Revisionist anthropology? I did use that term in a paper in *Current Anthropology* in 1981 (Kehoe 1981). There I challenged the standard view of American Indians as largely non-agricultural, arguing that our Eurocentric picture of agriculture obstructed our recognition of the alternative agricultural practices developed in America. Jennings (1975) had labeled colonist entrepreneurs' blindness to American Indian accomplishments the "cant of conquest," and Trigger (1980) made it quite clear that American archaeologists' conventional interpretations of American Indian history uncritically perpetuate racist images. Indians, like Americans of African descent, are relegated to castes labeled "primitive" and therefore to be without histories. Coupled with historians' reluctance to recognize historical knowledge in the discourse of Indians (cf. e.g., Berthong 1989) the first nations of our continent have been effectively muted for half a millennium.

In social anthropology, the work of Jane C. Goodale on *Tiwi Wives* (1971) published eleven years after the conventional analysis on the Tiwi by her fellow graduate student Arnold Pilling, and the more recent *Women of Value, Men of Renown* by Annette Weiner (1976) are certainly revisionist anthropology. In each case, a woman anthropologist worked among the same people studied by male anthropologists, and in each case she obtained the obverse of their pictures of the societies. Tiwi women, Goodale found, marry younger men. Kiriwina men, Weiner found, work to provide means for their wives to present themselves as persons of value. Women, it was demonstrated, were muted in the studies of male anthropologists, not so much because they as men were excluded from women's rituals, but more so because they paid little attention to women's activities, premising a priori that only men's activities would figure significantly in understanding the society. Goodale and Weiner threw off the shackles of this tradition when they gave voice to the muted class.

Victoria Claflin Woodhull dramatically proves that class, as well as gender and caste, biases mute much of human history. Claflin's father was a stablehand and horse trader, her mother a house servant. To earn a few bucks, the parents exhibited Victoria and her sister Tennie as imitation Fox Sisters on the mid-nineteenth-century county fair circuit. Entirely without formal education, Victoria became an effective orator, invited by Congressman Benjamin Butler to herself read before the House Judiciary Committee her memorial arguing that the recently passed Fourteenth and Fifteenth Amendments to the Constitution gave the vote to women. (Her interpretation rested on the fact that women are members of the human race, and race membership, she pointed out, cannot be used to deny the franchise.) Cady Stanton admired Claflin and attempted to link her crusades to the National Women's Suffrage Association. The Association would have nothing to do with the woman they denounced as a Free Lover and excoriated (quite inconsistently) as the accuser of Henry Ward Beecher, America's most-admired minister. (Claflin published, in her weekly newspaper, the adultery case brought by Beecher's assistant Theodore Tilton against his employer.) Stanton was forced to drop her alliance with Claflin. When it is remembered that the Woman's Suffrage Association membership overlapped considerably with the eugenics movement, the acceptance of these ladies' campaigns in the standard histories of the dominant class is obvious. Giving the vote to women threatened the rationale of dominance by literate propertied Western European men, but Anthony and Cady Stanton pleaded that their votes could strengthen their class's power. Claflin and her associates, on the other hand, demanded an end to the false consciousness fostered by that class. Challenging bourgeois cultural dominance was a truly subversive act, a real rebellion. Claflin was imprisoned and then induced into exile.

Gender, class, caste: each attribute is used to mute the presence of millions of persons destined to subordination under the ideology of the dominant class of propertied Western European men. Legal scholars are now discussing critical legal histories that one practitioner, Mari Matsuda, has termed "outsider jurisprudence." She says her term is preferable to "minority" because that "belies the numerical significance of the constituencies typically excluded from jurisprudential discourse" (Matsuda 1989, 2323n15). "Outsider jurisprudence" is a powerful departure from dominant discourse. "Minority" is part of the dominant structure—the word is meaningless without inclusion in the larger whole—and "revisionist" still tries to remain in the canon. "Outsider" asserts exclusion, it forces recognition that there *are* universes outside the dominant cosmology. The position is subtly and masterfully developed by Robert A. Williams, Jr., a Lumbee: "The ultimate goal of such a scholarship is to rediscover through this disinterring act our own discrete insurrectionist discourses suppressed by the tyranny of totalizing visions of knowledge and power" (Williams 1987, 104).

Another legal scholar, Joan C. Williams, emphasizes the insurrectionist foundation of outsider discourses when she claims that they attack and undermine the theory of possessive individualism central to modern dominant discourse. "The term," she explains, "refers to the liberal premises that society consists of market relations, and that freedom means freedom from any relations with others except those relations the individual enters voluntarily with a view to his own self-interest" (J. Williams 1989, 810; she takes the term from C.B. Macpherson, *The Political Theory of Possessive Individualism*, 1962). This theory of possessive individualism pervades mainstream anthropology, from the expectation that economic analyses will be prominent in ethnographies, to the lower evolutionary standing assigned to societies that seem not to privilege market relations and, at the extreme, the acceptance of sociobiology. Because it converts to subhuman status persons (slaves, serfs, peons, laborers, discriminated "racial" groups, women, children [Haraway 1991,145–47]) who are not free to enter into market relations with a view to their own self-interest, it promotes the continuing dominance of propertied European men. The damning evidence for the cruel self-interest maintained by the dominating discourse lies right in our Declaration of Independence and Constitution, where the authors write of the "self-evident . . . inalienable right to life, liberty, and the pursuit of happiness," then count slaves as three-fifths of a man and refuse the franchise or the full protection of the Constitution to women.

Dominant Discourse in Scholarship

Drawn largely from the professional and upper classes (Ryan and Sackrey 1984), academic researchers tend to accept the tenet of possessive individualism as naturally as Kabyles accept their habitus (cf. Bourdieu 1977, 72–95). The "marketplace of ideas" is more than a metaphor; scholars' ideas are indeed their working capital (Barnes 1977), and the relations of competition premised in the Western concept of the market lie unconformably with the ideal of selfless cooperation once propounded by Robert Merton. Cartels in academia are most visible in citation cliques (Cribb 1980), but they build through a more fundamental exclusionary strategy, the definition of what is to count as relevant discourse.

Alasdair MacIntyre's hegemonic strategy can be glimpsed even in the recent book *Engendering Archaeology*, edited by Gero and Conkey (1991).[5] The editors declare that in 1987, "There was simply no archaeological literature to cite as contributions, nor was there any defined circle of experts to fall back upon"; only "A tiny smattering of literature identified the *existence* of women in prehistory" (Gero and Conkey 1991, xi, their italics). Presumably the smattering consisted of the six studies focusing on inferring gender from prehistoric archaeological data, selected for recommendation in the article "Incorporating Gender into Archaeology Courses," (Spector and Whelan 1989) published after a three-year, well-publicized development project begun in 1985. That article cited, of course, the path-breaking methodological paper presented at the 1977 Plains Conference by Janet Spector and subsequently published in the resulting volume, *The Hidden Half*, edited by Albers and Medicine (1983). *Choice*, the librarians' journal, selected *The Hidden Half* as one of the top ten academic books in its field published in 1983. The research tradition inaugurated by Spector's paper was reinforced at the 1987 Plains Conference in a session organized by Marcel Kornfeld and published as Memoir 26 of the *Plains Anthropologist* (Kornfeld 1991). That same year, a session at the American Anthropological Association annual meeting featured five papers on inferring gender from the archaeological record, and this session, too, has been published (Nelson and Kehoe 1990). Mesoamericanists' work "engendering archaeology" saw print in 1988 as *The Role of Gender in Precolumbian Art and Architecture*, edited by Virginia Miller. And most obviously, Marija Gimbutas's explicitly gendered *The Goddesses and Gods of Old Europe* had been published in 1974 (second edition, 1982). There was, in 1986, no "defined circle of experts" on archaeological identification of gender roles in prehistoric societies, but there were a number of concerned researchers.

Ironically, it was in the landmark volume *The Socio-Politics of Archaeology*, co-edited by Gero (Gero, Lacy, and Blakey 1983), that Wobst and Keene described "Archaeological Explanation as Political Economy" (Wobst and Keene 1983). They emphasized the "superb fit" of precisely the research for which Conkey is noted with the "political economy" of the profession of archaeology, describing the strategy she used, of selecting "the Paleolithic of the periglacial Upper Pleistocene," as likely "[t]o be particularly successful . . . in achiev[ing] control . . . [and causing] other archaeologists . . . to have become enmeshed within a cone of dependence, deference, and predetermination where before they had enjoyed relative explanatory independence." The greater one's success in this political economy, they state, "the higher will be one's citation count" (Wobst and Keene 1983, 82–84). Gero and Conkey invited "researchers who had a solid and demonstrated working knowledge either of specific classes of archaeological data (e.g. ceramics, botanical remains, shellfish) and/or of particular perspectives in prehistory (e.g. complex hunter-gatherers, early agricultural societies)" (Gero and Conkey 1991, xii). Exactly as Wobst and Keene outline (1983, 81–82), this strategy toward control of a career field chooses "classificatory behavior" (cf. Reiss 1982) from which "a series of statements is then contrived." How this constrains archaeological research and interpretation is confessed, in the Gero and Conkey volume, by Ruth Tringham, "My wish to retain respectability and credibility as a scientific archaeologist was stronger than my motivation to consider gender relations" (Tringham 1991, 95). Conkey elsewhere (1991, 111–12) cites Wobst and Keene's paper to explain archaeologists' obsession with "origins," but seems not to recognize the reflections of the strategy they outline in her own career.

What must be foregrounded in our discussions of feminist critiques and gender-focused research in archaeology is the fundamental issue of alternative discourses (Haraway 1991, 147; Wobst 1989). The "cone" strategy of commandeering discourse that Conkey discusses very well, if not reflexively, in her 1991 article is an exclusionary maneuver useful in the maintenance of dominance. From the perspective of outsider jurisprudence, who dominates—white upper-class male or white upper-class female—is beside the point. We can reject the hierarchy of dominance, the "defined circle of experts," in toto. We can reject the early-modern Western worldview with its insistence on a monolithic centered discourse, and in its place, stipulate the kind of decentered, multiplex, dynamic interplay congruent with modern evolutionary biology and physics. We should assert the validity and viability of "emergent, differentiating, self-representing, contradictory social subjectivities, with their claims on action, knowledge, and belief," as Haraway (1991, 147) passionately urges. Not a canonical literature, but a praxis of research and stimulating discussion, an "archaeology of humans" (Wylie 1991, 22) should be the goal nourished by a feminist consciousness.

Back in the beginning of archaeology as a professional discipline, Sir John Lubbock pursued the strategy for hegemonic control, omitting citation of work he plagiarized in his establishment of the canon for prehistory (Kehoe 1991a). Lubbock was a member of a small self-selected dining club of men openly plotting the takeover of the Royal Society, and in chronicling this group, historian Ruth Barton (1990, 72, 81) remarks, "The X-Club devoted enormous energy to gaining power. It is less clear what the Club did with this power: the records are patchy [but] . . . the greatest symbolic achievement of the X-Club was . . . a conflation of science, church and state," no less! Anthropology, even archaeology, are not the spinning-out of truth within ivory towers. From Asad (1973), Leacock (Etienne and Leacock 1980; Leacock and Safa 1986), and the burgeoning wave they set in motion in social anthropology, through the more recent reflective studies in archaeology (e.g., Fowler 1987; Hinsley 1981; Kehoe 1985, 1989, Kristiansen 1981, 1985; Schávelzon 1988), the clear connection between the practice of mainstream anthropology and service to the dominant class in Western states has been amply, though far from exhaustively, demonstrated. In his brilliant critique of the New Archaeology, Gibbon (1989, 180) concluded "that archaeology is a more uncertain, open, challenging and perhaps anxiety-ridden enterprise than our positivist heritage has indicated."

An outsider archaeology above all recognizes the severely pauperized nature of the archaeological record. In the best of preservation conditions, we have no more than the material residue of behavior. Every such trace is a privileged key, a lesson we have slowly absorbed as researchers have demonstrated the power of flotation and refitting techniques, using minute organic remains and stone flakes not only to obtain knowledge of human behavior in the past, but also to refine our knowledge of taphonomic processes affecting sites. Another lesson, more painful, demands that we archaeologists, as scientists, stringently distinguish between our observations and our inferences from them. The distinction is between *syntagm* and *paradigm* (Ardener 1971; Kehoe 1991b, 430), what actually appears in the archaeological record and the labels we then supply—for to name is to categorize, to link into conceptualized classes. Here, when phenomena are recognized as data and identified as constituents of known behavior, is the consequential moment for the archaeologist intent on liberating the discipline from its racist, elitist chauvinism.

Opening our practice to outsiders' labeling, outsiders' paradigms, is certainly inviting anxiety. Brumbach and Jarvenpa, for example, admit (1990, 41) that the local informant may prove to be a "'wild card' who may provide information that is unexpected and unforeseen in any research design." Their experience collaborating on sites with Chipewyan and Cree residents of the district moved them to realize how much of anthropological tradition is, as they put it, our own "folklore." They learned that "obvious" landscapes, parameters of sites, and tool types looked otherwise to the people whose families had occupied the lands. Their comfort in knowing what they had mastered through years of academic study shattered under the teaching of their Indian collaborators. Two "cultural grammars" were available, the academic and the Indian. The archaeologists became translators, compelled to accept their collaborators' well-sustained identifications and compelled also to correlate these with the accustomed discourse of colleagues within the discipline.

A good example of archaeological folklore is the practice of labeling bifacially flaked, symmetrical pointed stone artifacts "projectile points": the tradition goes back to the nineteenth-century beginnings of our discipline, when "savages" were envisioned leading short, nasty, and brutish lives, constantly defending themselves from fearful beasts. A century and a half later, we can identify artifact usage from techniques of edge-wear analysis and lithic reduction processes, yet it remains common at professional meetings to see slides of artifacts casually labeled "projectile points" when many appear to be knives or reworked implements. The consequences are more than a neglect of information on artifact functions; since most bifacially flaked stone artifacts lie in or near habitation remains, it would be most parsimonious to infer that they were knives and that they represent the tools of women processing food and raw materials. The conventional label "projectile point," elicited from gross morphology of the artifact, links into the paradigm "hunter," normally construed as male. In effect, archaeological convention peoples the past with men and robs women of their artifacts (Bird 1988).

The grand gesture of embedding quotes from designated muted classes in our dominant discourse will neither absolve us from the moral obligation to listen, nor assist us toward deeper understanding of our species and ourselves. As scholars, we must resist control by favored schools of research, their mapped-out modes of discourse and quoting circles, as earnestly as we seek to uncover field data. Pure science is a virgin mother: either a miracle unlikely to be met in our lives or a chimera. Cold appraisal of the lovely vision is discomfiting but necessary if we are not to simply replace one elite group with another politically astute privileged X-Club.

Conclusion

When we as anthropologists struggle to throw off the shackles of tradition, to hear the muted groups, to see the obscured, we are fighting for the recognition of human worth to which Franz Boas committed his energies. Let us remember that in 1919, the traditionalists nearly cast out Boas from the American Anthropological Association (Pinsky 1988). Woman or man, we as anthropologists betray the best of our discipline if we blindly hew to the imperialist doctrines still embedded in the theories and only slowly fading from the practice of mainstream anthropology. We who are women particularly should engage in the historically sensitive, emic anthropology developed by Boas and his colleagues, so many of whom were, because of him, women. Women are supposed to listen; we, and then men who will stand with us among the heterogeneous multitude, can open opportunities for collaboration with our fellows from diverse backgrounds. We can listen to those who will speak among the myriad, and present the worlds of a variety of cultural traditions, not as singly definitive, but as multidimensional. There are galaxies outside our own, and we can see them if we subdue the blinding glare of Western positivist structures.

Boas was an outsider. I think we might, following Matsuda and Rob Williams, say we are engaged in outsider anthropology. We risk never getting prestigious positions, seldom getting cited, seldom invited to participate in popular symposia, but outsiders do get to meet some of the world's most interesting and admirable people. After all, outsiders are by far the largest component of the population of planet Earth.

NOTES

This article was originally printed in Exploring Gender Through Archaeology, Prehistory Press, 1992.

1. Eller had asked me, although we were not acquainted, to vet the archaeological material in her manuscript. To my pleased surprise, she had mastered the relevant material; I found only two, very minor, bits to correct. The book is a strong contribution to feminist anthropology.

2. Originally published in 1972 as "Belief and the Problem of Women," in *The Interpretation of Ritual: Essays in Honour of A.I.Richards*, edited by Jean La Fontaine. London: Tavistock. Note: A. I. Richards was Audrey Richards. Wikipedia states, "Though she was widely regarded for her academic accomplishments, Richards never held a chair in anthropology." The entry then lists administrative and Reader positions, and that she was the first woman elected President of the Royal Anthropological Society, 1964–65. https://en.wikipedia.org/wiki/Audrey_Richards#Academic_career, accessed 6/11/23.

3. Full disclosure: The students had invited Robert Hall, but he wasn't able to attend at the time. He recommended that they invite me in his place. They did, warning me that my presentation would not be published because I was not on their planned list. No matter, it was my first conference abroad, first visit to Cambridge, and eye-opening to meet and hear these young scholars hatching out of their student nest.

4. https://www.therai.org.uk/archives-and-manuscripts/manuscript-contents/0189-anthropological-institute-of-great-britain-and-ireland-wellcome-medal-ms-189?highlight=WyJ3ZWxsY29tZSIsIndlbGxjb21lJyJd, accessed 6/10/23.

5. In Conkey's own research specialty, none other than the revered doyen l'Abbé Breuil published in 1949 a series of views of a remarkably gendered prehistory where women can be seen doing many activities they are later denied by modern archaeologists. Perhaps his experiences with one of his most eminent pupils, Dorothy Garrod (Boyle et al. 1963), raised his consciousness of the importance of prominently considering gender roles in human history. Perhaps we are seeing the quiet influence of Miss Mary Boyle, the Abbé's constant companion.

REFERENCES

Albers, Patricia and Beatrice Medicine, eds. 1983. *The Hidden Half.* Washington DC: University Press of America.

Ardener, Edwin. 1971. "The New Anthropology and Its Critics." *Man* 6:449–67.

———. 1975. "The 'Problem' Revisited." In *Perceiving Women,* edited by Shirley Ardener, 19–27. London: Malaby.

Ardener, Shirley. 1978. "Introduction." In *Defining Females,* edited by Shirley Ardener, 9–48. New York: John Wiley and Sons.

Asad, Talal, ed. 1973. *Anthropology and the Colonial Encounter.* London: Ithaca Press.

Barnes, Barry. 1977. *Interests and the Growth of Knowledge.* London: Routledge and Kegan Paul.

Barton, Ruth. 1990. "An Influential Set of Chaps: The X-Club and Royal Society Politics 1864–85." *British Journal of the History of Science* 23:53–81.

Berthong, Donald. 1989. "Berthong Speaks." *Meeting Ground* 21:3–4. Chicago: D'Arcy McNickle Center for the History of the American Indian/The Newberry Library.

Bird, Caroline. 1988. "Woman the Toolmaker." Paper presented at the Stone Tool Conference, University of New England, Armidale, Australia.

Bourdieu, Pierre. 1977. *Outline of a Theory of Practice.* Translated by Richard Nice. Cambridge: Cambridge University Press.

Boyle, Mary, Dorothy Garrod, M. C. Burkitt, Henry Field, Kenneth Oakley, and Glyn Daniel. 1963. "Recollections of the Abbé Breuil." *Antiquity* 37 (145): 12–18.

Breuil, Henri. 1949. *Beyond the Bounds of History.* Translated by Mary E. Boyle. London: P. R. Gawthorn.

Brumbach, Hetty Jo, and Robert Jarvenpa. 1990. "Archaeologist-Ethnographer-Informant Relations: The Dynamics of Ethnoarchaeology in the Field." In *Powers of Observation: Alternative Views in Archaeology,* edited by Sarah Nelson and Alice Kehoe, 39–46. Washington DC: Archeological Papers of the American Anthropological Association, No. 2.

Christenson, Andrew L. 1989. "Introduction." In *Tracing Archaeology's Past: The Historiography of Archaeology,* edited by A. L. Christenson, 75–77. Carbondale: Southern Illinois University Press.

Conkey, Margaret W. 1991. "Original Narratives." In *Gender at the Crossroads of Knowledge,* edited by Micaela di Leonardo, 102–39. Berkeley: University of California Press.

Cribb, Roger L. D. 1980. Comment on Eugene L. Sterud's "Changing Aims in American Archaeology: A Citation Analysis of *American Antiquity.*" *American Antiquity* 45 (2): 352–54.

Daniel, Glyn, ed. 1981. *Towards a History of Archaeology.* London: Thames and Hudson.

Etienne, Mona, and Eleanor Leacock, eds. 1980. *Women and Colonialization.* New York: Praeger.

Fowler, Don. 1987. "Uses of the Past. Archaeology in Service to the State." *American Antiquity* 52:229–48.

Frank, Francine Wattman, and Paula A. Treichler. 1989, *Language, Gender, and Professional Writing*. New York: The Modern Language Association of America.

Gero, Joan M., David M. Lacy, and Michael L. Blakey, eds. 1983. *The Socio-Politics of Archaeology*. Amherst: Research Report Number 23, Department of Anthropology, University of Massachusetts-Amherst.

Gero, Joan M., and Margaret W. Conkey, eds. 1991. *Engendering Archaeology*. Oxford: Basil Blackwell.

Gibbon, Guy. 1989. *Explanation in Archaeology*. Oxford: Basil Blackwell.

Gimbutas, Marija. 1974. *The Gods and Goddesses of Old Europe: 7000–3500 BC*. Berkeley: University of California Press.

Goodale, Jane C. 1971. *Tiwi Wives*. Seattle: University of Washington Press.

Grene, Marjorie. 1986. "In and On Friendship." In *Human Nature and Natural Knowledge*, edited by Alan Donagan, Anthony N. Perovich, Jr., and Michael V. Wedin, 355–68. Dordrecht: D. Reidel.

Haraway, Donna J. 1991. *Simians, Cyborgs, and Women*. New York: Routledge.

Hinsley, Curtis M., Jr. 1981. *Savages and Scientists*. Washington DC: Smithsonian Institution Press.

Jennings, Francis. 1975. *The Invasion of America*. Chapel Hill: University of North Carolina Press.

Kehoe, Alice B. 1981. "Revisionist Anthropology: Aboriginal North America." *Current Anthropology* 22 (5): 503–9, 515–17.

———. 1983. "The Shackles of Tradition." In *The Hidden Half*, edited by Patricia Albers and Beatrice Medicine, 53–73. Washington DC: University Press of America.

———. 1985. "The Ideological Paradigm in Traditional American Ethnology." In *Social Contexts of American Ethnology, 1840–1984*, edited by June Helm, 41–49. Washington DC: American Ethnological Society.

———. 1989. "Contextualizing Archaeology." In *Tracing Archaeology's Past*, edited by Andrew Christenson, 97–106. Carbondale: Southern Illinois University Press.

———. 1991a. "The Invention of Prehistory." *Current Anthropology* 32:467–76.

———. 1991b. "The Weaver's Wraith." In *The Archaeology of Gender*, edited by Dale Walde and Noreen Willows, 430–35. Calgary: University of Calgary Archaeological Association.

Keur, Dorothy. 1941. *Big Bead Mesa*. Society for American Archaeology Memoir 1. Menasha: Society for American Archaeology.

Kornfeld, Marcel, ed. 1991. *Approaches to Gender Processes on the Great Plains*. Plains Anthropological Society, Memoir 26.

Kristiansen, Kristian. 1981. "A Social History of Danish Archaeology." In *Towards a History of Archaeology*, edited by Glyn Daniel, 20–44. London: Thames and Hudson.

————. 1985. *Archaeological Formation Processes*. Lyngby: Nationalmuseet.

Leacock, Eleanor, and Helen I. Safa, eds. 1986. *Women's Work: Development and the Division of Labor by Gender*. South Hadley MA: Bergin and Garvey.

Lewis, Thomas M. N., and Madeline Kneberg. 1941. *Prehistory of Chickamauga Basin in Tennessee*. Knoxville: Tennessee Anthropological Papers No. 1. University of Tennessee

Matsuda, Mari. 1989. "Public Responses to Racist Speech: Considering the Victim's Story." *Michigan Law Review* 87:2320–23.

Macpherson, C. B. 1962. *The Political Theory of Possessive Individualism: Hobbes to Locke*. Oxford: Oxford University Press.

Miller, Virginia E., ed. 1988. *The Role of Gender in Precolumbian Art and Architecture*. Washington DC: University Press of America.

Nelson, Sarah M., and Alice B. Kehoe, eds. 1990. *Powers of Observation: Alternative Views in Archeology*. Washington DC: Archeological Papers of the American Anthropological Association, Number 2.

Pinsky, Valerie. 1988. "Archaeology, Politics, and Boundary-formation: The Boas Censure (1919) and the Development of American Archaeology During the Inter-war Years." Paper presented at the first International Summer Institute in the Philosophy and History of Science, Berlin.

Reiss, Timothy J. 1982. *The Discourse of Modernism*. Ithaca: Cornell University Press.

Rossiter, Margaret W. 1982. *Women Scientists in America*. Baltimore: The Johns Hopkins University Press.

Ryan, Jake, and Charles Sackrey, eds. 1984. *Strangers in Paradise*. Boston: South End Press.

Schávelzon, Daniel. 1988. "Las Excavaciónes en Zaculeu (1946–1950): Una Aproximación al Analisis de la Relación entre Arqueología y Politica en América Latina." In *Recent Studies in Pre-columbian Archaeology*, edited by Nicholas J. Saunders and Olivier de Montmollion, 167–90. Oxford: BAR International Series 421.

Spector, Janet. 1983. "Male/Female Task Differentiation among Hidatsa: Toward the development of an Archaeological Approach to the Study of Gender." In *The Hidden Half*, edited by Patricia Albers and Beatrice Medicine, 77–99. Washington DC: University Press of America.

Spector, Janet, and Mary Whelan. 1989. "Incorporating Gender into Archaeology Courses." In *Gender and Anthropology*, edited by Sandra Morgen, 65–94. Washington DC: American Anthropological Association.

Trigger, Bruce G. 1980. "Archaeology and the Image of the American Indian." *American Antiquity* 45:662–76.

Tringham, Ruth E. 1991. "Households with Faces: the Challenge of Gender in Prehistoric Architectural Remains." In *Engendering Archaeology: Women and Prehistory*, edited by Joan M. Gero and Margaret W. Conkey, 93–131. Oxford: Basil Blackwell.

Weiner, Annette. 1976. *Women of Value, Men of Renown*. Austin: University of Texas Press.

Willey, Gordon R., and Jeremy A. Sabloff. 1980. *A History of American Archaeology*. San Francisco: W. H. Freeman.

Williams, Joan C. 1989. "Deconstructing Gender." *Michigan Law Review* 87:797–845.

Williams, Robert A., Jr. 1987. "Taking Rights Aggressively: The Perils and Promise of Critical Legal Theory for Peoples of Color." *Law and Inequality* 5:103–34.

Wobst, H. Martin. 1989. "Commentary: a Socio-politics of Socio-politics in Archaeology." In *Critical Traditions in Contemporary Archaeology*, edited by Valerie Pinsky and Alison Wylie, 136–40. Cambridge: Cambridge University Press.

Wobst, H. Martin, and Arthur S. Keene. 1983. "Archaeological Explanation as Political Economy." In *The Socio-Politics of Archaeology*, edited by Joan M. Gero, David M. Lacy and Michael L. Blakey, 79–89. Amherst: Research Report Number 23, Department of Anthropology, University of Massachusetts-Amherst.

Wylie, Alison. 1991. "Feminist Critiques and Archaeological Challenges." In *The Archaeology of Gender*, edited by Dale Walde and Noreen Willows, 17–23. Calgary: Archaeological Association of the University of Calgary.

PART 5. The Themes that Bind

Fundamentally, the power to succeed in American archaeology lay in accepting Manifest Destiny. Accepting that WASP invaders were fulfilling the destiny decreed by their Creator as they superseded First Nations, accepting that their Creator had caused their Civilization to evolve beyond any others. Normal science in American archaeology assigned sites to bands, tribes, or chiefdoms, unmapped, foraging, illiterate, and animistic. As John Locke had explained in 1689 (Kehoe 2009), their labor had no value.

White Patriarchy wasn't perceived; like fishes in water, archaeologists were enveloped in it. Nancy Lurie, who became the American Anthropological Association's president in 1984, was mentored by W. C. McKern, archaeologist and then director of Milwaukee Public Museum, ever since her father brought her as a young girl to the museum on Saturdays. After she finished her PhD as McKern had advised, she applied for a curator position in the museum. When she walked into his office to discuss her application, he burst out, "Nancy! The curator position! A woman! NO!"[1]

Archaeology was popularly seen as a rich man's pursuit, not a job. Year after year my students' parents would tell me, "I wanted to be an archaeologist, but of course I had to earn a living." Until the midcentury explosion of students with the G. I. Bill, few colleges or universities offered majors in anthropology, and fewer still the PhD. Some that did refused to advance women and non-white men beyond the MA degree; this was still happening in the 1980s. Very few Jews became archaeologists, perhaps in part because until 1951, the Ivy League schools had a quota of not more than 15% of their undergraduates could be Jews. American archaeology was a cocoon. Its pupae lived in a racist, segregated society where Manifest Destiny felt obviously true.

When the Cold War followed America's glorious victories in 1945, General Eisenhower warned of the military-industrial complex devoted to the hard sciences that had created their munitions and factories. In vain: Los Alamos's white men scientists led the creation of a National Science Foundation that would dominate scientific research in the United States for the rest of the century. Numbers, measurements, statistics—hard masculine "things"—prevailed over interpretations based on historical data. The University of Michigan dominated American archaeology from Leslie White teaching that counting joules controlled by humans revealed the evolution of civilization, Albert Spaulding insisting that statistics' results were more reliable than human judgment, through Elman Service explaining the clear progress, in numbers of people organized, from small bands through tribes and chiefdoms to states. Grant proposals to NSF by men, couched in hypothesis-deductive method with measurable results, were funded. These successful white men earned tenure, supervised students, recommended, or did not recommend, applicants to their colleagues.

For two generations, this was academic American archaeology. Neither professors nor students recognized the dogma. John Yellen, director of archaeology at NSF, heard Joan Gero expose the blatant bias against women in grant funding, had her analysis checked, promised to rectify the injustice, and forty years later, nothing of this had changed except Gero's death. The Cold War waned. Currents from the underclasses swelled: President Nixon created a bill that in 1975 made clear the sovereignties of both parties to U. S. treaties with First Nations. Desegregation and affirmative action opened mainstream schools and employment to non-whites, and academic archaeology slowly was swamped by culture resource management companies. The tipping point was NAGPRA. Academic archaeology could no longer take for granted that WASP Manifest Destiny had (of course) overcome the primitive race.

With the new millennium came women, Indians, Blacks, Latin American immigrants' children, Asian Americans, and working-class whites. CRM needed staff. We could say that capitalism broke down the class-based power of traditional American archaeology. "Heritage management" replaced "cultural resource management" as the tag for the business, moving it from something to be mined to a humanities box. After a quarter century, students assumed that of course they would be collaborating with the communities around sites or their descendants. Meanwhile in the ivy towers, administrators cut staff and budgets, demanded faculty bring in outside funds, moved libraries of books to distant storage and laboratory support to the remunerative sciences. Tall white men remained disproportionately full professors, for it takes a generation for change to appear. Meanwhile, a CRM company owner and then a Choctaw Nation citizen were elected presidents of the Society for American Archaeology, an Asian-American woman became its Executive Director, and women predominated its board. Power slowly has shifted in American archaeology from academic WASPs with a Y chromosome to a wider range of employments and families of origin. Power in archaeology had to acknowledge the power of capitalism as it shifted from industrialism to commerce and tourism.

What About Truth?

Alison Wylie, our only dedicated philosopher of archaeology, published an essay, "The Interpretive Dilemma," in 1989 in *Critical Traditions in Contemporary Archaeology*, edited by herself and Valerie Pinsky. The two were young women from North America studying at Oxford and Cambridge, respectively. Experience on both sides of the Atlantic honed their skill in comparing standpoints and theories; Wylie built a career in philosophy of science that in 2011 carried her to the presidency of the American Philosophical Society. Pinsky, tragically, fell victim to a degenerate disease not long after she earned her doctorate, cutting short her promising work in history of American archaeology.[2]

Wylie's essay firmly established her position as a very well-informed and balanced critic of archaeological interpretive work. Neither Kuhnian "paradigms" nor efforts to deduce general regularities ("laws") sufficiently encompass the empirical data out there:

> [Archaeologists can] play evidential and conceptual resources off against one another in a way that may not guarantee convergence on a single truth but can provide grounds for assessing the degrees of plausibility and for rejecting (sometimes decisively) a good many alternatives. (Wylie 2002, 126)

Truth and power are often Janus-like: two faces of a single purpose. Persons focused on achieving power seem often to claim, and to apparently even believe, that they glimpse Truth. Their bounden duty is to reveal the Truth they have grasped. Plausibility is not enough, implausibility may not be enough; it is authority that supports Truth. Authority resides in offices, entwined with money and decision-making. Who is appointed to office depends upon tradition, reflecting cultural values. Those who do not manifest the criteria will be muted.

Among my excursions outside archaeology has been research into, first, Scientific Creationism and expanding from that, militant Christianity. In the 1970s, opposition to teaching organic evolution in school biology courses revived among conservative Christian churches. Local school boards were charged to eliminate evolution from curricula. In a suburb of Milwaukee, newly elected members of the school board planned to introduce a resolution to forbid teaching evolution as true. Several anthropologists in Milwaukee, myself included, carpooled to the evening open meeting of this school board, prepared to testify against the resolution. Four new board members were formally inducted, vowing to uphold the Constitution of the United States. Then they introduced their resolution. Not long before, a court case had been decided against such restrictions as contravening Constitutional freedom of speech and separation of church and state. This was brought up by a man in the audience who identified himself as a lawyer resident in the town. He declared that the resolution was clearly unconstitutional, and he would file a lawsuit against the board if they approved the restriction. That ended the attempt to mute Darwin.

For me, it was naked irrationality when these literate citizens, who surely had seen the Constitution while in school, proposed to curtail freedom of speech and exercise of personal beliefs. This wasn't the Deep South; these were not rural, uneducated people. Anthropologists had begun to organize against these efforts to impose religious beliefs upon the public. Laurie Godfrey, a biological anthropologist who had studied with evolutionary biologist Stephen Jay Gould, organized a session at an American Anthropological Association annual meeting about this rising threat to our teaching what the sciences of biology, geology, and paleontology had so well established as empirically founded and broadly consistent. Godfrey developed the session into an edited book, *Scientists Confront Creationism*, with leading evolutionary biologists explaining the strengths of their work. I contributed a chapter (Kehoe 1983b) on the culture of the Fundamentalist Christians who opposed the concept of organic evolution, maintaining it contravened the Word of their God. Other Christians, including in 1986 the Roman Catholic Church, reconciled the Bible with science by premising that God had instituted organic evolution.

The ethnography I did in local Fundamentalist churches was sometimes shocking; in most of the churches, men had the power roles, and women prepared food or provided music. After I retired from teaching, I researched more deeply, publishing in 2012 *Militant Christianity*, about the far-right Christian groups that later supported Donald Trump's MAGA campaigns. Make America Great Again by selling guns, denying marriage to same-sex couples, forbidding abortion, and so on—not least was opening huge areas of federal land to oil and gas exploitation, regardless of First Nations' traditional holy sites. These years of trying to understand truth claims based not so much on faith as on patriarchal authority, and excluding wider communities, made clear also how much of mainstream American archaeology accepted similar authority.[3]

An interesting insight into the issue of Truth is in Steven Gimbel's *Einstein's Jewish Science* (2012). Gimbel is a philosopher of science who had written a biography of René Descartes and a study of one of Einstein's supporters. He cites Robert Merton (born Meyer Robert Schkolnick) for arguing that the "scientific revolution" in the seventeenth century was led by Protestants rebelling against the Catholic Church's declarations of infallibility (Gimbel 2012, 4–5), and quotes Albert Einstein himself stating that "Jewish people" manifest their intellectual heritage in their interpretations, "what they think" (Gimbel 2012, 4). Gimbel's book, and correspondence we had, supported the critical stance my parents held as Jews against our dominant Christian society. It led me to look seriously at the secular Jewish culture, politically Social Democrat, in which Felix and Lucy Kramer Cohen[4] were immersed, how it led the Cohens to create the radical 1934 Indian New Deal, the 1941 *Handbook of Federal Indian Law*, and the legislation for the Indian Claims Commission. Felix Cohen was a leader of the Legal Pluralism approach to jurisprudence that denies that laws should be fixed and immutable (Tsuk Mitchell 2007).

Anti-Semitism is significant in understanding the history of American archaeology, because it was the often-unremarked background[5] to opposition to Franz Boas and his program for anthropology. Pinsky noted in discussing his 1919 censure, "The fact that Boas was Jewish, and *although not publicly acknowledged*, anti-semitism was rife during this time" (Pinsky 1992, 169, my italics). Boas, an immigrant, a Jew, a pacifist, and above all, a man determined to undermine eugenics policies by scientifically demonstrating that many "racial" criteria are environmentally malleable, was targeted for years by the WASP Eugenics Society, led by wealthy Madison Grant. Jews were seen as such a threat to America that the Ivy League universities limited enrollment of Jews to no more than fifteen percent of undergraduate classes (Synnott 1979). Grant and his lieutenants engineered the 1919 censure of Boas by the American Anthropological Association, abetted by the staff of the Bureau of American Ethnology, minus James Mooney, who was not informed of the scheme (Spiro 2008, 316–19). Removing Boas meant that he would no longer serve as anthropology representative on the National Research Council, prompting W. H. Holmes, chief of the Bureau from 1902–1909, to write to Smithsonian Secretary Charles Walcott,

> A new chairman of the [National Research] Council must be selected and it is most important that he should not be of the Hebrew kind. . . . [Clark Wissler] is . . . a two-faced Jew of the most cunning variety and an understudy of Boas (Secretary's Correspondence, Box 62, Folder 1–2, National Anthropological Archives).[6]

Wissler was WASP, descended through seven generations from a Massachusetts Bay Colony family.

In spite of the preponderance of WASPs in American archaeology, Boasian concepts of culture were accepted in the profession (Trigger 2006, 278–79), enabling American archaeology to be housed in departments of anthropology. Fundamentally, it was that "American Indians" were colonized, therefore archaeology of their sites should be in departments dealing with ethnographies of colonized peoples. Archaeology of literate nations resided in classical archaeology and art history departments, entirely separate from American archaeology (Trigger 2006, 216). Professionally, this produced the parallel organizations Archaeological Institute of America and Society for American Archaeology, the former founded in 1879 by wealthy collectors of classical antiquities, and the latter in 1934 largely in response to the huge increase in archaeological excavations produced by Roosevelt's New Deal program of thereby providing employment for laborers. AIA, in a *noblesse oblige* spirit, sponsors over a hundred local societies who host lectures by professionals, many working in Mediterranean classical archaeology, while SAA is organized as the professional organization for archaeologists, principally working in the Americas. In the mid-1980s, the president of AIA proposed to the president of SAA that the two meet jointly; SAA's president rejected the proposition although many SAA members, including the two presidents who succeeded that one, attended the Archaeological Congress that AIA organized in 1989.

Social class intertwines with religious affiliations, ethnic ties, and misogyny in American archaeology. None of these factors are normally considered or discussed in histories of American archaeology, except by Thomas Patterson, an avowed and well-read Marxist (Patterson, e.g., 1995, 2003, 2022). My own research on Daniel Wilson and the formation of "prehistoric" archaeology (Kehoe 1998) revealed it came from a matrix of Scottish middle-class reform politics, arguing for meritocracy instead of aristocracy. Daniel Wilson carried the politics as well as the practice of archaeology without documents to Canada when his merits could not win him a suitable position in Edinburgh. In Edinburgh, as in Boston, the wealthy wanted the relics of classical Greece, Rome, and Egypt, while Wilson and his sponsors insisted patriotically that Scotland's lithics, sherds, and tumuli should be displayed in its National Museum. In America, the class distinction is magnificently exhibited by a pair of museums abutting Central Park: on the east side, fronting on the mansions of the very rich, is the Metropolitan Museum of Art, and on the west side, in a middle-class neighborhood, is the American Museum of Natural History, where the art of American First Nations is displayed along with whale skeletons and dinosaurs.

Manifest Destiny vs. Historical Sciences

A world structured by hierarchical, oppressive social divisions . . .
becomes a world of unbridgeable epistemic solitudes.—Wylie 2012, 47

Standpoint matters, Wylie insists. She cites feminist scholar Nancy Hartsock's Marxist analysis, that "Those who must sell their labor, who lack control of the means of production and must navigate a class-structured world from a position of relative powerlessness, have direct experience of social realities that those in positions of structural advantage can ignore, and that are systematically obscured by a dominant ideology that serves to legitimate exploitative relations" (Wylie 2012, her summary of Hartsock's work).

My standpoint is clear. I do not apologize for it and have described my experiences that formed it (Kehoe 2022). I have also sought to understand the background and the experiences of American archaeologists who have ignored or rejected my work. Here, I will divide my observations into the question of Truth, and the question of Power: that "noble dream" of objective Truth, as historian Peter Novick (1987) saw it, and those exercises of power ranging from muting to brutal sexual assault. The social reality I have lived has never permitted me to occupy a position of power; at the same time, living "out on the tundra in the chilly climate" has afforded views of practice unconstrained by clique boundaries.

Bruce Trigger, in his magisterial *History of Archaeological Thought* (2006),[7] analyzes the post–World War II break between traditional "culture-historical" archaeology and the New Archaeology aiming to make the discipline "scientific." Not bamboozled by those claims of "science," Trigger saw the resurgence of a nineteenth-century "readiness . . . to believe that there was a pattern to human history and that technological progress was the key to human betterment." He saw the prosperity and international power enjoyed by Britain and Western Europe in their imperial epoch in the nineteenth century and by the United States following World War II, promoting this confidence in unilinear evolution toward Western Civilization (Trigger 2006, 386–87). The leader was Leslie White at the University of Michigan. His key was $C=ExT$, Culture equals Energy times Technology. Trigger, familiar with Marxism, stated firmly that White did not find this in Marxism; instead he reflected the zeitgeist of most Americans (Trigger 2006, 388).

I corresponded with two University of Michigan graduates who espoused cultural evolutionism, one who was in the heyday of G. I. Bill vets, the second in the next contingent in the 1970s. Each generously reconsidered his assumptions and what prompted them. The older man was Robert Carneiro (1927–2020), who received his PhD from Michigan in 1957. We exchanged letters in 2001, with a brief hiatus when the 9/11 attack on Manhattan kept Bob from his Lower Manhattan apartment for two weeks. All who knew him attest that Carneiro was friendly and helpful to younger colleagues, and that included even women. In his final letter, Carneiro concluded that a significant factor in his theoretical work was his experience, as a Catholic boy, of the hierarchy of authority in that church, from Pope down to his father. Hierarchy was everywhere; it was exclusively male (explicitly patriarchal in the Church); men contested for it, men fought for territory. Carneiro's well-known theoretical argument was that expanding populations led to war over circumscribed territories, the wars necessitating male leadership that became entrenched in hierarchically-controlled states (Carneiro 1970). There is a Malthusian flavor to this; Carneiro labeled his theory "ecological" and saw it answering the question of "*the* origin of *the* state" (Carneiro 1970, 733, my italics). "State" is a taxon that evolved inevitably, given the ecological circumstances he identified; male hierarchies are one feature of this taxon. Although Carneiro came to realize that these hierarchies seemed "natural" to him because they pervaded his world, he did not, in our correspondence, abandon the premise of a general rule deduced from a congeries of data.

This premise, taught by Leslie White and pushed by Lewis Binford as the hypothetic-deductive method of science, its aim being general rules, has outlasted Binford. My correspondence with a Michigan graduate a generation younger than Carneiro elicited an acknowledgment that "chiefdoms" might not be as pervasive as assumed since the 1970s, but that as abstract a concept as "power" can be observed and analyzed. This is an ontological position. In contrast to Carneiro, earlier, this younger American worries about power grabs, how power over others develops in human histories. Marshall Sahlins taught this generation of Michigan students not the simplistic mechanical power of harnessed energy, $C=ExT$, but to look at the manifestations of power over others in colorful societies such as Hawai'i. Those islands, inhabited so late in human history, originally had only a few settlers,[8] then expanded throughout all feasibly agricultural land. Why did the families permit a few to rule them? Why did they craft gorgeous headdresses and feather cloaks for the rulers? One can call them chiefs or kings, chiefdoms or kingdoms, from the point of view of seeking universals in human behavior—what is seen in Hawai'i can be seen in classical archaeology and many histories. *Does that make "chiefdoms" the manifestation of an evolutionary process?*

Back we go to basic science—empirical data. Data sit there, humans observe them, and some humans, intrigued by similarities and differences, suggest explanations for the apparent similarities and differences. It could be God's intelligent design. It could be Darwin's natural selection operating through Mendel's postulation of heritable elements. It could be fortuitous accumulations of compatible genes and mutations, on which natural selection *sometimes* operated (Kemp 2015 is a fascinating exposition of this view). Evolution is a graspable concept for bringing together vast amounts of data from all time and throughout the planet, the better to organize resources, sustain habitats, analyze medical conditions, and so on, and on. Yet it is not *empirical*. It is not a given. It should not be assumed a priori to account for archaeological data. Bruce Trigger characterized the 1960s seminal works by Marshall Sahlins and Elman Service as

> us[ing] ethnographic data to construct speculative, highly generalized sequences of unilinear development . . . the assumption that the greater selective fitness of technologically advanced societies ensured that progress had characterized cultural change throughout human history. (Trigger 2006, 389)

Exactly as Lewis Morgan said, "The railway train in motion, which may be called the triumph of civilization" ([1877] 1985, 553). From a postcolonial standpoint, even from a feminist standpoint, this postulated cultural evolution is pure Western racism.

"Evolution" persisted as the assumed process underling human history as well as organic changes. As the Cold War and STEM science waned—briefly, as it turned out—with the turn to a new millennium, some archaeologists became uncomfortable with the impersonality of the premised causal factors in cultural evolution, whether ecological adaptation or some inner drive toward overriding that with technology. Roger Green and Patrick Kirch revised their much-earlier article in *Current Anthropology* 28, a formulation of cultural development among Polynesians, explaining:

> Our more modest intention has been to ground the possibilities for evolutionary study within an integrative historical anthropology . . . . history in an evolutionary framework is contingency bound. . . . many and complex historical trajectories . . . condition multiple outcomes. . . . In anthropology, as in any science, history matters (Kirch and Green 2001, 284).

A Standpoint, Not a Contest

E. E. Evans-Pritchard, after working many years to comprehend the rational thinking of some Africans he came to know, taught his students,

> [Social anthropology] interprets rather than explains. The concepts of natural system and natural law, modelled on the constructs of the natural sciences, ... have been responsible for a false scholasticism which has led to one rigid and ambitious formulation after another. ... Released from these essentially philosophical dogmas, [social anthropology] can be really empirical and, in the true sense of the word, scientific. ... The feeling that any discipline that does not aim at formulating laws and hence predicting and planning is not worth the labour of a lifetime ... leads very easily to a misguided ethics, anemic scientific humanism or— Saint-Simon and Comte are cases in point—ersatz religion. (Evans-Pritchard 1963, 26–27)

Strong words.

Why would people *want* to live in a world that works by universal laws? Wait! *What* "people"? *Who* discovers these laws? *Who* says they are universal? Steven Shapin (1994) discovered that early modern Western science, taking shape in the seventeenth century, was markedly class-stratified. Gentlemen organized the Royal Society in England, where men of rank presented scientific data and conclusions to gentlemen. Experiments were set up by technicians employed by the gentlemen, and failures of experiments could be blamed on technicians. Shapin concludes that the apparent democratization of science has been a shift from authority propounded by titled men to authority set in institutions and exercised by their leaders. Professional conferences, like Robert Boyle's "public" demonstrations of his experiments to invited gentlemen in his mansion, are the venues where those titled with the PhD form a highly selective authoritative caucus. Until the late twentieth century, these elite groups did not admit women nor welcome men who were not white Christians. Western science developed within imperial powers imposing their laws throughout the worlds they controlled.

My standpoints, feminist and postcolonial, reveal the Manifest Destiny paradigm that still dominates American archaeology. I can also see the tidal shifts and rip currents that have undermined the dominance of WASP men.[9] The efficient cause has been the 1964 Civil Rights Act, though it took a generation for universities to realize it applied to them, given that their ruling paradigm was that dominance by WASP men is natural. As a generation of girls grew up playing organized sports and were encouraged to become professionals, and overt discrimination in graduate programs became rare, many dominant men saw their legacies could carry on through bright women. At the same time, with CRM providing the best opportunities to do fieldwork, and not requiring more than a master's degree, many men went directly into CRM jobs. Exclusion of women is recognized as illegal, and the shift of men to CRM—a separate movement with perhaps a class basis—seems under the radar.

On a larger ground, the dominance of America the Great's manifest destiny ideology has been supported by a series of rulings by a conservative-majority Supreme Court. On June 29, 2023, the Chief Justice wrote that expressly considering an applicant's race violates the "equal protection" clause in the Constitution. Ironically, that is in the Fourteenth Amendment of 1868, written to enforce the full enjoyment of citizenship to African-Americans. "Race" is a social construct developed by Enlightenment imperialists as they formally justified seizing land from First Nations and forcing a laboring class into unwaged servitude (Horsman 1986). Denying this history reinforces the dominance of the census class "white" and its usually unthinking acceptance of Manifest Destiny. If unilinear cultural evolution is taught to archaeologists, they are pushed into false doctrine and an ignorance of evolutionary biology.

Franz Boas was among the greatest scientists. He understood that the taxa of biologists are classification schemes, not empirically incontrovertible. He understood that to derive general rules, one needs a large sample, and *it is impossible to obtain a sufficiently large sample of humans to support* claims of general laws, other than Malinowski's "biological imperatives" of food, sexual reproduction, shelter, and so forth (1944, 91). Always concerned with sample size, he enlisted members of First Nations communities to be local correspondents recording texts and data to be archived, thus increasing the amount of data that would be available. Clark Wissler followed this for his Blackfoot studies, paying the school-educated David Duvall to interview, record, and commission traditional crafts to be made for the American Museum of Natural History. Frank Speck trained Gladys Tantaquidgeon to curate her Mohegan heritage. Ella Deloria, Archie Phinney, and Zora Neale Hurston were Boas's own students who would go on to work with their communities, Lakota, Nimiipuu, and Southern American Blacks. Additionally, Boas worked to support schools for archaeology to add data from the past. Throughout his forty years teaching at Columbia University, each year his students took his course on statistical theory, many of them twice because of its difficulty (Zumwalt 2022, 54).[10]

I want to emphasize that Boasian anthropology is keenly aware of the effect of limited samples of data. Compare the amount of data available to the Mediterranean classical archaeologist with the amount available to, for example, me working in the northern Prairies. Yet do the classical archaeologists derive general rules or laws from their material? No, they see historical particularities: contingencies hitting longue durée. What struck Stephen Jay Gould and Niles Eldredge so sharply: evolutionary histories show periods of stasis as much, at least, as they show change (Gould 2002, 36–37, 760–61, 1332–34). There are no derived general laws that will predict the actualities.

Historical sciences are fundamentally different from the physical sciences that experiment to find exact conditions that will regularly produce predicted results. You can't engineer human behavior. That would be morally repugnant—right? Not for the social sciences funded by the Rockefeller Foundation for much of the twentieth century (Baker 2022, 32–33). Bernard Barber, who became a well-known sociologist, wrote in Rockefeller's heyday, "The social sciences, like all science, are primarily concerned for analysis, prediction, and control of behavior and values" (1952, 259). This sentence, written in the shadow of Hitler and Stalin, is *fascist* (see Eco 1995). It was written while open anti-Semitism still prevailed in America.

The papers I have included in this volume developed from my formal education in the last years of *de rigueur* four-field Boasian anthropology in Barnard College, Columbia University, and Harvard. Suddenly this basically scientific discipline was assaulted by men insisting that it was unscientific because we were, as Boas scrupulously taught, very cautious in interpreting statistics; because we did not first propose hypotheses before doing fieldwork; because we sought as many data and as much a range of data as humanly possible; because we did not consider proposing general laws to be feasible; and because we did not believe humans belonged to a singular evolutionary series. Boasian anthropology is embodied in Kroeber's massive 1948 textbook, the book I read as a sixteen-year-old girl. It formed me. In the Acknowledgments that follow, I describe the scientists, the thinkers, who substantiated my way of perceiving and thinking.

For most American archaeologists, I am that woman who sees that the Kensington runestone authentically records a party of Scandinavians seeking furs inland in America in 1362. That woman who explains the possibilities and evidence for transoceanic voyages before 1492. That woman who—following leading archaeologists writing before the 1960s—sees a vast maize-growing Nuclear America as a trade ecumene, with Cahokia and Cholula one of its multiplicity of economic relations. Rather annoyingly, I am that woman who writes of First Nations not "tribes," seeing them as practical people not extraordinarily "spiritual." My badge should say: liberal Social Democrat Jewish woman Boasian anthropological archaeologist. Socially, culturally, atypical of American archaeologists. Atypically broadly trained, read, and experienced in histories, sociology, and philosophy of science. These relevant approaches to understanding the practices of mainstream American archaeology highlight its ideological foundation. They also explain why so much of my work has been rejected or ignored. I stand my ground, encouraged by the radical shift to collaboration with First Nations. Recognizing that multiplicities are what historical sciences must deal with, American archaeology should be able to rise out of Manifest Destiny.

NOTES

1. Personal communication with Lurie (1924–2017), an account she enjoyed sharing.
2. Pinsky is a great-granddaughter of Franz Boas. She avoided capitalizing on the connection, while enriching her research with family knowledge. A portion of her research was published (Pinsky 1992). Her dissertation, also 1992, is online, titled *Anthropology and the new archaeology: a critical study of disciplinary change in American archaeology*; https://doi.org/10.17863/CAM.19798.
3. A woman colleague eloquently described senior men in archaeology who similarly maintained dominance: "To maintain his faith that Indigenous people were practicing cultural resistance through the maintenance of deeply imbedded preconquest beliefs and practices, he had to ignore a lot of post-conquest elements in the communities he considered. When other researchers failed to

find those roots, he was sometimes abusive, telling them, and others, that they lacked sensitivity and the ability to see what was there. He crossed disciplinary borders only in limited ways. He was more or less ignorant of the natural sciences, even though he argued for an ecological hypothesis. He had a poor grasp of anything visual. He was good at languages, impressed and could often bully people into accepting his point of view or leaving the field. He left unstated, influences upon him of other anthropologists" (unnamed personal communication email message 6/19/23; I do not name my correspondent, nor the man she describes, because it is the type, not a particular person, that is of interest here).

4. Lucy Kramer Cohen was a student at Barnard College and then Columbia graduate school, studying under and assisting Franz Boas. She left as ABD in Anthropology in order to go with her husband to his position with the Bureau of Indian Affairs in Franklin Roosevelt's New Deal. Although Kramer worked full time for three years on the Indian New Deal and Handbook, she is not listed as employed because during the Great Depression, the federal government would not pay two salaries to married couples (Kehoe 2014, 74).

5. It is not generally recalled that Jews as well as Blacks were lynched in the South. Leo Frank, a young factory manager with a wife and two small children, was lynched in 1915 in Marietta, Georgia, by a white mob claiming he raped and murdered a white girl employee in his factory. No one was charged with his murder by lynching. Jews (recognized by looks or name) were not served in hotels or restaurants, redlined out of housing, not permitted in country clubs, and near Milwaukee, Wisconsin in 1929, a group of ten summer cottages for Jews was destroyed by arson (https://www.jta.org/archive/j-d-b-news-letter-377#:~:text =The%20cottages%20were%20destroyed%20in,This%20happened%20during %20the%20night).

6. I thank Valerie Pinsky for sharing this document with me.

7. Trigger conscientiously records that he wrote "from the perspective of ontological materialism and epistemological realism. These are positions that I am convinced any social scientist who believes in the evolutionary origin of the human species must adopt" (Trigger 2006, xix). He was, he states, "inspired by the work of Gordon Childe" (xx). An Ontario Canadian (1937–2006), he chose to live outside the power struggles south of that border. Instead, he followed the principles of Daniel Wilson, one of the first professors in University College, Toronto, and its first president when it became the University of Toronto: diligent, empirical, meritocratic, broadly experienced and knowledgeable, and kind and respectful toward everyone.

8. Polynesian colonizers did not arrive as egalitarian family groups. They were organized under chiefs to make the voyages and create settlements. Kirch and Green 2001 is a good source to understand the histories of Polynesian colonizations.

9. See even the third edition of Willey and Sabloff, wherein not one woman archaeologist is part of the history.
10. Zumwalt's two-volume biography of Boas is, as I write in 2023, the best biography available, but she is more interested in Boas's unceasing work for social justice than evaluating him as a scientist. For Boas's training in German science and his early field experiences as a scientist, the essays in Stocking, ed., 1996 are excellent.

Acknowledgments

Note: Use the Internet to find out more about the people I am appreciating.

At the core of this book is puzzlement: with all the claims and criticisms of who in archaeology is doing science, why are so few leading scientists and philosophers of science brought into the discussions?

In part this is a rhetorical question. I answer by asserting that mainstream American archaeology has been in thrall since the 1960s to Cold War scientism promoting STEM disciplines as Science. This I glimpsed as I researched American militant Christianity, the powerful role of the Rockefeller Foundation in the twentieth century, then had my insights confirmed by historian of science Mark Solovey and my anthropologist colleague David H. Price: thank you, Mark and David. Stephen Wolfram is another collegial friend who was there at the beginning of the Santa Fe Institute, challenged its version of science and goal of explaining "complexity," and countered its science with his own "computational science": thank you, Stephen, for your firsthand description of that meeting. How did I meet Stephen? Through his anthropologist mother, my colleague, Sybil Wolfram, founder of the *International Journal of Moral and Social Studies*.

Modest as my situation has been, living in Milwaukee and teaching unsupported in a Jesuit university, I have been extraordinarily blessed with the friendship of several really world-class scientists. First among all, Joseph Needham, whose meticulous and insightful work in biochemistry is pure science, from which his unceasingly open intellect recognized science in China rivaling much in the West. Intrigued by the bright, well-prepared students and postdocs from China in his and his wife's, Dorothy M. Needham, labs, Joseph learned to read and speak Chinese, and during World War II, he lived in China as liaison between Britain and the Chinese fighting Japan's invasion. After the war, he urged adding an S, Science, to the new UNECO (Educational and Cultural), and became its first Head of the Natural Sciences, struggling to bring in "peripheral" nations' scientists and research groups. He then returned to Cambridge with a bold challenge to Western imperialism: the series *Science and Civilisation in China*. Initially asking why China did not have a Scientific Revolution, he discovered that China had fostered scientific research for many centuries; it had not separated theoretical science from engineering and applied knowledge. *Science and Civ*'s nearly thirty volumes so far, ongoing although Needham died in 1995, are a platform for understanding the breadth of science and engineering.

In 1975, I was using the card catalog in the university library to find the series' call number, and noticed on the card that Needham was born in 1900. A long section in volume 4, called Nautics, discussed evidence for seafaring and possibilities for transpacific voyages before Magellan. For my longstanding interest in this, shared with David H. Kelley at University of Calgary, and realizing Needham at 75 might not be around much longer, I phoned Kelley to suggest we might try to organize a conference of archaeologists to discuss the pros and cons directly with this master of science and erudition. First of course we wrote to Needham, who replied he would indeed like to visit Mesoamerica with some of its archaeologists. A two-week peripatetic conference visited the Museo Nacional for Needham to talk with staff and discoverers of some of the artifacts of interest; El Tajín where Gordon Ekholm guided and discussed his work including the wheel-and-axle animal figurines; Monte Albán; and Palenque, where Merle Robertson and Kelley told us about reading Maya scripts and the history of that kingdom. At the conclusion of the conference, Needham said he and his collaborator Lu Gwei-Djen would write up their impressions and conclusions about the data, and each of the others should send in essays discussing the evidence and stating their own conclusions or questions. Needham and Lu, Kelley and I, and the other two who considered transpacific voyages probable, sent in drafts promptly; the four archaeologists not initially favorable *sent in nothing*. Not one page giving counter arguments. Conclusion? They cared more for their professional careers and reputations than for science and data. They had no arguments.

Needham and Lu eventually published their contribution as a book in 1985, dedicating it to me and David Kelley.[1] They encouraged me to visit them in Cambridge, which I did twice when in England, each time to discuss at length our common question on transpacific contacts. To follow Needham as he laid out data and inference and argument was an inestimable education in scientific thinking. And to be with him as a person was a profound moral lesson, for he did not allow his titles to be used, everyone must address him as "Joseph," as one human being with another. Even my eleven-year-old boy who accompanied us in Mexico: one morning as we all waited for our tour bus, my boy sat on a low wall reading *The Andromeda Strain*. Joseph noticed, left the men he was talking with, gingerly sat his six-foot-frame on the low wall, and discussed the biochemistry in the book with the kid. Whether that led to this boy becoming a pharmacologist passionately committed to evidence-based practice and real-world trials of drugs, I can only suspect.

Another friendship with world-class scientists came about when I received an email from someone I didn't know, telling me he and his wife had read my Kensington runestone book and wanted to say that they were impressed with the science in it. Nice, but who sent this? Did they know much about science? Ah, email address was UC-B, that would be University of California-Berkeley. I Googled UC-B and the name, David Wake. David Wake was Distinguished Professor of Evolutionary Biology; his wife Marvalee Wake was department chair. Yes, this couple knew science! Replying to the email with thanks began a correspondence, and twice when I was in the Bay Area, beget afternoons talking with David in his lab. Again, as with Needham and Lu, I basked in the sun of a marvelously informed and reasoning mind speaking without pretense. David's special research was in the evolution of salamanders, and I was able to reciprocate a little by sending him our mapping of a Saskatchewan boulder outline construction of a salamander. A tiger salamander, we had been told. David said this was correct, tiger salamanders are the northernmost salamanders and their thick body reflects Bergmann's law. David died in 2021, and I continue occasionally messaging with Marvalee. They had picked up my runestone book when visiting family in the Kensington area.

One more person I want to acknowledge among the superb minds whose caring kindness has given me understanding of an empirical, scientific approach to our world: Robert Goodvoice. Mr. Goodvoice was a Wahpeton Dakota at Sioux Wahpeton Reserve outside Prince Albert, Saskatchewan. I met him the night his sister Florence and her husband, Joe Douquette, took me to learn about Wovoka's Good Tidings (Ghost

Dance; see my book).[2] Several times more I visited him on the Reserve to listen to his teaching; he wanted to guide me, as a mother who would be guiding the children I had with me. Eloquently he conveyed the reality known to his people and others among the First Nations. Now, thanks to a Saskatchewan historian who discovered tapes he had recorded, you can read the history of his nation and his discourse on their knowledge and celebrations in *The Red Road and Other Narratives of the Dakota Sioux*.[3]

My Colleagues

First among my colleagues working on history of archaeology is, of course, Bruce Trigger. His death so soon after retirement has been a real bereavement for me. We had in common our friend Daniel Wilson, the poor lad from Leith Walk whose talents were recognized by the Edinburgh reformers striving to establish a meritocracy. Daniel introduced the word and the concept of "prehistory" to the English-speaking world in 1851, immigrated to Toronto in 1853 to teach in the new college there, and after summer trips with Anishinaabeg and travels to see sites, wrote the excellent *Prehistoric Man*, published in 1862. When Bruce praised my *Land of Prehistory*, my confidence in my work was established. Most of all, I miss his comradeship.

Canada is outside the arena where ambitious archaeologists battle for prestige. At the University of Calgary, Jane Holden Kelley and David H. Kelley, Gerald Oetelaar, Brian Kooyman, Dale Walde, Geoffrey and Sharisse McCafferty, and Donald B. Smith (in History); in Edmonton, Jack Brink and my Harvard classmates Ruth Gruhn and Alan Bryan. In CRM in Calgary, that master of ground-truthing and knapping, Eugene Gryba. In Saskatchewan, Bruce McCorquodale.

In the Eastern Woodlands, Robert L. Hall, bringing Mahican understanding to intelligently scientific archaeology; David Overstreet and James Clark; Dale Henning; William Gartner; James Gallagher; Guy Gibbon; Lynne Sullivan; Robbie Ethridge; Nancy M. White; Donald Blakeslee; Dena Dincauze.

Mesoamericanists: Andrea Stone; Joe Mountjoy; Alan and Pamela Sandstrom; Diana Zaragoza; Linda Manzanilla; J. Charles Kelley.

Among feminists: Sarah Nelson; Ruthann Knudson; Deni Seymour; Carole Crumley (primarily an historical ecologist); and my fellow girl archaeologist at Plains Conferences, Patricia O'Brien.

Among First Nations citizens: Beatrice Medicine; JoAllyn Archambault; Darrell Robes Kipp; Carol Tatsey Murray; Stewart Miller; Joe Watkins; Bernard Perley.

WAC comrades: Kristian Kristiansen; George Nicholas; Koji Mizoguchi; Hirofumi Kato; Daniel Schavélzon; Peter Schmidt; Bettina Schulz Paulsson.

Those who recognize the probabilities of transoceanic voyages before 1492, in addition to Needham and Lu: Stephen Jett; Carl Johannesen and George Carter; Terry Jones; Gordon Ekholm.

My colleagues in Europe: the Edinburgh Strong Programme members Barry Barnes and David Bloor; Jiri Svoboda; Hans Müller-Beck.

My former students Alan Kolata and Alex Barker, and David Wilcox who always insisted that Tom and I were his teachers. (Wilcox was my field assistant the first season at François's House fur trade post, and then worked at Gull Lake bison drives with Tom.)

My teachers: Richard and Nathalie Woodbury; Glenn Black; Stuart Piggott.

My husband and field partner, Tom Kehoe.

Lastly, I thank my editor, Matthew Bokovoy, who proposed this book after working with me on my memoir, *Girl Archaeologist*. Matt quickly accepted that the memoir would not follow the standard formula of a wounded, suffering woman on a quest, instead letting me tell that I wouldn't let the bastards keep me down. Something of that in Matt, too, prompted him to suggest publishing those rejected papers, with opportunity to tell the bastards what good historical science is. Once the text was submitted, the University of Nebraska Press's superb production staff made the process more and more gratifying: Taylor Martin, Kayla Moslander, Hannah Gokie, Tish Fobben, Nathan Putens, and editor in chief Bridget Barry, who suggested the inclusion of a dramatis personae for this unconventional project.

NOTES

1. *Trans-Pacific Echoes and Resonances; Listening Once Again* by Joseph Needham and Lu Gwei-Djen, published in 1985 by World Scientific. "Nautics" is in volume 4: Physics and Physical Technology, Part III: Civil Engineering and Nautics, of *Science and Civilization in China*, published by Cambridge University Press. The 1977 conference is reported "Early Civilizations in Asia and Mesoamerica" by Alice B. Kehoe, *Current Anthropology* 19 (1):204–5.

2. *The Ghost Dance: Ethnohistory and Revitalization,* by Alice B. Kehoe, published originally by Holt Rinehart in 1989 in their Cultural Anthropology series; the second edition was published in 2006 by Waveland Press in Long Grove IL.

3. *The Red Road and Other Narratives of the Dakota Sioux* by Samuel Mniyo and Robert Goodvoice in 2020, edited by Daniel M. Beveridge, published by the University of Nebraska Press.

References

Adams, Henry [1907] 1931. *The Education of Henry Adams*. New York: Random House. Reprint, Modern Library edition.

Anderson, Benedict. [1983] 2006. *Imagined Communities: Reflections on the Origins and Spread of Nationalism*. London: Verso.

———. 1992. *Long Distance Nationalism: World Capitalism and the Rise of Identity Politics*. Amsterdam: CASA.

Ardener, Edwin. 1971. "New Anthropology and Its Critics (The Malinowski Lecture, 1970)." *Man* VI (3): 449–67.

———. 1975. "The 'Problem' Revisited." In *Perceiving Women*, edited by Shirley Ardener, 19–27. London: Malaby.

Ardener, Shirley. 1978. "Introduction." In *Defining Females*, edited by Shirley Ardener, 9–48. New York: John Wiley and Sons.

Aristotle. 1946. *The Politics*. Translated by Ernest Baker. London: Oxford University Press.

Arthur, Kathryn Weedman. 2019. "Ethnoarchaeoalogies of Listening: Learning Technological Ontologies Bit by Bit." In *Archaeologies of Listening*, edited by Peter R. Schmidt and Alice B. Kehoe, 25–46. Gainesville: University Press of Florida.

Baker, Erik. 2022. "From Planning to Entrepreneurship: On the Political Economy of Scientific Pursuit." *Studies in History and Philosophy of Science* 92:27–35.

Barber, Bernard. 1952. *Science and the Social Order*. Glencoe IL: Free Press.

Barr, Juliana. 2011. "Geographies of Power: Mapping Indian Borders in the 'Borderlands' of the Early Southwest." *William and Mary Quarterly* 68 (1): 5–46.

———. 2017. "There's No Such Thing as 'Prehistory': What the Longue Durée of Caddo and Pueblo History Tells Us about Colonial America." *William and Mary Quarterly* 74 (2): 203–40.

Benedict, Ruth. 1943. "Franz Boas." *Science* 97 (2507): 60–62.

Bergerbrandt, Sophie. 2013. "Preface." In *Counterpoint: Essays in Archaeology and Heritage Studies in Honour of Professor Kristian Kristiansen*, edited by Sophie Bergerbrandt and Serena Sabatini, 755. Oxford: Archaeopress.

Binford, Lewis R. 1980. "Willow Smoke and Dogs' Tails: Hunter-Gatherer Settlement Systems and Archaeological Site Formation." *American Antiquity* 45(1):4–20.

Boas, Franz. 1932. "The Aims of Anthropological Research." *Science* 72(1983):605-613.

Bourdeau, Michel. 2023. "Auguste Comte." In *The Stanford Encyclopedia of Philosophy*, edited by Edward N. Zalta and Uri Nodelman. https://plato.stanford.edu/archives/spr2023/entries/comte/.

Bradley, Richard. 2015. "Repeating the Unrepeatable Experiment." In *Material Evidence*, edited by Robert Chapman and Alison Wylie, 23–41. London: Routledge.

Brown, Jennifer S. H. 1980. *Strangers in Blood: Fur Trade Families in Indian Country*. Vancouver: University of British Columbia Press.

Bruchac, Margaret M. 2018. *Savage Kin: Indigenous Informants and American Anthropologists*. Tucson: University of Arizona Press.

Carpenter, Stephen M. 2020. "Mesoamerican-Mississippian Interaction Across the Far Southern Plains by Long-range Toyah Intermediaries." *Plains Anthropologist* 65 (253): 1–32.

Carneiro, Robert L. 1970. "A Theory of the Origin of the State." *Science* 169 (3947): 733–73.

Chadwick, Robert E. L. 2013. "The Olmec-Xicallanca of Teotihuacan, Cacaxtla, and Cholula: An Archaeological, Ethnohistorical, and Linguistic Synthesis." In *The Olmec-Xicallanca of Teotihuacan, Cacaxtla and Cholula*, 55–65. Oxford: BAR International Series 2488.

Chapman, Robert, and Alison Wylie, eds. 2015. *Material Evidence: Learning From Archaeological Practice*. London: Routledge.

Collingwood, Robin G. 1939. *An Autobiography*. London: Routledge.

———. 1946. *The Idea of History*. Oxford: Clarendon Press.

Crumley, Carole. 1987. "A Dialectical Critique of Hierarchy." In *Power Relations and State Formation*, edited by Thomas C. Patterson and Christine Ward Gailey, 155–68. Washington DC: American Anthropological Association.

———. 1995. "Heterarchy and the Analysis of Complex Societies." In *Heterarchy and the Analysis of Complex Societies*, edited by Robert M. Ehrenreich, Carole L. Crumley, and Janet F. Levy, 1–6. Washington DC: Archeological Papers of the American Anthropological Society No 5.

Crumley, Carole, and William H. Marquardt, eds. 1987. *Regional Dynamics: Burgundian Landscapes in Historical Perspective*. San Diego: Academic Press.

Currie, Adrian. 2016. "Ethnographic Analogy, the Comparative Method, and Archaeological Special Pleading." *Studies in History and Philosophy of Science*. 54:84–94.

———. 2018. *Rock, Bone, Ruin*. Cambridge MA: MIT Press.

———. 2019. *Scientific Knowledge and the Deep Past: History Matters*. Cambridge: Cambridge University Press.

Currie, Adrian, and Kirsten Walsh. n.d. *Frameworks for Historians and Philosophers*. Penultimate version, forthcoming in HOPOS [HOPOS: International Society for the History of Philosophy of Science]. https://sites.google.com/site/adrianmitchellcurrie.

DeMallie, Raymond. 1985. *The Sixth Grandfather: Black Elk's Teachings Given to John G. Neihardt*. Lincoln: University of Nebraska Press.

Detienne, Marcel, and Jean Pierre Vernant. 1978. *Cunning Intelligence in Greek Culture and Society*. Translated by Janet Lloyd. Atlantic Highlands, NJ: Humanities Press.

D'Oro, Giuseppina and James Connelly. 2020. "Robin George Collingwood." In *The Stanford Encyclopedia of Philosophy*, edited by Edward N. Zalta. https://plato.stanford.edu/archives/win2020/entries/collingwood/.

Earle, Timothy K. 1997. *How Chiefs Come to Power: The Political Economy in Prehistory*. Stanford: Stanford University Press.

————. 2021. *A Primer on Chiefs and Chiefdoms* (Principles of Archaeology). Clinton Corners, NY: Eliot Werner Publishing.

Eco, Umberto. 1995. "Ur-Fascism." *The New York Review of Books,* June 22, 1995. http://www.nybooks.com/articles/1856.

Eddy, John A. 1977. "Probing the Mystery of the Medicine Wheels." *National Geographic* 151 (1): 140–46.

Eller, Cynthia. 2001. *The Myth of Matriarchal Prehistory: Why an Invented Past Won't Give Women a Future*. Boston: Beacon Press.

Eriksen, Thomas Hylland. 2016. "Ben Anderson: the Anthropologist." *Nations and Nationalism* 22:1–35.

Evans, Christopher. 1985. "Tradition and the Cultural Landscape: An Archaeology of Place." *Archaeological Review from Cambridge* 4 (1): 80–94.

Evans-Pritchard, Edward E. 1963. *Essays in Social Anthropology*. Glencoe IL: Free Press.

Flannery, Kent V. 1982. "The Golden Marshalltown: A Parable for the Archeology of the 1980s." *American Anthropologist* 84 (2): 265–78.

Gero, Joan, David M. Lacy, and Michael L. Blakey, eds. 1983. *The Socio-Politics of Archaeology*. Amherst: Research Report no. 23, Department of Anthropology, University of Massachusetts-Amherst.

Gimbel, Steven. 2012. *Einstein's Jewish Science*. Baltimore: Johns Hopkins University Press.

Gibbon, Guy. 2014. *Critically Reading the Theory and Methods of Archaeology: An Introductory Guide*. Lanham MD: Altamira.

Goldschmidt, Walter. 1959. "Preface." In *The Anthropology of Franz Boas*, Memoir 89, American Anthropological Association, v-vii.

Goldstein, Lynne, Barbara Mills, Sarah Herr, and Jo Burkholder. 2017. "Why Do Fewer Women than Men Apply for Grants After Their Ph.Ds." *American Antiquity* 83 (3): 367–86.

Gould, Stephen Jay. 2002. *The Structure of Evolutionary Theory*. Cambridge: Belknap Press.

Hall, Ryan. 2020. *Beneath the Backbone of the World: Blackfoot People and the North American Borderlands, 1720–1877*. Chapel Hill: University of North Carolina Press.

Howe, Nimachia. 2019. *Retelling Trickster in Naapi's Language*. Longmont: University of Colorado Press.

Hu, Di. 2012. "Advancing Theory? Landscape Archaeology and Geographical Information Systems." *Papers from the Institute of Archaeology* 21:80–90.

Jenkins, Ned J., and Richard A. Krause. 2009. "The Woodland-Mississippian Interface in Alabama, ca. AD 1075–1200: An Adaptive Radiation?" *Southeastern Archaeology* 2009: 202–19.

Horsman, Reginald. 1986. *Race and Manifest Destiny.* Cambridge MA: Harvard University Press.

Kaufman, David V. 2019. *Clues to Lower Mississippi Valley Histories: Language, Archaeology, Ethnography.* Lincoln: University of Nebraska Press.

———. 2023. "Contact between Mesoamerica and the Lower Mississippi Valley/ Southeast." Uploaded June 15, 2023. https://www.academia.edu/103305221 /Contact_between_Mesoamerica_and_the_Lower_Mississippi_Valley _Southeast.

Kehoe, Alice B. 1978. *François' House, an Early Fur Trade Post on the Saskatchewan.* Regina: Saskatchewan Ministry of Culture and Youth.

———. 1983a. "The Shackles of Tradition." In *The Hidden Half,* edited by Patricia Albers and Beatrice Medicine, 53–73. Washington DC: University Press of America.

———. 1983b. "The Word of God." In *Scientists Confront Creationism,* edited by Laurie R. Godfrey, 1–12. Boston: W. W. Norton. [Updated edition 2007. "Why Target Evolution? The Problem of Authority." In *Scientists Confront Intelligent Design and Creationism,* edited by Andrew J. Petto and Laurie R. Godfrey, 401– 25. New York: W. W. Norton.]

———. 1989. *The Ghost Dance: Ethnohistory and Revitalization.* New York: Holt Winston. [Updated edition 2006, Waveland Press, Long Grove IL.]

———. 1990a. "Points and Lines." In *Powers of Observation: Alternate Views in Archeology,* edited by Sarah M. Nelson and Alice B. Kehoe, 23–37. Washington DC: Archeological Papers of the American Anthropological Association No. 2.

———. 1990b. "'In Fourteen Hundred and Ninety-two, Columbus Sailed . . .': The Primacy of the National Myth in American Schools." In *The Excluded Past,* edited by Peter Stone and Robert MacKenzie, 201–16. London: Unwin Hyman.

———. 1998. *The Land of Prehistory: A Critical History of American Archaeology.* New York: Routledge.

———. 2000. "François' House, a Significant Pedlars' Post on the Saskatchewan." In *Material Contributions to Ethnohistory: Interpretations of Native North American Life,* edited by Michael S. Nassaney and Eric S. Johnson, 173–87. Gainesville: University Press of Florida and Society for Historical Archaeology.

———. 2005. *The Kensington Runestone: Approaching a Research Question Holistically.* Long Grove IL: Waveland Press.

———. 2009. "Deconstructing John Locke." In *Postcolonial Perspectives in Archaeology*, edited by Peter Bikouis, Dominic Lacroix, and Meaghan M. Peuramaki-Brown. Calgary: University of Calgary Archaeological Association.

———. 2012. *Militant Christianity: An Anthropological History*. New York: Palgrave/Macmillan.

———. 2014. *A Passion for the True and Just: Felix and Lucy Kramer Cohen and the Indian New Deal*. Tucson: University of Arizona Press.

———. 2022. *Girl Archaeologist: Sisterhood in a Sexist Profession*. Lincoln: University of Nebraska Press.

Kehoe, Alice Beck, and Thomas F, Kehoe. 1979. *Solstice-Aligned Boulder Configurations in Saskatchewan*. Canadian Ethnology Service Paper No. 48, Mercury Series, National Museum of Man, Ottawa.

Kehoe, Thomas F. 1958. "Tipi Rings: The "Direct Ethnological" Approach Applied to an Archeological Problem." *American Anthropologist* 60:861–73.

———. 1960. *Stone Tipi Rings in North-Central Montana and the Adjacent Portion of Alberta, Canada: Their Historical, Ethnological and Archaeological Aspects*. Bureau of American Ethnology, Bulletin 173, Anthropological Papers No. 62. Washington DC: Government Printing Office.

Kelley, J. Charles. 1955. "Juan Sabeata and Diffusion in Aboriginal Texas." *American Anthropologist* 57:981–95.

Kemp, Tom S. 2015. *The Origin of Higher Taxa*. Chicago: University of Chicago Press.

Kennedy, Roger G. 1994. *Hidden Cities: The Discovery and Loss of Ancient North American Civilization*. New York: Free Press.

Kent, Susan. 1993. *Domestic Architecture and the Use of Space: An Interdisciplinary Cross-cultural Study*. Cambridge: Cambridge University Press.

Keur, Dorothy Louise. 1941. *Big Bead Mesa*. Menasha WI: Society for American Archaeology Memoir No. 1.

Kipp, Darrell Robes. 2010. Opening address, Blackfoot History Symposium, Cutswood School, Browning MT, August 20, 2010.

Kirch, Patrick Vinton, and Roger C. Green. 2001. *Hawaiki, Ancestral Polynesia*. Cambridge: University Press.

Knudson, Ruthann. 2014. "Women in Reservoir Salvage Archaeology." In *Dam Projects and the Growth of American Archaeology: The River Basin Surveys and the Interagency Archeological Salvage Program*, edited by Kimball M. Banks and Jon S. Czaplicki, 180–201. Walnut Creek CA: Left Coast Press.

Kroeber, Alfred L. 1939. *Cultural and Natural Areas of Native North America*. Berkeley: University of California Publications in American Archaeology and Ethnology Vol. 38.

———. 1948. *Anthropology*. Rev. ed. New York: Harcourt and Brace.

Letiche, Hugo, and Matt Statler. 2005. "Evoking Metis: Questioning the Logics of Change, Responsiveness, Meaning and Action in Organizations." *Culture and Organization* 11 (1): 1–16.

Lopatin, Ivan A. 1960. "Origin of the Native American Steam Bath." *American Anthropologist* 62:977–93.

Lyman, R. Lee, and Michael J. O'Brien. 2001. "The Direct Historical Approach, Analogical Reasoning, and Theory in Americanist Archaeology." *Journal of Archaeological Method and Theory* 8 (4): 303–42.

Malinowski, Bronislaw. 1944. *A Scientific Theory of Culture and Other Essays*. Chapel Hill: University of North Carolina Press.

Marquardt, William H. 2019. "Dialectic in Historical Ecology." In *Historical Ecologies, Hierarchies and Transtemporal Landscapes*, edited by Celeste Ray and Manuel Fernández-Götz, 11–31. Routledge: London.

Morgan, Lewis Henry. [1877] 1985. *Ancient Society*. Tucson: University of Arizona Press.

Oetelaar, Gerald Anthony. 2014. "Better Homes and Pastures: Human Agency and the Construction of Place in Communal Bison Hunting on the Northern Plains." *Plains Anthropologist* 59 (229): 9–37.

Patterson, Thomas C. 1995. *Toward a Social History of Archaeology in the United States*. Fort Worth: Harcourt Brace.

———. 2001. *A Social History of Anthropology in the United States*. Oxford: Berg.

———. 2003. *Marx's Ghost: Conversations with Archaeologists*. New York: Routledge.

———. 2022. "Class Struggle and Contradictions in the Classic Maya World: The Applicability and Utility of Marx's Ancient Mode of Production." In *Pre-Capitalist Modes of Production and the Archaeology of Ancient American Civilizations*, published online at Academic.edu.

Pauketat, Timothy R. n.d. "The Maya and the Mississippi: On the Road to Medieval America." Unpublished draft of *Gods of Thunder: How Climate Change, Travel, and Spirituality Reshaped Precolonial America*. New York: Oxford University Press.

———. 2023. *Gods of Thunder*. New York: Oxford University Press.

Peace, William. 2006. "Introduction: The University of Michigan's Department of Anthropology: Leslie White and the Politics of Departmental Expansion." In *Retrospectives: Works and Lives of Michigan Anthropologists*. Ann Arbor: MPublishing, University of Michigan Library 16 (1).

Piggott, Stuart. 1981. "Summary and Conclusions." In *Towards a History of Archaeology*, edited by Glyn Daniel, 186–89. London: Thames and Hudson.

Pinsky, Valerie. 1992. "Archaeology, Politics, and Boundary-formation: The Boas Censure (1919) and the Development of American Archaeology During the Inter-war Years." In *Rediscovering Our Past: Essays on the History of American Archaeology*, edited by Jonathan Reyman, 161–89. Aldershot: Avebury.

Politis, Gustavo G. 2007. *Nukak: Ethnoarchaeology of an Amazonian People*. London: Routledge.

———. 2015. "Reflections on Contemporary Ethnoarchaeology/Reflexiones sobre etnoarqueología contemporánea." *Pyrenae* 46 (1): 41–83.

Price, David H. 2004. *Threatening Anthropology: McCarthyism and the FBI's Surveillance of Activist Anthropologists*. Durham NC: Duke University Press.

———. 2016. *Cold War Anthropology*. Durham: Duke University Press.

———. 2022. *The American Surveillance State*. London: Pluto Press.

Reisch, George A. 2005. *How the Cold War Transformed Philosophy of Science*. Cambridge: Cambridge University Press.

Sauer, Carl Ortwin. 1966. *The Early Spanish Main*. Berkeley: University of California Press.

Schmidt, Peter R., and Alice B. Kehoe, eds. 2019. *Archaeologies of Listening*. Gainesville: University Press of Florida.

Scott, Walter. 1815. *The Antiquary*. Edinburgh: Adam and Charles Black.

Shapin, Steven. 1994. *A Social History of Truth*. Chicago: University of Chicago Press.

Shapin, Steven, and Simon Schaffer. 1985. *Leviathan and the Air-Pump*. Princeton: Princeton University Press.

Simpson, George Gaylord. 1970. "Uniformitarianism. An Inquiry into Principle, Theory, and Method in Geohistory and Biohistory." In *Essays in Evolution and Genetics in Honor of Theodosius Dobzhansky*, edited by Max K. Hecht and William C. Steere, 43–96. New York: Appleton-Century-Crofts.

Smith, Donald B. 2021. *Seen But Not Seen*. Toronto: University of Toronto Press.

Solovey, Mark. 2012. "Senator Fred Harris's National Social Science Foundation Proposal: Reconsidering Federal Science Policy, Natural Science–Social Science Relations, and American Liberalism during the 1960s." *Isis* 103 (1): 54–82.

———. 2013. *Shaky Foundations: the Politics-Patronage-Social Science Nexus in Cold War America*. New Brunswick NJ: Rutgers University Press.

———. 2020. *Social Science for What?: Battles over Public Funding for the "Other Sciences" at the National Science Foundation*. Cambridge MA: MIT Press.

Stark, Miriam T., and James M. Skibo. 2007. "A History of the Kalinga Ethnoarchaeological Project." In *Archaeological Anthropology: Perspectives on Method and Theory*, edited by James M. Skibo, Michael W. Graves, and Miriam T. Stark, 93–110. Tucson: University of Arizona Press.

Steward, Julian H. 1990. *Theory of Culture Change*. Urbana: University of Illinois Press.

Stocking, George W., Jr., ed. 1996. *Volksgeist as Method and Ethic: Essays on Boasian Ethnography and the German Anthropological Tradition*. Madison: University of Wisconsin Press.

Stone, Peter, and Robert MacKenzie, eds. 1990. *The Excluded Past*. London: Unwin Hyman.

Strong, W. Duncan. 1940. "From History to Prehistory in the Northern Great Plains." *Smithsonian Miscellaneous Collections* 100:353–94.

Synnott, Marcia Graham. 1979. *The Half-Opened Door: Discrimination and Admissions at Harvard, Yale and Princeton 1900–1970.* Westport CT: Greenwood Press.

Taliaferro, Charles. 2023. "Philosophy of Religion." In *The Stanford Encyclopedia of Philosophy,* edited by Edward N. Zalta and Uri Nodelman. https://plato.stanford .edu/archives/sum2023/entries/philosophy-religion.

Trigger, Bruce G. 2006. *A History of Archaeological Thought,* 2nd edition. Cambridge: Cambridge University Press.

Tsuk Mitchell, Dalia. 2007. *Architect of Justice: Felix S. Cohen and the Founding of American Legal Pluralism.* Ithaca: Cornell University Press.

Tuck, Edward F., and Timothy K. Earle. 1996. "Why C.E.O.'s Succeed (And Why They Fail)." *Strategy & Business* 5:4–11.

Turner, Derek. 2007. *Making Prehistory: Historical Science and the Scientific Realism Debate.* Cambridge: Cambridge University Press.

Turner, Derek D., and Michelle I. Turner. 2021. "'I'm Not Saying It Was Aliens': An Archaeological and Philosophical Analysis of a Conspiracy Theory." In *Explorations in Archaeology and Philosophy,* edited by Anton Killin and Sean Allen-Hermanson, 7–24. Cham, Switzerland: Springer AG.

Van Engen, Abram. 2020. "How America Became 'A City Upon a Hill': The Rise and Fall of Perry Miller." *Humanities* 41(1). https://www.neh.gov/article/how -america-became-city-upon-hill.

Van Kirk, Sylvia. 1980. *Many Tender Ties.* Norman: University of Oklahoma Press.

Webb, Clarence H. 1968. "The Extent and Content of Poverty Point Culture." *American Antiquity* 33 (3): 297–321.

White, Leslie A. [1959] 2007. *The Evolution of Culture.* Walnut Creek CA: Left Coast Press.

Willey, Gordon R., and Jeremy A. Sabloff. 1993. *A History of American Archaeology.* New York: W. H. Freeman.

Williams, Robert A., Jr. 1990. *American Indians in Western Legal Thought.* New York: Oxford University Press.

Wood, Patricia Burke, and David A. Rossiter. 2022. *Unstable Properties: Aboriginal Title and the Claim of British Columbia.* Vancouver: University of British Columbia Press.

Wylie, Alison. 2002. "The Interpretive Dilemma." In *Thinking from Things,* 117–26. Berkeley: University of California Press.

———. 2012. "Feminist Philosophy of Science: Standpoint Matters." *Proceedings and Addresses of the* APA 86 (2): 47–76.

Zumwalt, Rosemary Lévy. 2022. *Franz Boas: Shaping Anthropology and Fostering Social Justice.* Lincoln: University of Nebraska Press.

Index

Ac ko mok ki (Akai Mokti), 26, 131
actualism, as principle in science, 110,
    177, 178, 180
Adams, Henry, 162
Adams, William, 176
AIA (Archaeological Institute of
    America), and SAA (Society for
    American Archaeology) compared,
    254–55
Albers, Patricia, *The Hidden Half*,
    229, 238
antiquarianism, in Scotland, 91
anti-Semitism, effects on anthropology,
    253–54, 263n5
archaeology, modeled on geology, 6
Ardener, Edwin, and syntagm/
    paradigm terms, 1, 16, 230–31
Ardener, Shirley, 230–32
Aristotle, 39, 53, 81, 129
Asch, Michael, 60–61
authority, power of, 251–52
Aveni, Anthony, 145

Barnes, Barry, 5
Barr, Juliana, 195, 206
Basque Country, 2
Bean, Lowell, 54, 56
Bernier, Bernard, 61–63
Big Towns (dispersed trading
    towns), 206
Binford, Lewis, 1, 6, 121–36, 257
Bird, Junius, 1
bison drives, 151–53
Black, Glenn, 1

Blackfoot (Peigans), 124–33, 138n2
Blakeslee, Donald, 130, 206
Boas, Franz: commitment to human
    worth and sound science, 242, 260,
    261–62; students of, 260–61
boulder monuments: in archaeology,
    150–51; astronomically-aligned
    boulder constructions, 153–54
Breuil, Henri (Abbé), 243n5
Brumbach, Hetty Jo, 241

Cahen, Daniel, site analyzed as syn-
    tagm and paradigm, 13
Cahokia, 159, 179, 193–96; downfall of,
    208–9; geography of, 205; interpret-
    ers of, 201; trade of, 207
cant of conquest (Francis Jennings),
    43, 44–48
capitalism, effects on American archae-
    ology, 251
Carneiro, Robert, 246, 256–57
Carter, George, 63–64, 98
Carter, Sarah, 32
Chandler, Joan, 65–66
Chesapeake Bay First Nations, early
    colonizations, 177
Cheyenne First Nation, 178
chiefdom, as term, 184
Childe, V. Gordon, 101, 179, 200
Cholula, Mexico (principal state and
    its capital), 193, 205
Christenson, Andrew, 3, 234
CIA (Central Intelligence Agency), 164
Civil Rights Act, 1964, 260

Claassen, Cheryl, 229
Clark, Grahame, 101
class, social, 255, 260
Cohen, Felix, 253, 263
Cohen, Lucy Kramer, 253, 263
Cold War, 163
Collingwood, R. G., 9, 11, 95n3, 110n3
colonialism, in archaeology, 7
Common-Sense Realism, 10, 12
communities of practice, as term for
    shared technologies, 210
continental core, 50–54
contingencies, in historical sciences,
    95, 110
Councils, governing First Nations,
    178–79
Cox, Bruce Alden, 31
CRM (Cultural Resource Manage-
    ment), 250, 260
Crumley, Carole, 98n5, 165–67, 173
Culhane, Dara, 170
Currie, Adrian, 95n2

Delgamuukw v. Regina, 99n3, 181–82, 223
Denevan, William, 98n5, 166
Dhegihan language nations, 201–3
Dincauze, Dena, 231
discrimination, in American archaeol-
    ogy, 249
Dixon, Roland, 155
Doctrine of Discovery, 104–6, 197, 227
dominant discourse, 238
Dumézil, Georges, 43–44
Dumond, Don, 66–68
Dunnell, Robert, site analyzed as syn-
    tagm and paradigm, 13

Earle, Timothy, 165–68, 173, 256
Eco, Umberto, 17
Eddy, John A. (Jack), 145, 153

Einstein's Jewish Science (Steven
    Gimbel), 253
Eller, Cynthia, 230
ethnoarchaeology, ethnohistory, ethno-
    graphic analogy, and direct ethnog-
    raphy compared, 92–93, 146
ethnohistory, as a discipline, 40
Etzanoa (dispersed trading town), 206
Evans-Pritchard, E. E., 259
evolutionism, unilinear cultural, 161–63,
    176, 198–99; and creationism, 252,
    256, 258, 260

fascist goals in America, 1930s–1950s,
    122, 261
Finlay, Jaco, 26
Fladmark, Knut, 68–70
food production, three zones in North
    America, 49–51. See also continen-
    tal core; latitudes, high; Pacific
    drainage
foragers: and idea of "nonproduced"
    food, 136; as inappropriate label for
    hunter-gatherers, 121–24, 135–36
Ford, James A., 1, 101, 194
François's House, 25
Freeman, Gordon and Phyllis, 33
French, David, 70–72
Fried, Morton, critique of "tribes"
    category, 200

"gender" archaeology, 230
Gero, Joan, 164, 239
Gibbon, Guy, 240
Gimbel, Steven, Einstein's Jewish Science,
    253
Godfrey, Laurie, 252
Goodale, Jane C., 235
Goodvoice, Robert, 267–68
Great Chain of Being, 197

Green, Roger, and Patrick Kirch, 259
Grene, Marjorie Glicksman, 233
Griffin, James B., 212

Hanson, Norwood Russell, 12
Haraway, Donna, 134
Healy, Paul, 72–73
Herder, Johann, 171
heritage management. *See* CRM (Cultural Resource Management)
heterarchy, as term for distributed leadership, 167, 173, 183–84
The Hidden Half (Patricia Albers and Beatrice Medicine), 229, 238
historical archaeology, oriented to documents, 6
historical particularism, as postcolonial, 212
A History of American Archaeology (Gordon R. Willey and Jeremy A. Sabloff), 234
Hopewell (Middle Woodland) culture, in Ohio, 33, 207
Howard, James H., 147

imagined community, as term for larger nations claiming unified culture, 159–60
Indian New Deal, 1934, 253, 263
Ingstad, Anne and Helge, 27
Iroquois in the West, Montana, and Alberta, 28
Isaac, Barry, 121

Jarvenpa, Robert, 73–75; ethnoarchaeology as two cultural grammars, 241
Jefferson, Thomas: excavated mound, 9; falsehood in Declaration of Independence, 168, 184n3
Johannessen, Carl, 109

Keeley, Laurence, site analyzed as syntagm and paradigm, 13–14
Kehoe, Thomas F. (Tom), 143–44, 147–54
Kelley, David H., 266, 268
Kelley, Jane, 102, 106, 268
Kelley, J. Charles, 2
Kensington runestone, 28, 159, 262, 267
Kent, Susan, 137
Keur, Dorothy, 234
Kipp, Darrell Robes, 122
Kirch, Patrick, and Roger Green, 259
Kneberg, Madeline, 234
Knorr-Cetina, Karin, 12
Kristiansen, Kristian, 166
Kroeber, Alfred, 41, 99, 184n10, 198

landscapes, cultural, 97–99
language, natural vs. scientific, 17
Lathrap, Donald, 101
latitudes, high, 50, 56–58
Latour, Bruno, 19
Lévi-Strauss, Claude, 31
Lewis, Henry, 76–77
Lewis, Meriwether, 26
literacy, linked to power, 5–6
Locke, John, 30, 104, 170, 197, 249
Loring, Stephen, on Ona impoverishment by commercial whalers, 138n5
Lubbock, John, 29, 198, 240
Lurie, Nancy, 249
Lux, Maureen, 33

maize, 39, 207
Majorville Cairn (Alberta), 33
Manifest Destiny, 109, 144, 159–60, 212, 249; Christian groups support for, 252; and Declaration of Independence false claim, 168–69; and preColumbian isolation, 171; and

Manifest Destiny (*continued*)
racism in American archaeology, 144, 260; and a Redeemer Nation, 161; and U.S. Constitution's denial of rights to women and enslaved persons, 237; and the White Man's Burden, 181
market systems, central to Western nation-states, 136, 237
Marquardt, William, 167
Marshall, John, ruling on "Indian tribes," 168–69
Matthews, Washington, 144
McEachern, Allan, and the *Delgamuukw* case, 29, 30, 181–82, 223–25
McGhee, Bob, 27
Medicine, Beatrice, *The Hidden Half*, 229, 238
Merchant, Tony, 226, 227
Mesoamerican–North American trade, 212
Metis (goddess), 89–90
Mississippian Ideological Interaction Sphere (South East Ceremonial Complex), 205, 210
Moore, John H., 31, 32
Moose Mountain (Saskatchewan), 14–15, 33, 145, 153–54
Morgan, Lewis Henry, 160–61, 198, 258
Mulloy, William, 137, 143
multiplicities. *See* contingencies, in historical sciences
Mvskoke (Creek) First Nation, 180

NAGPRA (Native American Graves Protection and Repatriation Act), 1990, 1, 200, 250
National Science Foundation (U.S.), 2, 163–64, 199, 249–50
Needham, Joseph, 265–67

North American First Nations, Europeanist interpretation of, 48. *See also* cant of conquest (Francis Jennings)
Nuclear America, 207

O'Brien, Patricia, 201
Oculgee, 210
Oetelaar, Gerald, 122
Old North Trail, 132
Olmeca-Xicallanca, 193–94
Osage nation, 179, 201–3
"outsider discourse," 237, 242–43

Pacific drainage, 50, 54–56
the past, as a "place," 9, 18–19
patriarchy, 249, 262–63n3
Patterson, Thomas, 255
Pauketat, Timothy, 195, 213n3
Peirce, C. S., 193
Pinsky, Valerie, 262n2
Plumb, J. H., 34
polis: described by Aristotle, 39, 42, 50, 129–30, 174; urban economy, 53
political economy of archaeology, 239
positivism, 162
Poverty Point, 194
Powell, (Major) John Wesley, 160, 185n11, 199
"prehistory," concept of, 91, 171
Price, David H., 265
"primitives," described in colonialist anthropology, 102–3
"projectile point," as label, 17–18, 242–43

Quetzalcoatl, in Mississippian America, 211

Ray, Arthur J., 225
Reid, Thomas, 10

Sabloff, Jeremy A., *A History of American Archaeology*, 234
Sahlins, Marshall, 2, 173, 257, 258
Sauer, Carl O., 97–101
Schaeffer, Claude E., 143, 147
Schiffer, Michael, analysis critiqued for syntagm and paradigm, 14
Schoenwetter, James, on Guila Naquitz data, 19
science, historical, 92–95, 176, 183, 213, 258, 261; abduction, 193; Enlightenment, 9–10, 103–4, 134, 171; fascist goals in mid-twentieth century, 261; modeling, 176; sample size, 261; worldview basis, 176
Service, Elman, 172–73, 175, 199
Shapin, Steven, 259
shell-tempered pottery, 210–11
Shipek, Florence, 77–79
Simpson, George Gaylord, 92, 183
Smith, Bruce D., 104n5
Smith, Donald B., 25
social class, 255, 260
social construction of reality, 17
Solovey, Mark, 265
Southeastern First Nations, kings recognized by Europeans, 177
sovereignty, of First Nations, 227n1
Spaulding, Albert, 7
Speck, Frank, 143
Spencer, Herbert, 198
Spiro site, 211
standpoint, affecting analyses, 255–56
Stanislawski, Michael, and direct ethnographic approach, 143
Stern, Theodore, 79–80
Steward, Julian, 198
Stocking, George, Jr., 40
Sturtevant, William, 176, 182
sweatbaths, 213

syntagm, 12–13, 15–16, 241

Thompson, David, 25–26
tipi rings, 144, 148–50, 174
Tlingit, 56
Tollan, Mexico, 196, 205, 206
Toltecs: in Mexico, 193; Toltec Mounds Plum Bayou site, 205
Totonacs, 194
trade language, Mobilian, 20
tribe, as term (vs. First Nation), 200
Trigger, Bruce, 256, 263n7, 268
Trudeau, Justin, 226
Trudeau, Pierre, 226
Tuck, Jim, 27
Turgeon, Laurier, 27
Turner, Frederick Jackson, 169–70
Tylor, Edward, 198

Uhlenbeck, C. C., 124
University of Michigan, archaeological programs of, 250

Vincent, Joan, 172, 175
voyaging: medieval, Asia to Mesoamerica, 108; Polynesian, 107, 263n8; pre-Columbian, 102, 104, 262

Wake, David, 267
Wake, Marvalee, 267
Watson, Patty Jo, 9
Wedel, Waldo, 99, 147
Weiner, Annette, 237
White, Leslie, 161, 162, 172–73, 175, 184n6, 256
Willey, Gordon R., *A History of American Archaeology*, 234
Wilson, Daniel, 29, 91–92, 169–70, 255, 263, 268
Wolfram, Stephen, 265

Woodbury, Richard, 1–2
Woodhull, Victoria Claflin, 235, 236
writing, necessity of, 184n5
Writing-on-Stone (Alberta), 33
Wylie, Alison, 91–92, 199, 251

Yellen, John, 164, 250

Ziman, John, 11

In the Critical Studies in the History of Anthropology series

*Invisible Genealogies: A History
of Americanist Anthropology*
Regna Darnell

*The Shaping of American
Ethnography: The Wilkes Exploring
Expedition, 1838–1842*
Barry Alan Joyce

Ruth Landes: A Life in Anthropology
Sally Cole

*Melville J. Herskovits and the
Racial Politics of Knowledge*
Jerry Gershenhorn

*Leslie A. White: Evolution and
Revolution in Anthropology*
William J. Peace

*Rolling in Ditches with Shamans: Jaime
de Angulo and the Professionalization
of American Anthropology*
Wendy Leeds-Hurwitz

*Irregular Connections: A History
of Anthropology and Sexuality*
Andrew P. Lyons and Harriet D. Lyons

*Ephraim George Squier and the
Development of American Anthropology*
Terry A. Barnhart

*Ruth Benedict: Beyond
Relativity, Beyond Pattern*
Virginia Heyer Young

*Looking through Taiwan: American
Anthropologists' Collusion
with Ethnic Domination*
Keelung Hong and Stephen O. Murray

*Visionary Observers: Anthropological
Inquiry and Education*
Jill B. R. Cherneff and Eve Hochwald
Foreword by Sydel Silverman

*Anthropology Goes to the Fair: The
1904 Louisiana Purchase Exposition*
Nancy J. Parezo and Don D. Fowler

*The Meskwaki and Anthropologists:
Action Anthropology Reconsidered*
Judith M. Daubenmier

*The 1904 Anthropology Days and
Olympic Games: Sport, Race,
and American Imperialism*
Edited by Susan Brownell

*Lev Shternberg: Anthropologist,
Russian Socialist, Jewish Activist*
Sergei Kan

*Contributions to Ojibwe
Studies: Essays, 1934–1972*
A. Irving Hallowell
Edited and with introductions
by Jennifer S. H. Brown
and Susan Elaine Gray

*Excavating Nauvoo: The Mormons
and the Rise of Historical
Archaeology in America*
Benjamin C. Pykles
Foreword by Robert L. Schuyler

Cultural Negotiations: The Role
of Women in the Founding of
Americanist Archaeology
David L. Browman

Homo Imperii: A History of
Physical Anthropology in Russia
Marina Mogilner

American Anthropology and
Company: Historical Explorations
Stephen O. Murray

Racial Science in Hitler's
New Europe, 1938–1945
Edited by Anton Weiss-
Wendt and Rory Yeomans

Cora Du Bois: Anthropologist,
Diplomat, Agent
Susan C. Seymour

Before Boas: The Genesis of
Ethnography and Ethnology in
the German Enlightenment
Han F. Vermeulen

American Antiquities: Revisiting the
Origins of American Archaeology
Terry A. Barnhart

An Asian Frontier: American
Anthropology and Korea, 1882–1945
Robert Oppenheim

Theodore E. White and the Development
of Zooarchaeology in North America
R. Lee Lyman

Declared Defective: Native Americans,
Eugenics, and the Myth of Nam Hollow
Robert Jarvenpa

Glory, Trouble, and Renaissance
at the Robert S. Peabody
Museum of Archaeology
Edited and with an introduction
by Malinda Stafford Blustain
and Ryan J. Wheeler

Race Experts: Sculpture, Anthropology,
and the American Public in Malvina
Hoffman's Races of Mankind
Linda Kim

The Enigma of Max Gluckman:
The Ethnographic Life of a
"Luckyman" in Africa
Robert J. Gordon

National Races: Transnational Power
Struggles in the Sciences and Politics
of Human Diversity, 1840–1945
Edited by Richard McMahon

Franz Boas: The Emergence
of the Anthropologist
Rosemary Lévy Zumwalt

Maria Czaplicka: Gender,
Shamanism, Race
Grażyna Kubica

Writing Anthropologists, Sounding
Primitives: The Poetry and
Scholarship of Edward Sapir,
Margaret Mead, and Ruth Benedict
A. Elisabeth Reichel

The History of Anthropology:
A Critical Window on the
Discipline in North America
Regna Darnell

History of Theory and
Method in Anthropology
Regna Darnell

*Franz Boas: Shaping Anthropology
and Working for Social Justice*
Rosemary Lévy Zumwalt

*A Maverick Boasian: The Life and
Work of Alexander A. Goldenweiser*
Sergei Kan

*Hoarding New Guinea: Writing
Colonial Ethnographic Collection
Histories for Postcolonial Futures*
Rainer F. Buschmann

*Truth and Power in
American Archaeology*
Alice Beck Kehoe

To order or obtain more information on these or other University of Nebraska Press titles, visit nebraskapress.unl.edu.

www.ingramcontent.com/pod-product-compliance
Lightning Source LLC
Chambersburg PA
CBHW031411270326
41929CB00010BA/1417